POWDER ROOM

The Untold Story of Indian Fashion

SHEFALEE VASUDEV

EBURY PRESS

An imprint of Penguin Random House

EBURY PRESS

USA | Canada | UK | Ireland | Australia
New Zealand | India | South Africa | China | Singapore

Ebury Press is part of the Penguin Random House group of companies whose addresses can be found at global.penguinrandomhouse.com

Published by Penguin Random House India Pvt. Ltd
4th Floor, Capital Tower 1, MG Road,
Gurugram 122 002, Haryana, India

Penguin Random House India

First published in Ebury Press by Penguin Random House India 2021

10 9 8 7 6 5 4

ISBN 978 81 8400 161 7

Typeset in Dante MT by Eleven Arts
Printed at Replika Press Pvt. Ltd, India

www.penguin.co.in

FSC www.fsc.org MIX Paper from responsible sources FSC® C016779

This is a legitimate digitally printed version of the book and therefore might not have certain extra finishing on the cover.

For my parents Indra and Harish Vaswani,
whose genes I wear to work

Contents

Introduction

When I quit my job in January 2010 as editor of *Marie Claire*, I didn't suspect that I was on my way to becoming its apologist. I had found the editorial climate of fashion magazines handcuffed by Bollywood and advertisers, from where fashion appeared to be a hostage to celebrities and the upper class. It seemed a very narrow matrix compared to the way the idea of clothing varies in India—from the barely clothed who spend their entire lives in hand-me-down rags to those who spend millions of rupees on wedding garments. Between the two classes lies the thriving middle class for whom 'fashion' is no longer a spectator sport. It, too, has begun to assess its worth through clothes, even as the rich look almost exhausted in their search for competitive ways of spending. There is a rising inequality between the middle class and the rich in education, employment, and entertainment in new India. Curiously, there is rising inequality in fashion affordability between these two classes. Further down, the lower middle class is just a disillusioned, sometimes resentful viewer of this unequal game. Featuring a luxury watch worth a million rupees alongside a lehnga, embroidered by a craftsperson who could not afford to send his children to school, would rattle my world view. I looked for conflict resolution. As a popular culture writer, I observed that divorce and fashion were two defining factors in the last decade. If 2000–2010 was the divorce decade, it was also India's dress-up decade.

Till I was in Class 12, I hadn't heard of Coco Chanel. Born and brought up in a middle class, liberal Sindhi family in the small town of Gandhidham in Kutch, I was raised simply. My parents, both teachers and Sindhi writers, had participated in India's freedom movement when they were young and carried the scars of Partition. In the India that remained, they wanted me to join the administrative service. Guided by Gandhian beliefs, my mother shunned expensive silks, precious jewellery, make up, perfumes, and everything 'artificial' (her favourite word for fashion). Even now, she doesn't know who or what Louis Vuitton is and what I mean when I rave about couture. Yet, she would indulge my childhood craze for new frocks and stitched them herself on an Usha sewing machine. I would cut out patterns from *Eve's Weekly* and *Femina*, choose the fabrics, and hover around while she sewed. No excess was permitted. Formal clothes were kept aside for weddings or festivals only. Old clothes became nightwear and a careful differentiation had to be made between 'home' wear and 'outside' wear. My parents would wear old clothes while travelling in trains (we always travelled Second Class) as clothes got 'spoilt in the train'. The recycling would never end, and after clothes were too worn out, the cotton ones would be cut and hemmed to make dusters. Yes, once in a while, my father who travelled often would pamper me with 'heel-wale sandals' from Bombay. Even so, 'fashion' was considered inferior to academic excellence and showing-off of any kind was plain bad manners. As an adolescent, I was scolded every time I asked if I could thread my eyebrows.

Later in life when my peers in fashion would tell me that their mothers had always used Chanel No. 5 or that they had grown up in a world of Estée Lauder powder and French chiffons, I would keep quiet. I still recycle my worn out clothes to wear at home and till this day haven't bought clothes or accessories from a single luxury label. Spending recklessly on clothes still makes me feel guilty.

So what am I doing writing about fashion? To be honest, curiosity drove me to research this book. I looked for threads that could stitch up the story of fashion in India through people who lived for and by it—from designers to weavers. What were the private lives and frustrations of designers like? What did their families think about them? Does fashion really help distract people from everyday problems?

The narrative of clothing and fashion in modern India seems to be a close indicator of new social behaviour, rifts inside families, generational differences, and the compulsions behind fanciful consumption. If the financial independence of Indian women has led to a large societal change and their sexual liberation, fashion has certainly added to tangible liberties. It appears to be India's biggest fantasy at the moment—the great new escape. Bollywood is its face, and the Indian wedding its alter ego. Its relevance and use as an end-goal in life may be a debate, but it drives a lot of what we see around us as urban culture. Also, there seemed to be a serious clash in the way media represents the fashion industry and what it actually is. We lampoon its malfunctions, allowing fantastical assumptions to gloss over the fact that clothes that reach mass brand retail stores or fashion collections we see at fashion weeks, take months to create. They are the culmination of serious business strategies combined with fiery creative imagination. Not all designers have had formal training; some have created large businesses by giving a free reign to their imagination. Anamika Khanna, one of the country's most critically applauded designers, never went to a fashion college, nor did the younger Anupama Dayal who managed to double her turnover between 2010 and 2011. Behind 'designer clothes' are armies of people: designers, karigars who sew crystals on saris for eighteen hours a day, tailors, and stylists.

Paradoxes leapt out of every subject I explored. Not only is India now a powerful retail destination for luxury and mass brands, but Manish Arora, the former creative director of French brand Paco Rabanne is one of the most popular designers at Paris Fashion Week. His design leadership has planted the words 'Indian Fashion' firmly onto the world stage. As have numerous showings, appearances on the Cannes red carpet and retail tie ups of other designers, some younger ones included. Our designers not only sell to bling-obsessed NRIs but also dress global celebrities.

Indian fashion sells in the Middle East countries as much as it does here. The world's terms of engagement with India as a manufacturing hub of fashion are still more or less the same—a sourcing centre for beautiful embellishments, embroideries, and affordable tailoring. At the same time, India's manufacture influence has inflated. Local designers and collectives now create entire prêt collections for brands like Kenzo, Ralph Lauren, and Tommy Hilfiger. In an opposite pursuit, Sabyasachi Mukherjee, one of the highest selling Indian designers has a vision of starting a clothing company that will make affordable garments for the middle class. Suneet Varma, an industry veteran, emphasizes the diversification of his expertise into design consultancies as one of the survival strategies in a market challenged by global brands.

The words 'fashion' and 'designer' are now conversational staples. They are bandied about in popular lexicon like a cloud burst, splashing every nuance. Stories of men and women I met in different towns strengthened the suspicion that outside magazines, fashion was hardly about the rich and the under-occupied. The black Sadri worn by BJP veteran Sushma Swaraj as her clothing statement; Mayawati's faux leather handbags; and the dramatic increase in the sales of black and coloured lingerie (as opposed to the stiff, white Libertina bras of our growing up years) in tier two cities; or Rajesh Pratap Singh, the Master of Minimalism in India fashion, designing the uniforms for the staff of Indigo Airlines—all provide insights into the way we have evolved.

While writing the book, I met and interviewed more than 300 people, from Nagaland to Ludhiana, designers to sponsors and directors of fashion weeks, and even those who have never opened a fashion magazine in their lives. The youngest weaver in the Salvi family that weaves the rare and now dying Patan Patola sari in Patan, Gujarat, told me he had quit a full time job as an architect to become a full time weaver and set up a private Patan Patola museum recording its history since the eleventh century. A gay stylist explained how fashion had helped him come out of the closet. A ladies' tailor told me that she dreamt of her masterji (cutter) and not her husband even when she was going through a messy divorce. In a memorable interview, an East Delhi girl told me how her priorities changed after she began working as a sales executive for a luxury brand at Delhi's Emporio Mall.

Equally compelling are the personal stories of designers who rebelled against their families to pursue their calling——regarded as 'not a lot better than a darzi's'. Young designer Rahul Mishra, a formidable talent, also a poster boy of responsible fashion, was born in a mud house in Malhausi near Kanpur. He was not sent to school till he was 6-years-old. When his father could afford seven rupees a month as school fees, Rahul's teachers realized he was too bright for Class One and promoted him to a higher class in a matter of months. By the age of nine, Rahul was in Class Six and scored full marks in mathematics. His father soon packed him off to study at the Maharashi Maheshyogi School in Lucknow. Many years later, when Rahul secured a seat at the National School of Design, Ahmedabad, his father was stung with shock. 'Darzi banoge?' he asked him. 'Yet it is because of my humble upbringing in a village that I respect the condition of weavers,' says Rahul who now ensures some of his weavers can afford laptops and save enough to buy a plane ticket when they travel to cities for collaborative projects. 'I don't mind if they plagiarizse my designs, they too need to get on with their lives,' he adds.

Not everyone is enamoured of fashion after all. Fashion magazines and their editors may well wield front row clout but fashion journalism is still considered inconsequential by a majority of mainstream Indian editors. No space is made for fashion in the main sections of newspapers as it might be good for Page 3 and the snippety glitterati pages of news magazines, but seldom for insightful, investigative big stories. It probably takes a Rohit Bal to have a heart attack for fashion to share front-page space.

Sociologist Prof Ashis Nandy who I met to make sense of the polarities that soaked my research, said he found these paradoxes germane to the narrative. 'It is those who forget that besides business, trendiness, and liberty, fashion is about aesthetics, become hostile towards it,' he said. To some extent this explains why issues around moral policing in our society are related to dressing. Farah Aziz of Aligarh Muslim University was assaulted in 2006 because she wore jeans to college without a sobering dupatta; the principal of a Chennai college accused young girls of distracting male teachers by wearing tight-fitting clothes. There have been so many such instances.

Somehow, the larger-than-life, uber-glamourous image and reasonable profitability of Indian fashion does not translate into an organized industry. Designers like Wendell Rodricks, Ravi Bajaj, Abu Jani–Sandeep Khosla, Tarun Tahiliani, Rohit Bal, Suneet Varma, and JJ Valaya have been working for more than two decades; Ritu Kumar, the matriarch of Indian fashion, has been around for more than thirty-five years, even official fashion weeks are more than a decade old. Sunil Sethi, the President of Fashion Design Council of India, is now on most annual power lists of various publications. Yet, neither the Ministry of Textiles, nor the Fashion Design Council of India officially monitors the worth and growth of the fashion industry and its many scattered but worthy mini-revolutions inside and outside fashion weeks. There are selection committees for fashion events but despite a burgeoning collective, there is no industry ethic, code, union, or agenda to live by. In the absence of norms, there is little accountability on pricing, quality or issues of plagiarism, copying and derivative design, and these are rampant.

Powder Room got written only because people (especially a couple of designers) shared their private experiences and realities with me. They left me a changed person and I must admit that if I was driven to this work out of a superiority complex as a fashion journalist, I have been cut down to size.

Real people still amuse me a lot. The term used by fashion media often hints at those who need makeovers to qualify as story subjects but still amuse a fashion magazine reader who might get bored with the details of Sonam Kapoor's wardrobe. These people too are driven by fashion, without being aware of its seasonal or technical perfection. Their stories fascinated me as much as those of socialites. I was curious to find out what fashion did for those who wore Dior gowns compared to those who could only afford Big Bazaar or Fabindia.

Chapter One charts the journey of Raakesh Agarvwal from being sexually abused in his childhood to becoming a commercially successful designer. Chapter two follows the story of luxury brands in India through Jennifer, a sales representative at the DLF Emporio Mall in Delhi. Chapter Three set mostly in Ludhiana highlights the Punjabi culture of 'show-sha' or conspicuous consumption and how it plays itself out through luxury labels. In Chapter Four, I have tried to examine the role of models and why male models are not the superstars of India's modelling business. The story of emerging designer Imcha Imchen and his bi-polar disorder runs as a metaphor to deconstruct the duality of attitudes in fashion in the North East in Chapter Five. Chapter Six profiles Rohit Bal and Sabyasachi Mukerjee who have left an indelible impression on Indian fashion. In Chapter Seven I throw light on the darzi culture in India and the role of boutiques in our lives. Rahul Salvi the youngest weaver of the rare Patan Patola sari in Gujarat helps me recreate the story of the cocooned Salvi family that doesn't want anything to do with the designer lobby, fashion weeks and government 'support' in Chapter Eight. Chapter Nine is about fashion media, how they operate and their role in Indian journalism. In the concluding Chapter Ten I have tried to examine the politics that exits within the fashion world and the various players involved in it.

My editor Milee Ashwarya found editing *Powder Room* quite challenging as the multiple layers within the fashion industry had to intertwine with stories of common people; we wanted to find a balance so that the book could find resonance not only with the fashion elite but also students and a regular Indian shopper.

I was often asked in this pursuit, whether my book will be controversial or negative. It is neither. I worked on it like a journalism assignment and have attempted to report the perplexities that clothe those who live by fashion in different cultures of India and through them reveal why the industry is not a mere sum total of designers, models, and fashion weeks. If at all, *Powder Room* might tell you why fashion is a form of zeitgeist and why the industry should not be judged by its clothes.

Dry Clean Only

'I'd wear any of my private attire for the world to see. But I would rather have an open flesh wound than ever wear a band aid in public.'

—Lady Gaga

Raakesh Agarvwal walked into the coffee shop at Radisson MBD in Noida, wearing shorts and a worn out T-shirt and gave me a big hug. Raakesh was freshly shaven, and a strong perfume wafted around him, but he looked gaunt and tired as always. 'If you see my call list, you'd think I am friends with Lara Dutta, Sonakshi Sinha, Anushka Sharma, Jacqueline Fernandes, Genelia D'Souza...' said Raakesh, showing me his BlackBerry. 'But how can I forget that there are no real friends in fashion,' he added, trying to diminish the effect of cheesy name dropping.

Just the previous evening, I had seen him on *UTV Stars* posing happily with Jacqueline Fernandes, one of his recent showstoppers. We found a table that looked out at the swimming pool. 'I am so sick of fake people in fashion that I long to meet and chat with those who are normal,' he added.

Raakesh has not been keeping well for the last couple of years and the word got around in the industry. A few days before we met at Radisson, he had attended a party hosted by a fashion magazine. Some socialites, who are also his clients, had walked up to him, curious to find out what was wrong. 'Where's your car, babe? Don't you drive a BMW now?' he drawled, mimicking what a lady had said to him. 'No I don't,' Raakesh had snapped back. 'I get distracted while driving and can't afford to keep a chauffeur driven car, so I take a Meru cab.'

Another walked up to him curious about his health. 'Babes, we heard you were on your deathbed, how nice to see you, are you okay now, sweetheart?' Before Raakesh could reply, the lady turned to air kiss and chat with someone else. 'This fake concern makes me sick. She asks me if I am on my deathbed, then doesn't even want to listen to my answer! Can you believe that?' Raakesh looked hurt.

He was used to being 'hurt' and 'sick'. In varying intensities, these feelings had helped him deconstruct his private life, his career, and the 'real face' as he would say, of the fashion industry. Sexually abused for fourteen years as a child, by a close male relative who lived in his home, while his mother feigned ignorance, Raakesh's story is one of pain and betrayal.

Raakesh Agarvwal, a product of National Institute of Fashion Technology (NIFT), Delhi, and now one of India's more successful young designers, has an endearing, thin-skinned personality. Feminine warmth defines his manner though he insists that he isn't sure whether he is gay, bisexual, or heterosexual. He is of medium height, has a dark complexion, and is always casually dressed in jeans and T-shirts. I have never seen him in a sharp suit or a bandhgala, even at the most formal functions. His best clothes would be a black shirt and black trousers. At parties and fashion shows, he is usually breathless and highly stressed, hair disheveled, as if he has just about managed to make it to the venue.

Raakesh waltzes from being a drama queen to an emphatic, overwrought designer openly livid about fashion week politics that has singed him more than once. He isn't anxious though about being judged for the misfortunes in his personal life. When he boasts about Bollywood heroines as his clients, he does it with naked earnestness. The divas he loves to talk about have worn his designs for magazine shoots and personal appearances many times over and some of them are his loyal customers. Shilpa Shetty wore a yellow jumpsuit by him for the cover of *L'Officiel* sparking off an order list as did his clothes made for Kareena Kapoor and Priyanka Chopra when they appeared on magazine covers. Reproductions of the 'Lara sari' as he calls one of his muddy brown creations with a bustier made from bronze chains, a showstopper piece worn by Lara Dutta, sold more than he could manage to make.

'I want to ask you something,' Raakesh said to me once. It was 9:30 am on a summer morning and I was in Raakesh's Noida factory to 'chat'. He was waiting for me outside the iron gates that open to his studio. The fittings section and tailoring wings were upstairs and the embroidery unit was in the backyard. He had been up all night and wore a pair of faded shorts, looking unshaven, exhausted, and ill. Nevertheless, he smiled warmly as always, and offered me kaju barfi the moment I entered.

'What's wrong with you? Not well?' I asked.

'I have had very high fever for the last few days, but I have a collection coming up so I worked through the night,' he said. Two of our former chat dates had been cancelled because Raakesh would get repeated bouts of jaundice and had been advised long periods of rest. His next question took me by surprise.

'Why do you keep coming back to me? You don't even like my clothes! *Marie Claire* barely featured me, when you worked there. So?'

Yes, I did keep going back again and again to meet him even though it meant driving past dirty, stinking open drains and over ruptured roads. Interestingly, this is where the rich come to order pricy bridal lehngas, Swarovski-studded bikinis, and stone-studded chiffon saris,

'I don't know why, but I feel drawn to you,' I said.

'You will be shocked if I told you about my personal life,' he said, looking me straight in the eye.

That morning, he told me about his childhood as the sun mocked us from the window, dappling his work desk moodily. He spoke of sexual abuse by a close family member, his growing fear that his mother would never believe him even if he told her every detail, that his worst fears about his mum turned out to be true; the solace he found in his elder sister's love; why he ran away from home to become a designer and how he got addicted to drugs.

Raakesh was born in an affluent and conservative Marwari business family in Adilabad, Andhra Pradesh. They owned cotton mills, traded in both raw material and loom cotton, owned crushers, oil mills, and had a transport company. His father died when Raakesh was in Class 10. He has two siblings, one brother and one sister. Due to expectations from uncles and elders, he joined the family business when he was in Class 9 and would go on to enroll in junior college in Adilabad.

He hated college even though he loved mathematics and economics. 'I am a true Marwari, numbers rock in front of me and I can interpret their moods and moments,' he told me. He knew nothing about fashion though, but the Miss India contest was his personal obsession. He would find every detail there was to know about it and roll it in his head hundreds of times. Later, I noticed how Raakesh liked speaking of award events; they stoked a feeling of awe in him.

The Agarvwal family was well-known in Adilabad as well as among the Marwari community in Hyderabad. Once, a group of students from NIFT, Hyderabad, came to meet them as part of a crafts documentation project. The Agarvwals put them in touch with local craftsmen and artisans. That interaction with fashion students left Raakesh curious for more. He was fired with dreams about working in the fashion industry. Almost overnight, he clamoured to study fashion and clung to the thought obsessively.

All this while, the sexual abuse at home had continued and he was also looking for a reason to escape his tormentor. 'I don't come from a glam background. Ours was a very disturbed and violent family, there were fights everyday. Given the conservative atmosphere, I couldn't confide in anyone, and fear and humiliation was killing me from within,' he said. 'I had to get out.'

Raakesh ran away from his family home for Delhi in 1997. He had very little money, no family support, and little idea about how he would survive. He was totally unprepared for the culture shock that life in Delhi would give him. 'From Adilabad, a village, to New Delhi of the late Nineties! My God, I can't tell you how I felt about the difference between the two.'

NIFT had gone through a survival struggle in the Nineties. In the previous decade, the garment industry was just a cluster of family businesses backed by manufacturing units of cotton mills. There was a strong need for expertise to meet increasing export demands. NIFT was set up to bolster this process. In 1986, a two-room centre in the shopping arcade in Delhi's Samrat Hotel was set up as the country's first government-run fashion institute offering three basic courses—Design, Manufacturing, and Marketing. This was in collaboration with the Fashion Institute of Technology (FIT), New York. Every faculty member at the Delhi NIFT was trained at FIT with the latter continuing to act as mentor in the initial years.

Soon, a nine-crore campus in Delhi's Hauz Khas area would mark the footprint of the country's premier fashion institute. But nobody—neither the government nor the industry—initially took fashion education seriously, recalls Rathi Vinay Jha, a civil servant and the founding director of NIFT. Mothers who wanted their daughters to do something respectable till they got married made enquiries as this was mostly perceived as a trendier version of the women's polytechnic. Designers in those days meant garage boutique owners.

In 1990, Jha was told by the Planning Commission that the then 4-year-old NIFT would have to be closed down. The government could not afford to divert the three-crore annual fund from the handloom budget for an elitist institution. Though NIFT was set up after the consistent efforts of handloom and cultural activist Pupul Jayakar, whose closeness to the Nehru–Gandhi family had shrunk the obstacles, Jha says it took an entire year to save NIFT.

By the time Raakesh enrolled to study (1997–2000), NIFT was a buzzing institute. It packed varied educational and fashion experiences for its students. Raakesh, on his part, was busy surviving the culture shock in his initial years in Delhi. He was jolted by the differences in fashion, food, attitudes, and lifestyle between Adilabad and Delhi. The many years of unresolved suffering and abuse had also left him temperamental, prone to fits of anger, sadness, and a lack of confidence. 'I didn't even have the guts to pick up the phone to talk to anyone in those days,' he told me.

Bottled anger and inner confusion foiled by a fast and reckless life in Delhi also led to creative outbursts and imaginative fashion projects. Raakesh took to drugs on the one hand and on the other began to create clothes that were noticed by the NIFT faculty.

'Why did I do drugs? No reason at all, peer pressure I guess,' he told me.

His graduation collection in 2000 got a big applause. The story he narrated through his collection was about a working executive from Japan and Raakesh showed multiple uses for his garments—a waistcoat that could be converted into a laptop bag for instance.

NIFT brought its own bag of experiences. When it was his turn to do his craft documentation project, he went to Kerala as the project was about Thayyam dancers who, according to folk and temple lore, embody the spirit of the deity as it possesses them during the dance. 'I felt like a Thayyam dancer. It was like experiencing an intense earthquake. I felt possessed too, broken almost by passion and anger,' he says.

'The abuse in my childhood has left me a troubled person—passionate, possessive, and stubborn. But I didn't know then that watching the Thayyam dance was a way of my past coming back to trouble me. I had no idea why I would suddenly burst into tears. Till date, I am easily hurt and heartbroken and can't take no for an answer or handle rejection. I want everyone's love,' he said. Raakesh did not cry as we talked quietly in his Noida factory, but I could feel that he was wailing inside.

'Are you gay, Raakesh?' I asked.

'I am not sure. I had a girlfriend in college for four years. Even when I went to train under Tarun Tahiliani after my graduation, I had a girlfriend, but I also had sexual relationships with boys. Drugs can destroy you, you don't know who you are, what you want,' hc said.

Raakesh slipped into an orgy of drugs, raves, and sex. He got confused about his sexual preferences and explored what came his way.

'What all did you do?' I asked him.

'Oh, don't even ask. Acid, ecstasy, cocaine, LSD—everything. When you do drugs, you do it all, you don't stop to choose. I would drink eighteen pegs of alcohol in one night. Sometimes these parties would go on and on, one after the other every evening. I was so addicted that I still get withdrawal symptoms even though I have been clean for quite some time now,' said Raakesh, recalling the time he took Acid and rode a waterbike in Goa. 'I had no idea where we went, who I was with, what I did. Finally the next morning, the saline sea water woke me up—I had passed out on some island,' he added looking sheepish.

Working under Tarun Tahiliani changed Raakesh's life, as he says, in many ways. 'There is no one like Tarun when it comes to cutting and draping.' 'He was a super boss. If someone has taught me fashion, it is Tarun,' said Raakesh.

Tahiliani Farms is an imposing area inside a private enclosure off Delhi's Vasant Kunj. 'Have tea, look around and I will be there soon,' Tarun Tahiliani told me over the phone when I reached the house and was shown into his study, a separate cluster of rooms in his farmhouse.

His study is like an artist's studio. It was summer when I visited him and a few hundred mogra flowers had been heaped into a large, open brass container, their riotous fragrance filling the room. Large windows looked out at lush trees swaying in well-manicured lawns. Everything inside the room was art: a huge Anjolie Ela Menon on the wall, mugs from Milan, a metallic figurine from a Venetian market. The lights hung like pieces of art and yet Tahiliani's larger than life presence loomed in the absence of his loud, flamboyant personality.

'Who doesn't know TT', quip people in the fashion industry. Fashion students new and old, interns and veterans, stylists and editors, models and make up artists, have-beens and wannabes talk about attending 'Tarun's show' as if he was their bum-chum and lived just round the bend. The reality is that 'everyone' may believe that they know him, but TT, as many people call him, can be very choosy about who he wants to know. Ensemble launched by Tarun and his wife Sal Tahiliani in Bombay's Fort area twenty-five years ago was not only the first multi-designer store with a distinct fashion vision, but also where the country's first ever fashion ramp was set up. The show mounted on that ramp is remembered till today as the first 'proper fashion show' by models and designers of that decade. Before that only mills organized fashion shows.

TT started his career after a business degree from Wharton. He is talented, arrogant, stylish, and hung-over with the fashion cool of the late Eighties. The parties he hosted in the past are like industry lore. But I must admit I have attended only those parties thrown by him which are sane and sophisticated—the kind where long-legged fashionistas hold champagne flutes and say no, thank you to snacks; where drop dead gorgeous women discuss subjects they have little idea about; where everything people wear is as beautiful as those who wear them. These are occasions when TT with his bulging eyes, penetrating gaze, deep voice, and boisterous presence is all over the place. His genteel and wise wife Sal and his smart sister Tina are always around, but he is clearly the star.

Down the years, TT began to resell himself to the media. This time as the new, reformed Tarun Tahiliani, who does yoga, drinks green tea and considers India as his biggest muse. I am not one of his old friends; I am barely a friend in fact, though over the years the two of us have struck a candid talking relationship. At times, after a fashion show, he tells me the difference between collegiate fashion and what must actually embody a full blooded fashion week show and his comments are very incisive. For all his arrogance, Tarun is more open to criticism than any other designer in the industry. He is a quirky mix of haughtiness and straightforwardness. He can bully you with his aggressive arguments. Yet, if his opponent is worthy, he will take a smack when it is his turn. Otherwise, he chews up those who argue with him and has mastered the art of ignoring those whom he dislikes. He can just look through people.

He is also a master of drapes, detailing, texturing, and tailoring even today, twenty-five years after launching Ensemble. If he is known as one of the more intelligent Indian designers, it is not entirely incorrect. He has academic acumen, and isn't just another street smart Sindhi businessman. Those who have worked with him say that he can write press releases in a flash and usually comes up with design interventions at his factory even before the gaps loom large. He is one of the very few designers in the country who know exactly what he is doing, and how many of his clothes sell from which store in India. I find him an exasperating interviewee as he attempts to answer questions without listening to them (verbal diarrhoea he calls it).

'You are a diva, the media's darling,' I told him when he finally arrived. 'Your image is bigger than your own clothes and it is the biggest injustice to your fashion and creativity,' I added.

He looked at me with his penetrating eyes, almost smiling but not quite.

'Yeah, okay, I was ahead of the curve and I got some lucky breaks,' he said. 'Growth has its own problems,' says the designer who was the first to make a big business out of fashion in India.

'If a Bollywood star is your best show stopper, it is a disservice to your clothes,' I went on.

He changed the subject.

In 2010, TT began seriously tracing his steps back to his roots after what he calls a 'decade long plateau of no creative movement'. His march back was through a show called The New Democrazy. It underlined the change of his brand ideology, from hair raising bling to a dominance of textile and craft. This was TT's defining moment. The kettle was on the boil in his mind for the last few years, but it acquired form and purpose with The New Democrazy. This became a point when he regressed just enough to become futuristic. He yanked his brand out of the lethargy of success to become rooted and alert. 'India' began hurting him in his guts and perhaps he reflected whether he was creating fashion for India or 'Indian fashion'. TT continues to court old moneyed families and nouveau riche Indians across the world, earning unbelievable amounts of money in the process, but realizes that a designer must also teach taste and aesthetic to the rich. Even in our infrequent conversations, I now notice his keen interest in philosophic questioning, his growing fatigue for the industry's vanities, and the fickleness of the retail market.

'What's happened to Indians? You can't tell where they are from anymore,' Tarun Tahiliani remarked emphatically as we continued to chat. 'Two decades ago I could make out where a woman came from, her region and cultural roots, by the way she draped her dupatta. But not anymore. I remember the Maheshwari saris we made nineteen years back for my show in

London, the very tension in the fabric was different. But we never invested time or effort in teaching the weavers how to strengthen this legacy,' he said a trifle regretfully, for once dropping his 'I Know Everything' shield.

TT claims that he hasn't only changed his approach to fashion but also his lifestyle. 'I am not getting a photograph kissing a model again for the media; I don't even want to invite journalists to my parties. I want to be seen as an Indian designer, do Indian things, create what Indians need. Every Tarun Tahiliani product should have an Indian personality,' he said, telling me about the jadau watches he designed in association with Timex.

From a life of partying (and overeating, he adds), he has transformed to doing yoga in the morning and following a healthy diet, which has revved up his energy and fired him to become a part of 'the new world order'.

TT is hard on plagiarists ('you copy me at your peril, I will come after you and drag you to court'), and is the first Indian designer to get a court order on fashion designers getting intellectual copyright in India. He is also intensely critical about fashion magazines putting international garments and brands on its covers. He was vindicated when Lady Gaga wore a Tarun Tahiliani ensemble for her press conference before her performance at Formula One in Greater Noida in October last year. TT told journalists that he was left stunned when Gaga didn't change her garment even for the performance and turned his drape into a pop singer's flamboyant performance piece as she sung for the Indian audiences. The very next day, TT's PR went into an overdrive, the Gaga story had to be told and sold. It was; everyone took notice.

Some time ago, he invited me to visit his headquarters to see the photoshoot of his look-book for the annual Bridal Exposition. The exposition is now a stand-alone fashion event that he hosts every July at Emporio Mall in Delhi. In 2011, he even took it to three other cities: Mumbai, Kolkata, and Hyderabad. The Bridal Exposition is like watching a decadent wedding procession, with an assembly of mannequins in heavy couture, bride and groom prototypes too, ready as if, to be called for the wedding ceremonies.

I was keen to see its look-book being shot. Tahiliani's headquarters in Gurgaon, is an imposing building, big enough to double up as a fashion college. It is flooded with natural light and bears Tahiliani's elegant touch although the venue of the shoot was understandably in a state of disarray. TT was barking orders to his staff while he led me to his study. Unlike the one at his farmhouse, this one is styled like a fashion professor's den. There were hundreds of books around but I was distracted by a framed, Swarovski sample card standing up on his writing list like a wine menu. It had crystal samples in a few dozen hues alongside the shade name. I fell for a midnight blue crystal.

'You are a Sindhi, my dear, bling is in your blood,' said TT when he saw me eyeing it.

Outside the study, models—male and female in full make up—were getting ready to pose for the camera. No one smoked, giggled, or hung around idly. A traditional Rajasthani costume artist that TT had brought from a village was helping tie the turbans on the men. TT is fastidious when it comes to his work. That day, he had a number of assistant stylists fussing around him, but I felt he trusted only himself. Clear about the statement his couture must make, his orders cracked like whips as he styled his models. Luxe, classic, opulent, embellished, old guard parading as the modern sophisticate, dainty Basra pearls, sensuous chiffons, half covered rounded breasts, the big red bindi, the maang-tikka, slender models in red, white, and black. His brides were glossy-lipped, hinting sexual promise, not announcing it. They were maharanis in Swarovski, damsels in net blouses and organza gowns. 'Garments must be as luxurious inside as outside,' said TT, showing me the rich fabrics he had fused inside the heaviest of lehngas. 'People must feel luxurious the moment they wear something like this and long before they step out for the wedding.' TT's wedding garments are constructed with functionality in mind; he spends hours figuring out how the crinoline must be fitted on the inside of a lehnga. 'A bride must be able to pick up the lehnga and go for a pee without feeling restricted,' he explained telling me about Italian cutters who work with him to help him get the construction right. The grooms he had styled for his shoot were heterosexual but not macho. They were good looking gentlemen with a day's stubble, never a beard or a moustache, who wore safas, bandhgalas and necklaces.

TT is fixated with the classical ideal of feminine beauty. The Big Daddy of Indian fashion may be eating healthy food and experimenting more with textiles than with crystals these days but I realized that there is no radical change in his approach to fashion. His ideal showstopper is a sweet, mildly sexy woman in chiffon drapes. As he went about directing his models, it was hard to believe that he had an emergency intestinal surgery just two days ago. His stitches hurt, but he took painkillers and carried on grumbling and working nevertheless. Despite all this, his staff clearly adored him.

So does Raakesh. 'Whenever, wherever we travelled for work, Tarun treated us like his own kids.' 'We would eat and drink what he ordered for himself. He is egalitarian and very democratic,' said Raakesh. 'He would work hard and party equally hard,' he added, slightly ruefully this time.

Partying, drugs and long hours at work have taken their toll on Raakesh's fragile body and mind. In the last few years, he has had hepatitis, many episodes of severe flu and viral fever, diagnosed with Crohn's disease, and was in and out of hospital numerous times. His hepatitis was medicine-induced, his physician had told him. He had been indiscreetly treated with harsh steroids for an ongoing skin problem earlier by a dermatologist who had not explained the significance of tapering steroid doses. Raakesh would be put on and off oral steroids as and when his skin problems were aggravated. He would take six tablets one day and nothing for the next one month leading to a series of side effects.

Going by his recent medical history and his distressed demeanour, I'd wonder how this 32-year-old was churning out collections for fashion weeks, participating in travelling fashion shows to different cities, getting Bollywood divas to walk as his showstoppers, and expanding his retail base to notch up decent business. He would be in the hospital one day attached to a saline drip and the next, working through the night with his tailors and embroiders, doing fittings for his shows, giving last minute touches to clothes that looked like they had emerged after a dip in a sea of crystals and sequins. Every fashion week, even now, he gets several attacks of Crohn's Disease.

'I love bling. I am bling,' he had told me cryptically a year ago when I had done a story for *The Indian Express* on why Indians were crazy about glittering ensembles. 'Bling has saved my business from going bust. If the nouveau riche didn't fall over themselves to buy embellished garments, designers like me would be nowhere,' he had said, showing me crystal-studded itsy-bitsy swim suits now popular with brides. These would be worn either for pre-marital bachelorette parties or during honeymoons on beaches.

Raakesh does live by bling. The crystal craze is his saviour. His 2010 collection was called Premier Class. 'If I didn't want to impress fashion editors, I would call my line "Clear in Crystal",' he says candidly. 'Beneath it all, there is mukaish and resham chikankari but my customers have no idea. They are all busy counting Swarovskis,' he adds. He had taken me to his workshop to explain how many karigars did authentic resham embroidery on fabrics and took his sketches along to explain how, after the first cut, the blouses or pre-dyed lehngas are embroidered again, then re-draped according to the original design before the final finish.

Raakesh's karigars were working on a shaded sari, painstakingly embroidering the different hues on its field with coloured crystals, a project that could take weeks. Threatened by client deadlines, sometimes he has to hurry up these orders and puts fifteen karigars on one piece; even so, it takes a minimum of twenty hours a day for fifteen days. 'We have to offer super glam stuff to Indian clients; otherwise they don't understand designer wear. Even now customers come, bargain and argue about the simpler pieces saying, 'so what's the big deal in this? I can get my tailor to make it after buying material from the whole sale market in Nehru Place.' They don't comprehend the stages of colouring, dyeing, measurement, cut, embroidery, fittings that go into designer wear. They size the worth of a garment by the crystals or the embellishment on it. The Indian market is on a Swarovski high,' he said.

The most popular debut on India's fashion stage in the last decade is of Swarovski crystals. Like Louis Vuitton, it stormed into the shopping wish lists of Indians and staged a palace coup. Swarovski usurped our embroideries and upstaged real, gold zari to become a metaphor. It stands for bling-at-large; a subculture in our style statement. 'India is a natural market with its history of adornment, all we had to do was drop the penny,' said Sanjay Sharma, former director of Swarovski India Pvt. Ltd. 'Till five years ago, we focused on the high end market because buying designer wear here is like saying I have arrived. Now we have found ways to integrate Swarovski crystals even with traditional wear,' he added.

In December last year, a shining celebration to commemorate ten years of Swarovski's success in India was held at the Austrian Embassy in Delhi. Crystal World, the theme of the evening, comprised art and live exhibits that mapped the company's milestones in the country.

Designers basked in the Swarovski glory. 'We are not here to replace but to add on,' said Sharma whose marketing genius gave brand value to what are actually just three dimensional pieces of glass. In 2009, the recession year when every other global and local fashion brand was financially hit, Swarovski recorded a double digit growth in India.

Raakesh had earlier told me how the rich women of Hyderabad would buy traditional Kanjeevaram saris and send them to designers like him to further embellish them with crystals. 'I create Kanjeevaram sari sets with sexy blouses and belts. Babes, South India wants to glam up!' he said.

To meet his customers 'who count Swarovskis before agreeing to the price of a lehnga', Raakesh invited me yet again to his Noida studio.

There I saw a would-be bride and her mother arguing hotly about where the girl would tie her wedding lehnga. The duo had flown in from another city for the fitting of the bridal ensemble, which would cost them Rs 5 lakh. The ensemble consisted of a lehnga which had to be fitted at the waist and a choli created from only about 60 cms of cloth, I figured.

'Isn't it too sexy for a bride?' I whispered to Raakesh.

'There is nothing like "too sexy" anymore,' he responded, patting me on the back reassuringly. 'From Meerut to Hyderabad, every bride including those from Marwari families only want backless itsy-bitsy cholis. That's why I have to give wine to the mummies,' he said winking.

'I want my tattoo to show, so I will tie it here,' the young girl yelled, indicating where she wanted the lehnga, way down below her belly button.

'How can you tie it *there*?' said the mother losing her cool. 'What will people *say*?'

'Let them say what they like, I don't care. It's my life, my wedding, my lehnga, you take a chill pill, mama,' the girl shouted back.

The mother went and sat on the couch and sulked.

Raakesh smiled indulgently but didn't intrude. Such slanging matches were a routine in his studio and he had learnt not to leap into the battle. Instead, he had smartened up his selling tactics and ordered wine and pizza when he expected rich customers for fittings.

'They spend a few lakhs on each ensemble, I can't have them driving out of my studio for a good lunch. So water to begin with then wine and Italian food, that's the least I do when I have clients shopping for lavish weddings,' he said.

Most affluent weddings in India now are like the Baroque court where wealth, power, and status are served up in a flaming pudding of excess. The lehnga, the sartorial centerpiece of this ritual of profusion, is the show stopper. Its materials are sourced from all over the world. Then come the embellishments on it—new stones riding piggy back on old embroideries. It is couture in the way it is handmade, involves intensive labour, days of work on one garment, fittings and intimate designer-client interaction. Raakesh was right, it must be sampled over food and wine in a studio setting that attempts to replicate a luxurious palace. These garments were a rage even in the Middle East market where crystal studded couture made the Sheikhs swoon.

Raakesh was one of the most avid users of Swarovski crystals. But he could not afford to buy genuine Swarovski pieces. Instead, he bought his sequins, stones, crystals from private vendors abroad who sold them for 30 percent cheaper than the Austrian company and also gave him a credit of forty-five days.

When I asked Tarun Tahiliani what drove Indians to look like Karan Johar baraatis, he defended India's obsession with bling. TT had recently even created a jewellery line in association with the Austrian crystal brand. 'Bling is in our tradition. The nouveau riche prefer it because they think it makes them noticeable. Taste comes with time. But why look only at embellishments? Look at the way we measure, sculpt a sari, gown or lehnga around a customer. It is not as if we are only stitching crystals on to saris. I have French tube tops with sari drapes; I have hired specialists to do this job, so that a wedding ensemble is cut like a global garment but made from Indian fabric. The vocabulary is Indian, the cut is European. This is the definition of contemporary Indian couture. Once you accept it, even if grudgingly, it is easy to see why the multi-hued Swarovski crystals mirror the story of our transition.

By the end of 2011, Raakesh too was in a transition phase in his life. We had had many intimate chats and I realized he exaggerated his optimism before me. He seemed to borrow his words from his dreams, hoping perhaps in the heart of his hearts that things would turn out the way he envisioned them. He was lucky that whatever he would brag about would eventually come at least half true. Once, he told me about the hundreds of orders he was getting from clients in Hyderabad and why he had opened a studio there with a manager. I found it difficult to believe it but when I visited Elahe, a popular fashion retail store in Hyderabad that stocked known designers, its owner Smita Shroff told me a similar story about cling, bling and value that must be 'visible on a designer garment'. Hyderabad is a growing market for blingy designer wear; people there have a new fascination for big labels (both global and local) and Raakesh's clothes were indeed popular. 'The Reddys are the Punjabis of South India,' Shroff said, simplifying it for me.

If anyone simplified life for Raakesh and understood, supported, nourished and accepted him as he was—besides his older sister—it was his partner Apurbe G. Tewari. A mild-mannered, middle-aged gentleman, who can easily pass for Raakesh's elder brother, took him home to live with him, his wife and kids. Apurbe may formally be Raakesh's partner and mentor, but he is actually his anchor and friend, and really the only reason why Raakesh can still call himself a designer.

'Anyone else would have thrown me out after the number of temperamental outbursts, anger fits, drinking and drug binges that I got into,' says Raakesh. He had flitted from having a girlfriend to having male sexual partners and was taken for psychological counseling by his older sister and Apurbe. But it was the latter who held him through when he completely broke down. Business suffered severely.

Raakesh wasn't just doing drugs but after having quit working with Tahiliani in 2005, he floated on as a derivative designer. He had no individual statement, nothing to distinguish his USP in fashion. One day, Sabyasachi walked up to him at a Lakme Fashion Week stall and advised him to dump his western silhouettes and obsession for western wear and create what India wants.

'Had it not been for Sabyasachi, I would have battled with silly esteem issues, believing that Western wear is edgy and Indian wear meant being regressive as a designer,' he said. 'I was inspired by Sabyasachi, look at how Indian his clothes and silhouettes are, how true he is to himself, to the craft of our country and by that to his customers,' said Raakesh. 'If Valentino can remain loyal to gowns and Karl Lagerfeld can make Chanel jackets and Fendi dresses; if Roberto Cavalli doesn't change himself for anyone, why should an Indian designer make a living out of Western wear?' said Raakesh to me at his factory.

This made Raakesh change his design focus towards Indian garments, making sequined saris with sexy cholis, kurtis, tunics, and lehngas. Having learnt construction at Tarun Tahiliani's he was always good at it and now included draping in his design. To stay afloat and grow, he would invest in a two dimensional plan: embellished garments and use of fluid fabrics that draped well.

'I made leather bustiers and dresses for two seasons but I went bankrupt,' he said.

While Sabyasachi, his inspiration, worked with stiff khadi and low twill Benarasi silk; Raakesh wanted to be associated with sexy glamour. He fantasized about Hollywood, the Oscar awards would keep cropping up in his conversations. As part of Tarun Tahiliani's team, he had dressed up Aamir Khan for the Oscar Awards ceremony in 2002 when *Lagaan* had been nominated and was fascinated by the most-watched red carpet in the world. He wanted to make Hollywood-like garments for Bollywood heroines and filmi bling for customers from Punjabi Bagh. 'If Bollywood girls want to look like their Western counterparts, people from conservative but rich communities want to look like film heroines; it is a continuous chain and I wanted to become the link.' This meant using charmeuse lycra, silk lame jersey fabric, tulle lycras, foiled chiffons, georgette, rayon jersey, velvet, sometimes soft leather for bustiers. No Indian textiles. The words 'Indian sexy' stuck and became his calling card.

Till this design turnaround would uplift their business in late 2009, Raakesh and Apurbe were almost bankrupt. 'We didn't pay salaries for some months, it is only now that we have begun to break even,' he told me. Raakesh, who was going through countless disturbances in his life, both at personal and professional fronts, told me he had to really shake himself up after he realized that he had no money to pay his staff. 'People's livelihoods and family lives depended on me and I was letting them down,' he said.

Around the same time, his best friend betrayed his trust and dumped him. Raakesh hasn't learnt how to recover from betrayal. 'Whatever my psychologist may tell me, I am very bad with betrayals,' he said. Even before he could accept the loss and deceit of his best friend, came the diagnosis of Crohn's disease.

Raakesh had a long prescription list staring at him. He was asked to lose weight that he had put on during his drug, alcohol, and food abuse days; address the scars left over from childhood sexual abuse, and hit an exit cycle from his victim mentality as well as put his business back in order. He weighed 97 kilos and felt like deadweight. Things went from bad to worse when a film he had signed with JP Dutta as the style director too got floored. Again, he says, it was Sabyasachi who advised him to show bridal wear on his ramp. 'Once I showed my bridal line at a fashion show, there was no looking back. Orders came in multiples.'

Things started to get better after he moved into Apurbe's house and the latter's kids became 'Raakesh Chacha's' life and purpose. 'I am their chacha, not "uncle". Everyone is an uncle, I am more than that. Any mother, anywhere in the world can leave their kids with me and I will make sure they don't cry. I am not just good with kids, I adore them.'

A dietician, a general physician, a psychologist, and a reworked business plan with a new design aesthetic stretched ahead of him. He quit parties and drugs, would watch movies at home with Apurbe's kids, eat homecooked food strictly monitored by the dietician, sleep early, wake up in the morning to exercise and reach the factory at 9:30 am sharp. He lost about 10 kilos and become disciplined about work.

His 'glamourous bling' (his own words) began to be noticed on his ramp shows. Soon, the clients he had made friends with during his time at Tarun Tahiliani began to call him. 'Now everyone comes to me,' says Raakesh who drops names easily. 'Koel and

Kalli Purie, Tanisha Mohan, Feroze Gujral, Queenie Singh, Harathi Reddy, everyone, everyone; we are doing glamourous, sexy clothes and everyone wants them.'

'Have your clients ever told you why they like your clothes?' I asked Raakesh.

'No, not really. People like looking sexy and glamorous I guess. Why don't you ask them?' he responded.

I took his suggestion seriously and asked for an appointment with Queenie Singh, former Miss India, and now a prominent socialite and party hostess in Mumbai. In September last year, Queenie had hosted a party for American socialite Paris Hilton at Mumbai's JW Mariott and before that for Naomi Campbell.

My informer chided me on not knowing how the A-grade vs B-grade grammar worked among party hostesses and socialites. 'There are four rungs of hierarchies, each come for a different price and can be worked out through different networks of connections,' she said. Another publicist I checked this out with reiterated similar politics. 'Oh, and huge money is involved. Now even a C-grade socialite doesn't host a party or attend an event for Rs 50,000. It is all in lakhs and then there are categories,' she said. 'Brand fit' and 'networking success' led a hostess to seal what Queenie had managed during Paris Hilton's arrival. She didn't respond to my messages or my email about the Paris Hilton visit, so I would never know how she worked it all out.

All the same she didn't look stung with this gossip, nor did Hilton. Both posed happily for the paparazzi that had gone berserk in the few days that Hilton was in Mumbai. The American heiress wore a Rocky S dress and Jewels By Queenie.

Jewels By Queenie is a niche jewellery store in South Mumbai. A small staircase leads up from the showroom to a smart little office with a low ceiling. I waited there for the lady who was formerly known as Queenie Dhody. This was a year before Paris Hilton's visit to Mumbai and a year after Queenie's separation from her spouse Raja Dhody, after which she went to be with Raja's close friend Dr Farhad Taraporevala, an orthopaedician. It had been scandalously reported by the media and I wondered how Queenie would have survived it.

Raakesh had told me that he had been to Queenie's Mumbai home for parties and once, in a drunken stupor had passed out in her master bedroom. 'She was kind. She didn't wake me up to say get out now the party is over. In fact, I badgered her to get me cocaine by hook or by crook as I was losing it once again but she said no, she had no idea where to get it from. She never did drugs and politely refused to indulge me. Yet, next morning, when I rose with a giant hangover, she made tea for me and was nice and warm. That's not the side of her you see in her photographs,' he had said.

When Queenie strode in in her Jimmy Choo stilettos with her glistening skin and nude lipstick, wearing a pink, printed shirt tucked into blue jeans, long chains on her neck, big cocktail rings on her fingers, her hair ready to attend any party in the world, I could see why magazines loved her. Youthful, despite her forty plus years, slim and toned, she had the with-it-ness to carry off a Madonnaesque leather jacket or a feminine Rohit Bal choli. She looked like an excessively caked Barbie doll in her pictures. In magazines, Queenie sinks well into a shape issue, age issue, power issue or a best dressed list but is never spotted in any nuanced life story. You will never read a first person account by her about how she survived her turbulent personal life. When I saw her, I felt that make up and magazine fashion did her a disservice: she would be ravishing without both.

'Are you a fashion victim?' I asked her.

'Yes, but in a comfortable sense of the term. I enjoy it, I have the feel and flair for it, I can spend endless hours shopping in Champs Élysées in Paris as much as walking down the stalls of GenNext designers at fashion weeks. I can wear a Hervé Léger dress, Christian Louboutin boots, an Issey Miyake drape or substitute them all with khadi harem pants,' she said.

There is an edge of tiredness in Queenie's world view, and weariness in her made up eyes that never shows in her pictures. Her conversation was laced with what she called 'the matte and gloss of life'.

Queenie told me about her collection of hundreds of shoes, bags and ensembles that range from high street T-shirts worth Rs 1000 to couture garments worth a few lakhs and that she enjoys partying if the host is right. She told me that as a young Miss India in 1988, she believed fashion was about flamboyance, bling, glamour, and wealth. Later she understood its essence lay in a personal voice. 'As the competitiveness among social classes becomes intense, people start latching on to fashion for the wrong reasons. They think fashion is about buying a Hermès Birkin bag,' she said. She surprised me. I found Queenie to be sensitive to the nuances of fashion and of life.

Harathi Reddy of Bangalore, another of Raakesh's client had another surprise in store for me. When I called the prima donna for time, she told me she was writing a book of Andhra recipes recording everything that was cooked in their native village and their homes for the last five generations and would welcome me to a home cooked meal.

When she opened the door to her luxury flat in Bangalore, I felt I was looking at an Andhra Cate Blanchett, a South Indian Miu Miu model, a Prada customer, and a Tarun Tahiliani woman all at once. Harathi is a tall girl and wore loose white linen slack pants, a white, off shoulder see-through top in stretch fabric styled to reveal a magenta pink bra strap on one side. Her hair was pulled back in a long black ponytail and her eyes were lined long in a retro look. She blended into her surrounding yet stood out.

Envision a Good Earth store with white lilies in tall glass vases, white candles all around, artifacts in matte silver, open spaces widened by wall to wall mirrors in the dining area, sofas wearing textured white fabrics, a large, minimalist dining table—that's Harathi's home.

It is in her kitchen where her best ideas are cooked. She served a meal of rice and coconut prawn curry, an old family recipe, with beans and sprouted salad in tiny separate silver bowls. A jaggery payasam followed. 'I understand the true value of everything,' said Harathi, a real estate manager who runs her own company with her husband. For many years she was a hospitality executive at the Taj group of hotels. 'I buy fashion but less is a hundred times more for me. I don't do ladies' lunches either because they become congregations of women wearing designer clothes, all carrying Birkins,' she said, eager not be judged by her wardrobe.

She needn't have worried. She had her labels—Lady Dior bags, Cartier Bleu watches and Rohit Bal garments—yet she stood taller than her things. Luxury had its uses, she confessed quietly.

However, a nagging reminder that bags and shoes worth 2.5 lakh in a country like India are at best an indulgence few can afford, has left her undecided about the right balance She admired her mother who lived in the US, yet wore Kanjeevaram saris everyday at home with diamond clusters in her ear, a mangalsutra, a bindi on her forehead, her hair in a long black plait.

'Do you judge people by their clothes?' I asked Harathi.

'Yes, I do judge people for their sophistication, cleanliness, and style but not by the money they spend on their looks.'

Raakesh's life, in more ways than one is symbolic of the many realities that also exist in the Indian fashion industry. Perhaps any fashion industry in the world. Consider its nuances. Raakesh comes from a small town, was a victim of child sexual abuse, got a cultural shock when he came to Delhi, became dependent on drugs, parties and alcohol, is unsure about his sexuality, trained under one of the most commercially successful designers, then was inspired by Sabyasachi whose arrival and designs changed wedding retail in India. Raakesh now feeds into the growing market for embellished wear, has Bollywood heroines endorsing his clothes and some of the most noticed socialites around India wearing his garments. No one story could bring in all these aspects together in one tapestry as Raakesh's does.

He is now busy with the planning, construction, and design of what he calls his super studio and headquarters in Noida. 'All glass and wood, pure luxury, just like my clothes,' he explains. He is off drugs, but does drink, and smoke often, he tells me. He is happiest when he's with Apurbe's kids who love 'Raakesh

Chacha' to bits and don't eat their breakfast till he feeds them before they go to school. He spends hours playing video games with them or taking them to parks and playgrounds while Apurbe takes business decisions.

His sister has been taking the news of Raakesh's success back home for the last couple of years and recently, the entire family decided to own up to the mess they had created in his life. 'My abuser still lives in that house but I am trying my best to forgive him,' said Raakesh. 'My mother is very unwell now, who knows how long she will live? My brother's adolescent children need an anchor to support and guide them. My brother didn't study beyond Class 10, nor did his wife, and I feel the family needs an educated person who understands the ways of the world to lift it out of its disturbed consciousness,' he said.

'Was it easy coming face to face with your abuser?' I asked Raakesh.

'No.' he said simply.

Raakesh is slowly coming to terms with the reality of the fashion world after getting 'a dose of everything' as he says. 'I spot fake people more easily now than I did earlier,' he says. He has no close friends in fashion and wants it to stay like that. He sees a counsellor regularly and needs a general physician to monitor health issues related to poor immune function. He still looks exhausted most of the time even though hc has started putting on weight again. His bling has set out on a procession of its own. He believes he will never be bankrupt enough again to not pay salaries.

His alma mater NIFT is inclusive too. In 2010, a decade after Raakesh passed out, NIFT Director General Rajeev Takru's sole mandate was to follow the Supreme Court's ruling and make the institute democratic and inclusive. NIFT's rapid expansion to 15 centres, including Kangra, Kannur and Rae Barelli was to evolve a non-elitist agenda by accommodating 54 percent more seats over three years for OBC and other quotas. The national level topper of the final year NIFT exam in the year the Supreme Court put out that ruling was from a village in Bihar.

Price on Request

'What does luxury mean to you,' I asked Silvia Venturini Fendi at the Fendi Pallazzo in Rome in April 2008.

'Freedom,' she said.

The girl pulled out a bunch of tissues in the scented ladies room of New Delhi's high end DLF Emporio. 'You know what?' I heard her say to another girl as she wiped her hands, 'I heard a young pretty lady got a Fendi Peekaboo handbag customized and invited her friends to Zest to celebrate it. Aish hai na; bas paisa hona chahiye.'

I turned and smiled at her. She didn't smile back.

Later when I introduced myself, she gave me only her first name, Jennifer*. 'Ma'am, I will lose my job if you interview me,' she said and politely excused herself.

The 'young and pretty' Fendi customer who Jennifer had heard of was Payal Sen, editor of the lifestyle store Roseby's magazine, *Enhance* and the shop's trend forecaster. I had gone to the Fendi store to ask who had ordered the Peek-a-boo but they refused to divulge customer details. I found Payal instead through the grapevine. When I asked her on the phone if I could come by to see her made-to-order handbag, she laughed and invited me home.

30-year-old Payal looks a little like Twinkle Khanna; both share the same immaculate grooming, classic style, and lady-like poise. She was dressed in a pair of jeans, an ivory chikankari kurti and slippers when I visited her at her opulent home in Delhi's Jorbagh. The drawing room was rich with art, silver, crystal, and silken rugs. Low-cal brown bread sandwiches sat on white plates and were brought on a carved wooden tray by a uniformed butler. The Fendi bag had been discreetly left on the floor near a sofa wearing turquoise silk.

Payal told me that she was extremely picky about what she bought and never gave in to impulse shopping. Made-to-order luxury products were her ultimate indulgence. For the customized

Peek-a-boo, she had chosen red leather with black stitching and gold hardware; her name had also been etched on the inner lining with the date and city of make—Rome.

The beautiful young woman was offended to hear that there was idle gossip among salesgirls about a party at Zest, which she said she never had. She also refused to tell me what she paid for the bag.

I went back to find Jennifer, hoping that it wouldn't cost the girl her job. She worked as a sales executive in a luxury store at Emporio and agreed reluctantly to talk to me. 'We can't sit here. Let's meet at Khan Market,' she said.

Jennifer is a dark skinned, slight looking girl. She came to Latitude, the Good Earth café in Delhi's Khan Market, wearing a pale blue, chest print T-shirt with black jeans and black metallic hoops in her ears. Her thick, raven hair was pulled back by a hair clip, making her look like a teenager. Without her store uniform—formal black trousers and a well-tailored lilac shirt with black, kitten heels—she looked younger than her 23 years, similar to the girls I would see on the Delhi metro every day.

She has a warm sunny disposition and an earnest, extremely polite manner—and if you observed closely, a subtle refinement which put her a few notches above the regular Delhi Metro Girl. One of three siblings, she belongs to a middle class family from Patparganj in East Delhi. Her sister was in higher secondary school and her older brother worked in a Costa Coffee shop.

Two years after finishing a pass course at Delhi University and some odd jobs later, Jennifer was short listed by a head hunting firm for a luxury brand store. After an interview with its Indian representative, she was recruited and put through rigorous training sessions. 'They presented the brand to us through photographs and CDs. We learnt about its ethos, history, all the product lines, prices, and also how to handle customers,' she told me. She was given grooming and make up tips by a visiting consultant who also coached the team on language and articulation. 'The trainer reminded us that the store was not a beauty parlour and a lady customer should *never* be addressed as didi,' she said.

Training sessions such as the one Jennifer described are an intensive process handled by a team of professionals. Prasanna Bhaskar, who formerly worked as Regional Director, South East Asia and India, for Salvatore Ferragamo, would lead similar sessions for her staff in India. She would fly down from Hong Kong where she was based for this. Prasanna, who was trained by and worked for Louis Vuitton when it first arrived in India in 2003, told me that LV was like an academy when it came to training its employees. Most candidates who sought work with luxury brand stores as sales staff belonged to middle class families and needed to change the way they thought and behaved.

Jaideep Sippy, the founder and CEO of Style Kitchen, a Pune-based company that markets healthy eating solutions, was once the corporate trainer for LV's Middle East and India stores. Never, ever address a customer by the first name, Jaideep would tell his store staff, not even when you are invited to. Hindi was a big no-no. Everyone from the youngest sales girl to the store manager was encouraged by the brand to 'believe' that they weren't just representatives of the brand, but were Louis Vuitton themselves. 'If a customer is Tarun Tahiliani, you are Louis Vuitton,' was Jaideep's way of empowering his store team. He had been similarly empowered during his training period.

Paris or New Delhi, sales staff are taught how to walk across a shop floor. French elegance isn't incidental. It is learned. Teams at these stores get specially tailored clothes made for them and during fittings they are also taught the importance of wearing the right size, even for undergarments. Some brands now hire grooming consultants to teach new staff as in the case with Jennifer. The right choice in lipstick and make up, personal hygiene, use of deodorant and perfumes, how to greet the customer—everything has to be taught and drilled in.

Prasanna, like Jaideep, found role playing a useful tool. She would enact a customer, both the well-mannered and the fussy one and then turn into a store manager to explain to a trainee how to greet them, show them around the store discreetly, and handle objections. Details are harped upon; a sales person selling a shoe must know how to bend down on one knee and help a customer slip on the shoe.

'It was during these sessions that I realized that Indian boys and girls don't bend down easily,' said Prasanna laughing.

The 'Act' as Prasanna called a new recruit's relationship with the brand, must then eventually become a part of her life. 'They should stop acting the act and slip into it naturally the moment a customer enters a shop,' she said.

While junior recruits like Jennifer are trained in India, those who manage stores, select merchandize or work at a country manager level are flown to brand headquarters from wherever they are in the world and encouraged to mingle with workers inside factories to understand the brand's sensibility. Everything from the vision of the chief designer to the positioning of a brand in advertising commercials is explained to them. Some brands insist that store managers physically experience the brand they sell by stitching a part of a shoe, cutting leather, driving a fine nail into a handbag in a factory, or if it is a beauty brand, participate in laboratory processes to see what goes into the making of a lipstick or an age-defying cream before it is packaged and sealed.

Human resource trainers of luxury brands are prepared for the class divide between a brand and its employees, especially in new markets and recruits are culturally immersed in the brand. Prasanna would show new trainees images of the Italian countryside, the view from a train going from Milan to Florence, and the Palazzo Spini, the building that houses the Ferragamo offices and museum in Florence. Jaideep showed his students exactly where LV offices were located across the world through Google maps, which was the nearest airport, which river flowed past. Recruits were made to pronounce street names correctly and to remember the tourist sites near the stores. Since many Vuitton products are inspired by places, Jaideep would also give the occasional geography class so that his trainees could understand why a collection was titled Manhattan by Marc Jacobs or another was inspired by a rain forest. Soho, Hudson, Russia, Canal Street—everything was explained, as was the peculiarity of fine, French cuisine. What is fondue? What is nouvelle cuisine? Sales teams were enabled to answer all these.

Prasanna's training sessions were scheduled once every fifteen days from seven till nine in the morning before the Ferragamo store at the Emporio mall opened. Team scenarios would be reconstructed and at Friday breakfast meets every week, everyone had to present a recap of what they did. That's how most brands function.

It was at one such recap meeting that Jennifer was asked to walk across the shop floor. Her manager wasn't happy with the way she noisily dragged her footwear and wanted her to correct it. While role playing, Jennifer stumbled and slipped. The trainer was beside her in an instant. She taught her how to pick herself with grace, brush her clothes lightly even if they were not dirty and then smilingly move towards the customer apologizing without making a big deal about it.

After attending some of these sessions, I began to understand where Jennifer learnt her refinement. She had been working at the store for ten months and during this time, not only had she been put through the training process, but the brand she worked for had flown her to Dubai for a workshop for sales staff from the Middle East and India. She came back armed with a new goal—to work in the luxury sector in Dubai where she was told shop assistants were paid much more as when compared to their Indian counterparts.

In 2010, Jennifer earned about Rs 27,500 each month. She was occasionally stung by the disparity between the world of luxury and her life back home. 'We can't spend this kind of money even on medical care,' she said, the sincere, bright smile never leaving her face as she sipped her mango panna. Only a couple of belts and small items cost less than her monthly salary; sometimes, she said they sold products worth five or seven times of what she earned. I wondered if she was resentful. If she was, she succeeded in concealing it well.

'What would you buy for yourself if you could afford it?' I asked her.

'A Louis Vuitton Canvas Monogram Neverfull bag,' she said, without a blink, her hand unconsciously touching her faux leather handbag.

French fashion house Louis Vuitton Malletier—part of Louis Vuitton Moet Hennessey (LVMH), the world's biggest luxury conglomerate—came to India in 2003. It was one of the first luxury brands to come in. Long before their launch, Vuitton monitored Indians who shopped abroad to compile a customer database. They added to their list, new, high-net-worth individuals who were their potential customers. Product viewings over champagne and tours to the company's private museum and special orders workshop at Asnières near Paris were arranged for potential converts to the brand.

In consonance with its old affinity with Indian royalty, LV appointed Tikka Shatrujit Singh, the great grandson of Maharaja Jagatjit Singh of Kapurthala, a prominent LV customer in his day, as its India advisor. An old trunk made for the Maharaja of Kashmir was displayed at the first LV store at Delhi's The Oberoi Hotel. Events hosted by the brand would invariably have younger members from erstwhile royal families as guests. It was clear even for a novice to figure that the royalty associated itself with Vuitton. The company used its royal heritage to connect with India's new elite: CEOs earning big salaries; NRIs wanting to come back and settle at home and closet spenders like politicians and bureaucrats who would lavish extraordinary amounts on luxury goods but never announce it publicly.

A combo of brilliant strategies followed—a highly-publicized friendship with Bollywood, patronage of Indian art and heritage, and capturing the imagination of the newly emerging fashion media in India. The company made sure that new products (initially the Indian store only stocked accessories) were launched in India simultaneously with its flagship store at Champs Élysées in Paris reassuring even the most discerning customers in the country that they were at par with their global counterparts. Today, if we have to think of one object that stands for global luxury in urban India, it would be the monogrammed Louis Vuitton bag.

'Show and tow,' as Amira Sethi* calls it. She and I did a power yoga class together. She was plain-looking; medium built and appeared to be about 30. She barely said a word to anyone at the class but as if to make up for her silence, her platinum polished gold bangles would jingle as she struggled with yoga postures and the diamond pendant on her slim chain would forget its place on her neck.

Two things were constant about her. She only wore dresses and all the accessories she carried were LV—her handbag, gym bag, wallet, make up kit, even her hair clips. 'Why do you always wear LV?' I once asked her in the changing room. 'You have your job and other distractions with it. At least, I have my Louis Vuitton,' she said looking up. 'Why don't you talk to my sister Brinda about labels? She is obsessed with them.'

The slim corridor outside the lift on the seventh floor flat of the Nadkarni home in Juhu, Mumbai, looked like a kitschy pop art gallery. Tall painted flower pots had been put on the two sides of the door to the lift, masks and street art hung on the yellow painted walls. Every time the lift doors parted, a fake Husain (or, was it real?) would split into two.

'Come in, come in,' said 46-year-old Brinda Nadkarni*, greeting me brightly when she answered the door. 'Amira told me you are researching Louis Vuitton,' she said. 'Everyone has it, fake or real,' said Mrs Nadkarni, yelling for her house help to bring me nimbupaani.

The small drawing room in the Nadkarni house had everything from everywhere. Leather sofas on wooden floors, coloured glass vases, shiny leather ferns, checked rugs, paintings, sea shell decorations and hard bound books with gold spines.

'Who is fond of reading?' I asked Mrs Nadkarni.

'No one. The books are for show. The interior decorator suggested we put them for an intelligent look as they go well with wooden floors. But I didn't like what that girl did with my drawing room, so I added more. You see my husband has been wearing Hermès ties ever since he went to study architecture in Paris; I know a good product when I see one,' she added, tucking my bra strap back into my kurti in a friendly way.

As I tucked into the homemade bhel, I asked her why she bought so many luxury brands. 'Status bhai. Aur kya? You can't get status with an Images bag can you?' she laughed and said.

Mrs Nadkarni had lately become a fan of Bagsutra, a luxury bag rental service and told me how her kitty party gang as well as friends of her daughter rented bags from there.

'They deliver the bag home after you order it by the phone or the Internet. You can use it for one party or keep it for a week,' she said explaining how the bags were not to be left on the floor and had to be protected from cigarettes and eatables that could leave stains. Bag rents went between Rs 1000 to Rs 3000.

'At least they are originals, not fake. I hate fake, it is so cheap. Why not buy Zara instead?' she said indignantly, asking me why I was carrying a cheap bag (a Rs 2800 camel-coloured Hidesign satchel).

Jennifer would have agreed. 'You don't look like the former editor of *Marie Claire*. For the sake of your status you should at least buy one nice handbag. I can advise you on which one,' she had told me. I remember laughing loudly.

This It-Fever had not caught on when Rajesh Mehta, a businessman now settled in London and forgotten by the media, first brought international brands to the Beautiful Boulevard in Mumbai in the mid-Nineties. His was a franchisee enterprise with entry level products from Lanvin, Tiffany & Co, Omega, Lancôme, Longines, Breguert, Lalique, Givenchy, Longchamp and Godiva among others. These were mostly beauty products or watches and wallets. The counters at Beautiful Boulevard looked enticing but the rich still bought luxury during their trips abroad. In those days, buying a Longines watch in India didn't bring the same thrill that buying it abroad did, a veteran watch collector told me.

Then in 1999–2000, the government relaxed its export-import policy and permitted import of watches below Rs 35,000. The taxes were still at 50 percent but the elephant was in the room. A year on in 2001, the elephant literally walked into the room with American supermodel Cindy Crawford atop it, for a lavish launch of Omega watches at Delhi's Imperial hotel. Shah Rukh Khan was made Omega's first Indian brand ambassador. A year later in 2002, Tag Heuer, a division of LVMH watch and jewellery, entered the market and within twelve months poached SRK from Omega. 'We would have done anything, paid Shah Rukh Khan any money he asked for. Our agenda was simple. Steal the thunder from Omega,' a former Tag Heuer employee told me.

Three years after that, Tag Heuer, which had been averaging a 40 percent growth in India since its arrival, hosted an all-night party in Goa. A select guest list culled out from India's partying republic wearing the most sought-after luxury labels participated in the celebrations. It thundered that December night. Champagne glasses tinkled over Goan fish fry as SRK emceed a bikini contest and played volley ball. Everyone who read about that event wanted a Tag watch.

So did Abraham. I met the 22-year-old college student in pursuit of a story at Slip Disc, the dance club of Voodoo, a notorious hangout in Colaba. It was a pickup joint, frequented by men and on the day I went, a young boy wearing red lipstick and an orange two-piece bikini was seductively squirming on the floor.

Abraham, in blue jeans and a pale yellow dhakai shirt stood by, enjoying the tease. 'I am a model. I have done auditions for Prahlad Kakkar and Prabuddha Dasgupta and modelled for *Man's World*,' he told me. I fell for Abraham's charm instantly even though I was his 'aunty's' age. Sexy would be an unimaginative way to describe him. He was an Adonis with curly hair, broad shoulders, and a strong, determined jaw line. A businesswoman from Hyderabad had once offered him a modelling contract and a visit to her bedroom. He had been selling his libidinal skills to rich, middle-aged women since.

He held a palm top in his hands and I noticed a Tag Heuer watch on his wrist. 'Oh, women give me anything I want,' he said following my gaze. 'I love branded watches and Gucci shoes,' he added. On the palm top, he showed me the photo of his girlfriend, a 36-year-old housewife from Jaipur. 'Isn't she gorgeous?' he asked. Abraham's girlfriend was buying time to elope with him and leave her 6-year-old son and businessman husband behind. 'She gifted me the Tag watch,' said Abraham.

If Louis Vuitton is one of the most selling brands in *India Today*, it is partly because they entered the market in 2002 and 2003, three years before most of the other brands came in. From 2001, the economy was booming and a new affluent class was being minted. The Household Income Survey done by the National Council of Applied Economic Research (NCAER) in 2005 found that there were 53,000 Indian families with annual incomes of more than Rs 1 crore. In 2000–01, the number was 20,000. In the early 2000s, the average Indian salary surged by 14 percent (18 percent for IT professionals), the highest wage growth in Asia, as recorded by Hewitt Associates, a global human resources company. There were 1.6 million Indian households that spent an average of $ 9000 a year on luxury goods, according to The Knowledge Company, a management-consulting firm in New Delhi. Indians from wealthier families were not only competing with the purchasing power of their European or American counterparts, some were even eclipsing them. According to the McKinsey Global Institute's charts, the number of the ascending Indian middle class would go up to 583 million by 2025.

This statistic, however, does little to bridge the gap between the brand and its employees. Jennifer told me how her first disagreement with her boyfriend emanated from the disparity in their personal and professional lives. It happened during the shooting of the film *Aisha* at the Emporio mall in Delhi. 29-year-old Devendra; six years older than Jennifer, worked in a LG showroom in East Delhi and had taken the day off because she had convinced him to come to see the shooting. She had told him to wear the clothes he wore for his brother's wedding so that he looked like a customer and could gain entry easily into the exclusive mall. Later Jennifer admitted that her suggestion had led to an argument.

Entry was restricted during the shoot and the place was crawling with bouncers and camera crew. Devendra could not get in due to the commotion outside the mall. When asked by the guard which store he was going to visit, he had fumbled, then dropped the charade. Instead, he pleaded with the guard to let him in, saying he had taken a day's leave for it. This enraged the guard further who shouted that he never got a day off. Chutti meant pay cut for him. He cursed Devendra for behaving like a sahib when he was not.

Devendra left in a huff, later accusing his girlfriend of having no self-respect as she worked in a place where those who didn't wear expensive clothes or speak French were frowned upon. Jennifer admitted it was her fault; she had forgotten to tutor her boyfriend better about the French and Italian brands.

Jaideep Sippy explained to me the complexities that emanated out of class differences. He told me that recruits, who have a clear sense of self, are individualistic, stubborn or have a strong love for their country's culture and its conventions are not ideal candidates for luxury brands. They resist the process of transformation through mentoring.

'So you look for blank slates while hiring; people who are easily impressionable, who wouldn't resist your ideas?' I asked.

'Well, yes, but remember no brand wants a dumb person, only those who don't mind being told how to think and behave like an Italian or French person,' said Jaideep. His words made me remember my experience at the Hermès store at Delhi's The Oberoi Hotel. I had noticed that if a piece of merchandize had to be plucked off the shelf to hand over to a customer, the sales person first slipped on delicate white gloves. When the Birkin bag was handled, the staff would hold it like a newly born deer.

Jennifer was only too happy to be a blank slate. She had begun to understand the difference between fashion and luxury but it was difficult for her to convey this to her family, even to most of her friends. They were all smart girls and many of them aspired to own products they saw in magazines, but they couldn't understand why a pair of shoes should cost Rs 50,000. 'My mom who saves every penny possible just cannot understand why people pay lakhs of rupees for bags and designer garments. I often show photographs of some of our customers when I spot them in *HT City* to my mother. But she turns away, totally uninterested,' she said.

After their fight on the day of the *Aisha* shoot, Jennifer told me that it was all very well for Devendra to chide her, but he did not have the humility to work with a luxury brand. 'He is so arrogant,' she sighed. Her job was leading to repeated arguments with her boyfriend and more intermittently, with her siblings too. 'They love the stuff when I show them pictures in brochures or magazines but then they accuse me of sucking up to foreigners,' she said.

Jennifer hadn't realized that she was beginning to change, not only in her behaviour but also in her expectations of others. She didn't like the toilet at her home with its bucket, mug, and plastic stool and told me she hated the iron drum kept in a corner for storing water. She was afraid they would get dengue but her mother wouldn't listen. She asked her parents to get a shower fitted with her next salary and they had an argument. She was getting used to scented loos and fresh napkins at work but her mother was unable to provide them at her home. She had also begun to find the 'lousy' manners of her friends at restaurants irritating and her younger sister's childhood habit of borrowing her comb and lipstick irked her. Hygiene and privacy were beginning to make sense in her mind, but she couldn't find them in her life. She steadfastly refused to let me visit her at home.

In January 2006 the Indian government allowed foreign companies to open single brand stores in India and have a controlling interest of 51 percent in a joint venture with an Indian partner. Nike, Calvin Klein, Marks & Spencer, all opened shop with a local partner. Later the floodgates opened. Chanel, Dior, Armani, Jimmy Choo, Gucci, Fendi, followed by Hermès, Cartier, Piaget, Kenzo, Tiffany, Moschino, Ermenegildo Zegna, Hugo Boss, Dolce & Gabbana, Just Cavalli, Bottega Veneta, Canali, Versace, Tod's, and Ferragamo came on each other's heels. They came prepared to bleed, having pencilled in big marketing budgets, upto 40–60 percent of total expenditure. This would include Bollywood stars as ambassadors, brand trips for fashion media, advertising, and marketing.

The seduction had begun. A two-way fascination began to get recorded. Magazines wrote about Christian Louboutin's fascination with Delhi's Lodhi Gardens, Chola bronzes, and Ayurveda. Italian designer Roberto Cavalli told me in an interview for *Marie Claire* that he was dumbstruck by the costumes of Indian royalty, 'My god! The clothes and jewellery I have seen of the Indian royalty just took my breath away! I wish I could copy and create a Cavalli version and put them on the ramp!'

Anna Zegna, the image director of Italian luxury brand Ermenegildo Zegna, had once told me how she felt drawn towards India and described it as her 'calling'. 'As an adolescent, I wanted to come to India, there was something about this country that beckoned me, a part of me belonged here, maybe I am connected by a previous birth,' she told me over lunch at a restaurant near her office at Via Savona in Milan. It was only after Anna completed college that her father allowed her a trip to India. A spiritualist and yoga master, she first found her way to Mt Abu to meet the Brahmakumari sisters who ran a religious cult there. The experience left her deeply affected, pulling her back to India again and again. Now she supports Care & Share an organization for underprivileged children near Vijaywada in Andhra Pradesh.

On the other hand, much as we loved Louboutin loving our country, we wanted everything that was not from India. All this while LV continued to emphasize the seriousness of its new relationship with India to the world. In 2006, Espace Louis Vuitton, the top floor art gallery of the brand's store at the Champs Élysées in Paris pulsated with photographs, videos, sound and visual montages by French and Indian artists for an exhibition called India of The Senses. The brand released a commemorative notebook with watercolours by French artist Florence Asch, depicting scenes from Mumbai including a dhobi ghat, vendor selling rat poison, a bored cow in a No Parking slot, and the making of a Bollywood film.

In 2010, Salvatore Ferragamo threw open his family villa in Florence for the wedding of a couple from one of India's known industrialist families—Sajan and Sangita Jindal. Directed by Vandana Mohan, one of the country's most popular wedding managers, the event hosted guests from all over the world. The first wedding ever to take place at the Ferragamo villa (apart from the family's own weddings), it was the result of intense discussions between Prasanna Bhaskar and Mohan. The former wanted Indian customers to experience the brand at its home in Florence; for the latter it would be one of the most unusual and aspirational venues she could suggest to a client. No pictures were ever featured in fashion glossies as there had been a strict contract between the family and the event managers. But those who attended said it was one of the most stunning events they had seen; dholak beats pulsated amid Italian luxury and Dior gowns sat at high tables with Sabyasachi lehngas. In those three days of wedding celebrations, the Ferragamo store in Florence did four months' worth of business. Everything that flew off the shelves was bought by Indians, NRIs, or those who had travelled from here.

Manishi Sanwal, GM, Indian sub-continent, LVMH watch and jewellery, who went on to join the brand's Duty Free Shopping division told me that if SRK was one big reason behind the brand's success in India, the other was their CEO Jean Christopher Baba. An India fan like Anna Zegna, Baba had backpacked across the country long and frequently enough to hear the shopping heartbeat of the Indian customer closely. Delhi's Chandni Chowk or Haridwar's Lakshman jhoola, he knows it all like the back of his hand and as Sanwal said 'understands why Indians, like the Chinese, are eager to cross the road even when the light is red'.

India's growth as a potential market has also made it a muse for design, like none other. Hermès has had a long relationship with India not only through close family friendships with the Sarabhai family in Ahmedabad, but also through the many India-inspired themes for their scarves, as well as an open admission by Jean Paul Gaultier, their former creative director, of his love for Indian textiles and drapes. In October 2011, a few months after opening a 3,000 square feet store at Mumbai's Fort area, they launched the Hermès sari. Limited edition saris made by a French saddler brand especially created for the Indian market is a new step. 'Designing these saris for India is like a light homage to the country,' said Patrick Thomas, chief executive of Hermès International to Indian journalists over lunch at the store. 'Hermès admires India and has a lot to learn from here,' he said strategically. Later to help Indian customers warm up to the dexterity they bring into their craft with the work of veteran artisans, Hermès brought down artisan Valerie Vasquez-Pascual to display how a Hermès Bearn wallet was made.

Other brands have also been paying homage to India in their own ways. Gucci, exactly like Hermès, displayed an artisan's corner in its Mumbai and Delhi stores. Open days for all customers were inaugurated after lavish cocktail evenings for their regular customers and the media. Gucci's PR in India filled the inboxes of journalists with old, black and white images displaying the artisanal strength of the brand. Bottega Veneta launched the Knot India clutch. Tomas Maier, the creative director of the brand, made a knotted box blending conventional Indian embroidery with new laser-cutting. In 2010, Tod's too launched an India clutch during Diwali and Dior dedicated a new limited edition watch—the Mumbai Christal with eight time zones—to Mumbai city. The launch coincided with the opening of the new Dior store in the Taj Mahal hotel. Canali brought in the Nehru jacket, Etro too launched India jackets and Hublot, an India watch. Louis Vuitton, in association with noted heritage expert Rajeev Sethi, created a Diwali 2010 collection of dresses made from Indian vintage saris, designed by Marc Jacobs. In 2012, Louboutin announced Bollywood style heels when he opened a store at DLF Emporio.

One day as we were changing after the yoga class Amira, referring to our earlier conversation, said, 'Babe, Karan Johar uses LV trunks as props on Koffee with Karan. He even gifts away LV products to his guests. Have you noticed?' Nobody could turn a blind eye to Bollywood's infatuation with LV. And yes, I had not only noticed the set decorated with LV trunks but had also heard from a LV insider that Johar was trying to exchange unused LV wallets given to him for his guests for 'other products'. It was a piece of gossip that I could never verify. Under CEO and Chairman Yves Carcelle, an astute strategist and an ardent Bollywood fan, LV had introduced a flurry of aspiration in Bollywood and KJo was just one of the devotees.

It wasn't just LV. Roping in Bollywood became a fail-safe blitzkrieg for most luxury brands. Tod's, Armani, and Hermès remained noticeable exceptions but by the end of 2011, Tod's gave in by inviting Kalki Koechlin and Kangna Ranaut for their events. For others, Bollywood is the least common denominator even today. Global CEOs of most luxury companies are sent detailed briefing reports about India that include 'bomb scares, developments on the Kashmir issue, visits of global political dignitaries, music launches, films and fairs, the weather and everything that makes it to the 9 o'clock news,' an insider said. The headline of these reports remains the same: What Bollywood Did Next. Ferragamo even invited Priyanka Chopra to choose a shoe style which they wanted to dedicate to her (and through her get to the flush Indian market). Priyanka picked a bejewelled stiletto studded with Swarovskis.

Most celebrities like KJo, love these products and the attention they get from luxury brands. A PR person told me how executives working in the luxury industry tend to quit their jobs as they are essentially turned into sophisticated riders who must take merchandize to the houses of film stars for trials. Once, a publicist intervening between me and her client—a cover girl who had been miffed at one of our shoots, because we didn't get the clothes she wanted—told me that the best way to make up was to gift her a luxury product. I sent a Jimmy Choo Tube mirror leather clutch. It worked. Representatives, however, told me not to get swept away by the perception that Bollywood stars were their biggest customers.

Jennifer, who is disdainful of them, spoke angrily of their rudeness. 'They don't respond to us when we greet them,' she said and complained that they wanted everything for free.

In obeisance to India, *The International Herald Tribune* called luxury giants and select designers to a conference on Sustainable Luxury at the Imperial in New Delhi in early 2009. The newspaper's fashion editor Suzy Menkes, one of the most respected fashion writers in the world, was the master of debates as designers Nicholas Ghesquiére, Dries Van Noten, and François-Henri Pinault, the CEO of PPR's Gucci group, among some of the biggest stars of global luxury, talked about working with India and 'responsible luxury'.

Sari or Starry was the dress code of the dazzling party that Pia Singh, director of DLF Universal which owns Emporio, threw for the conference members. Mogra flowers, earthen lamps, diyas on colourful rangolis and scented tea lights danced everywhere. Roberto Cavalli was so enthralled by the vintage Indian costumes displayed at the party that he could barely talk between his exclamations, and Anna Zegna of Zegna shone in a Hermès sari dress and jadau earrings.

That party opened my eyes to the infectiousness of luxury. This was a World Wide Web of desires, necessitating a certain lifestyle: rich and famous friends, lavish parties, common stories of global travel. A Bottega Veneta knotted clutch without a five star champagne evening would be miserable; as would be a Dior couture gown if it didn't have a red carpet to walk on.

But maybe I was wrong. 'Everyone is our target audience,' said Armani's former India GM, Atul Midha in rebuttal to my thesis. As with Tag Heuer and LV, the trickle down had really begun in earnest. Jennifer agreed with Midha. 'You are wrong, ma'am; all kinds of rich people now buy luxury goods. We are dependent on the business class from West Delhi more than the women you see in magazines. I have a list of customers from Punjabi Bagh who I have to call every few weeks with information on new arrivals. We also send things to their homes for viewings,' she told me.

One of the biggest client bases for luxury remains Punjab. Delhi is the biggest market for luxury goods because it pulls wealthy customers from the state, most notably from Ludhiana and Jalandhar. The Tag Heuer sales figures prove as much—its sales in Delhi between 2008 and 2010 were way ahead of all its other centres put together. At the same time, no brand underestimates the spending power of small towns like Haridwar or Sitapur in UP. Manishi Sanwal, of LVMH watches and jewellery, told me that an IAS couple from Sitapur who wanted to gift their son-in-law a luxury brand had recently bought a steel-gold watch for Rs 79,000.

There is also a demurring acceptance among global luxury brands to engage with our market on desi terms. Huge seasonal discounts, theme sales, press viewings, family sales, trunk shows in small towns, flying in big customers to luxury malls for private viewings of new collections or taking goods to the doorstep of customers—everything is now fair game for luxury in India. Now press releases sent by luxury houses pitch luxury products as gifts for Diwali, Raksha Bandhan, Holi, even Onam, Ganesh Chaturthi, and Navratri, with specific suggestions on what to buy.

Luxury watches, also the highest selling luxury products in India, are considered top choices as wedding return gifts to guests and as birthday presents sent to 'government officials'. All purchases are made in cash. (Incidentally, it was Jennifer who pointed out to me that most people who bought luxury paid in cash, not by credit card.) About hundred Dior watches sold every month in 2010. During the recession, watches above Rs 1 lakh were slightly affected but the category of Rs 60,000 to Rs 80,000, remained a very sought-after segment. Cash happy buyers gave luxury brands confidence. LVMH brought in haute couture Dior watches in yellow sapphire, amethyst and diamonds inspired from Dior couture. A limited edition watch for Rs 12,00,000 sold in 2010 as did two watches from the Sharon Stone limited edition line priced above Rs 9,00,000.

This was almost fifty times Jennifer's salary. As I got to know her better, I realized that the future played constantly on her mind. She was saving for her parents, to try to go to Dubai, and to get a credit card soon. She often mentioned marriage, though when I asked if Devendra had proposed to her, she would change the subject.

After two weeks of cold war—'not even a single sms, not even a word on Facebook,'—Devendra and Jennifer patched up. He went to pick her up after church one Sunday and promised to take her to see *Aisha* after it was released. But before that, Jennifer said she had to do a lot of apologizing.

'I took a red rose, an Archies card, and a Van Heusen shirt as a gift for him. I was guilty, it was my mistake,' she told me. Devendra was pleased. He told her that he was saving to buy her a good watch for her birthday. There was no luxury watch on Jennifer's wishlist. She just wanted an Espirit.

When I called to wish her on her birthday, I asked 'Did Devendra gift you that watch finally?'

'No, no, he had to contribute money for his younger brother's college admission. He was really sad about it,' she said defensively.

Which college? I asked.

'Kirori Mal in Delhi University,' she replied.

'The tuition fees there is barely Rs 3000 for a day scholar for the whole year,' I remarked.

'He said he will give me the watch after our first time,' she said her voice turning into a whisper.

'First time? You mean he will gift it to you when you have sex with him, is that what he is saying to you?' I asked, my feminist instincts ruffled. She changed the subject. 'Ma'am, do you think Sabyasachi will take an order for a white gown with a veil for my wedding?' 'He only makes lehngas and saris, no? And how much will it cost? I don't want to be a burden on my brother, he was fired from his call centre job during recession and had to take up this Costa Coffee thing.' Devendra was no longer her favourite subject.

Jennifer's blank slate was obviously being written upon. What had first started as a dislike for Bollywood stars had grown to include certain rich people. She had started getting hassled with the tantrums some wealthy people threw in stores. 'They think they are also buying us.' There was clearly a battle in her mind, probably fuelled by Devendra who never lost an opportunity to remind her that she was a 'foreigner logon ki chamchee'.

'Maybe this is the time you can attempt to understand Devendra's feelings and why your siblings tease you,' I said to her as she had begun bringing up the class divide a little too often. 'No, you don't understand, ma'am,' she said, changing the subject yet again and telling me how a lady had stormed out of their store a few days ago after an angry tirade on why the Delhi store never had new stuff.

By the end of 2011 the Indian government took a decision to allow foreign brands to take 100 percent ownership of stores that sold a single brand. But the Indian market has turned out to be a classical mousetrap according to luxury retailers. Dashing all presumptions that it will be another big party after China, the cultural complexities and fiscal laws here have thrown some brands off their track. Huge capital costs, high custom duties, steep rentals for retail spaces, media spends, the difficulty of finding suitable staff, which can be trained and retained, paucity of shopping spaces that allow for the creation of a luxury environment, and fickle customers who migrate from one brand to another make selling luxury in this market an uphill climb.

Society hostesses don't always carry original brands all the time, a well-known PR person told me. She named some who she knew brought back copies from Thailand and wore them as medals during parties. It's not just the Page 3 set. The parallel market is a huge threat; particularly in India.

Besides, limiting luxury brands to high end malls of which there are only a few, has hurt profits of many brands. That's why, said Patrick Thomas of Hermès, they set up shop in one of the old colonial buildings of Mumbai, away from what are seen as shopping ghettos. There are perhaps only four luxury spaces in India: Delhi's DLF Emporio Mall, which has a total retail space of 350,000 square feet, Bangalore's UB City Mall, spread over 10 acres and Mumbai's Taj Palace and Palladium, Phoenix Mills. Other stores are scattered, mostly in five star hotels like Chanel's first store at the Imperial. But now, even five star hotels are not seen as the best locations for brands as its stifles the brand positioning. At the same time, the biggest brands are reluctant to open shop alongside non-luxury ones in premium markets. In France, Hermès has a shop at Cannes on the beach road as well as in Manila on a shopping street. But in India, Bangalore's

Commercial Street, Mumbai's Bandra Bandstand or Colaba, or Delhi's Khan Market are still not seen as luxury environments.

Prasanna Bhaskar says that India was a marketing case study of a unique kind. 'The customer is caught between announcing the logo she invests in and the need to graduate into a mature buyer. Customers are still migrating from one brand to another and the merchandizing strategy has to be tweaked from season to season.'

Jennifer's assessment that a majority of shoppers at luxury malls including those who came from Punjab bought some brands just for the heck of it, not because they understood its sensibility, was validated by brand representatives. The shopping budget of some ladies was exhausted within an hour of reaching Emporio. Then with the remaining cash, they would go to stores of Indian designers. The purchase depended on the visibility of the logo rather than its authentication card.

Migrating customers mirror the confusions of a new market. Jennifer had earlier told me that one lady had offered her Rs 2000 for the day as fees if she guided her about how to shop or what to shop for. It was a good opportunity for her to make money on the side, but she was unable to do it on a working day.

'Who was the lady?' I asked. 'Why did she need a shopping assistant?'

'The lady was almost bald, ma'am, she had such thin hair and you could see patches of bare scalp through it, but she wore a beautiful Just Cavalli dress.'

After that offer, Jennifer made up her mind to try shopping assistance on her off days. Not at Emporio, but at other malls. She had a long list of customers from her store to start dialing and ask if someone needed a shopping guide. 'I can do some research on other brands too,' she said excitedly.

She looked the part too. Since our first meeting there had been a subtle change in her dress sense. Her look had moved on from ordinary middle class casual to casual chic. She had invested in strappy, silver-coloured Gladiator sandals. She would often use a dark blue pencil (M.A.C. she said) under her eyes and had got her hair trimmed in a jagged, modern cut. The clip from her hair had vanished as had metallic hoops from her ears. She would wear faux pearl studs, white shirts with blue jeans and had acquired a pair of Ray-Ban aviator sunglasses.

All luxury brands give five to seven pieces of accessories to their staff free of cost. This is to enable them to experience the brand and be seen in it. Additionally, each staff member can buy seven more pieces (accessories or clothes) each season on a special staff discount. For seniors like store managers, these discounts go up to forty percent. For Jennifer it would be twenty five percent, but she couldn't avail of the facility much as her salary didn't allow her to. Yet, she enjoyed what the store manager would give her and proudly showed it off to her friends and to me.

She looked happier than I had first seen her and had greater confidence. The very way in which she would order her cold coffee told me that Jennifer was ready to slug it out alone in Dubai.

Prasanna's words echoed in my mind. 'You won't believe the transformation some of these people go through once they start taking their career in luxury seriously,' she had said.

I believed it because it was right in front of me.

Once when I went to Emporio for a store event, Jennifer introduced me to one of her friends, the same girl I had seen with her some months back in the ladies' room. Archana worked in an Indian designer's store on the third floor of the same mall and there was a marked difference in the way the two girls behaved, ate, sipped water or sat. Jennifer was clearly the more sophisticated of the two, while Archana wore costume jewellery with her uniform and her nail paint was chipped.

Since Jennifer treated me as a confidante, I asked the girls whether some of them working at Emporio came looking for jobs at this mall not as careers but to find rich men to marry. This is what I had been told by a very senior brand manager who had had repeated staff issues. 'DLF Emporio is becoming a pickup joint,' he had said.

Jennifer was visibly hurt. A thin veil of tears formed in her eyes while Archana looked accusingly at me. 'I didn't expect this from you, ma'am. We are middle class people but we have our values,' she added. I apologized profusely.

Despite the hiccups, the size of the luxury market in India has grown. It is estimated to be worth $30 billion by 2015. India's domestic sales of high end jewellery, handbags, shoes, watches, and clothing are estimated at $2.2 billion, just a fraction of the sales in China. Yet the annual sales growth is 20 percent. 'Despite terrorism and the market downturn, the India numbers are impressive,' Atul Midha told me. One day, I walked into the Bottega Veneta store at Emporio without any appointment and chatted with the sales person. He told me that most clutches were sold long before they arrived in the shop and showed me the order list. The Caba, priced above Rs 3 lakh, as well as the Mineral Knot priced between Rs 80,000 to Rs 3.75 lakh were among the hot picks. You could see the seasonal look-books or choose one from a photo album with the rich and famous carrying Bottega clutches. There were pictures of Preity Zinta, Shilpa Shetty, Sonali Bendre, and Nita Ambani carrying them.

It was Louis Vuitton that had surged ahead in India and elsewhere. By July 2010, the group had 2,468 stores worldwide with 495 in Asia where it recorded the strongest growth momentum and profitability in the last few years. In India, the growth rate was pegged above 20 percent in the last year.

Nevertheless LV has a challenging time ahead. The company initially announced that they were going to set up a Vuitton store in every Indian city with a population of 10 million plus by 2010. But that didn't materialize. China has thirty LV stores; India has only four. The success of its 'loud' bags (LV sales people can point these out with a snap of their fingers) has become a cliché. Once loved as a luxury brand by the aristocracies, its democratization has distanced the classes from it. Most Indian designers, too, seem underwhelmed by the LV logo on bags, saying it looks jarring with embellished Indian couture.

The Indian market is evolving fast, migration from brand to brand notwithstanding. Those who hankered after LV bags now don't want to be seen wearing them. Some customers are leaning towards timeless brands like Hermès and the Birkin, visible among the Indian socialite circle. It may become—if it hasn't already—as commonplace as the monogrammed LV bag.

India has one of the largest numbers of retail outlets in the world. Overall, clothing is now a $33.2 billion dollar industry and the second largest segment of India's spending chart. From the setting up of India's first mall in 1999, there has been a steady migration of retail from the traditional to the organized format, the trend sharp and visible in the urban areas. A report called The Bird of Gold on the rise of India's consumer market by international major, McKinsey and Co, predicted that there would be more than 570 million middle class Indians by 2025 and India would become the world's fifth-biggest consumer market, seven places up since the mid–2000s. At the Mint Luxury Conference 2012, Neelesh Hundekari, principal at management consultant firm AT Kearney said that the market was growing at 20 percent and it would be about $15 billion (around Rs 76,500 crore today) by 2015.

The most discerning luxury buyers are no longer interested in being seen in magazines or at events which are beamed on Page 3; they have moved on to a completely upscale tier of spending. A brand representative told me that the King of Morvi wanted only exclusive Chaumet watches. Tag, Zenith, and Dior were beneath his status and taste. 'You will never find out what the really rich, really want,' he added.

Unfortunately, while LV did a lot to position itself through art, culture, royalty, and Bollywood, it has perhaps forgotten that its distinction lies in its old values. Once when arguing with Amira about LV—she the good cop and I the devil's advocate—I relented and told her about the brand's test laboratories, which are high-tech torture chambers for its goods.

I recalled my visit to Asnières, LV's private museum and special orders workshop near Paris, telling her about the long hours of hand-stitched precision that went into the making of a single bag. At another LV factory, handbags are bombarded with ultraviolet rays to test their resistance to fading. Zippers on bags are tugged open and shut 5000 times. An artificial hand with a Vuitton charm bracelet on the wrist is shaken vigorously to make sure none of the charms fall. Another arm lifts a handbag off the floor, and drops it. The bag, loaded with weight, is lifted and dropped over and over again, for four days, to test the journey it will undertake as our companion.

Unlike provocative Vuitton campaigns that show celebrities and models draped over luggage seducing the viewer into a good life, this agnipariksha was a captivating way to understand the brand's worth. Amira became google-eyed and looked at the white and black LV Damier bag in her hand fondly adding that she wished magazines told customers about all these things. But to retain loyal fans like Amira, LV will have to re-strategize its moves in the Indian market and elevate itself from simply being the most visible brand.

Luxury sellers find India a country of perplexingly shifting sands. A line from a resoundingly powerful Louis Vuitton Core Value campaign video Where Will Life Take You may work as a metaphor: 'A true journey is one that brings us face to face with ourselves.'

Jennifer had to face up to the truth. Her relationship with Devendra wasn't going anywhere. They had repeated fights over her job. He asked her to choose. She kept her job. After they broke up, she won a Vodafone SMS contest and got a free holiday for two to Goa. She went with her sister.

The last time I phoned her, she said she had quit her job at Emporio and was making preparations to move to Dubai. She recently wrote me an email; there was a quote by Coco Chanel at the end of her note, beneath her signature.

*Names changed

The Ludhiana Ladies

'Fashion is the science of appearances, and it inspires one with the desire to seem rather than to be.'

—E. H. Chapin, in the *Living Words*

Maharaja Hotel, Ludhiana.
10:30 am

As I entered the hotel lobby, I saw a lady in a scarlet dress and gold stilettos. She was led by an oversized Fendi bag. The diamonds in her ears were sparkling bullets and a series of solitaires glided on her arms as two diamond bangles. Her mahogany hair was prettily blow dried, her nails spoke French, and her make up was flawless. She didn't have the air of a visiting NRI nor did she seem to have walked out of Pankaj Mishra's *Butter Chicken in Ludhiana*. Before I could place her, I saw another slim built and tall woman, her white Armani shirt tucked into a pair of clinging True Religion jeans and cinched with a Coach belt. Jimmy Choo heels and a Gucci Bag added to her elegance. Her glistening hair was pulled back in a long ponytail. A gorgeous sardarni, she could be from anywhere in the world, I said to myself; except for the giveaway diamonds in her ears and a pair of diamond bangles on her wrists.

Customers at Radhika Dhawan's First Row, a travelling exhibition of designer wear, these two Ludhianvi women stormed into my notes like gusty hot wind on a summer afternoon in Punjab. They left me speechless, groping for words.

In the next few hours, I saw more international brands in the form of shoes, bags, pins, clips, sunglasses, T-shirts, jeans, belts, watches than I had seen in months. I had seen LV wraps only in magazines before this, but I saw one here. Groups of fashion obsessed women seemed to have walked out of magazine pages into the small banquet hall. Roberto Cavalli tops, Dior bags, Jimmy Choo shoes, Armani dresses, Rock & Republic jeans, Gucci belts, Chanel clutches, Bvlgari sunglasses, Burberry scarves, Vertu phones. Most wore six different labels from head to toe. A majority wore tight fitting designer jeans with the top tucked in and a belt. The rest wore dresses. Watches were mostly Cartier with gold or metallic straps. Infants were wrapped in Burberry blankets and mothers-in-laws came in Monisha Jaising kurtis carrying LV bags.

Everyone wore diamonds on their ears, fingers, arms. A pair of diamond bangles was a constant. As were Swarovski crystals. On T-shirts, cell phone trinkets, shoes and chappals, even on bra straps. One lady wore a sexy, off-shoulder indigo blue Cavalli dress with Swarovski bra straps on display.

'Hello, hello, listen, where did you get these bra straps from?' I overheard someone asking her.

'Bangkok,' came the reply.

'Do you have an extra pair you can sell me?' said the inquisitive first voice.

'No, but I can get it for you next time. You will also find them in Manish market in Mumbai,' said the lady before striding away on her silver heels, flicking back her hair self-consciously.

I looked around. *They all* looked like clones of each other.

Where was Divya Dhanda, I sighed, collapsing on a plastic chair near the payment counter.

I felt miserably out of place. In a white and gold Dhakai sari with a green Sabyasachi blouse, I didn't know if I was over-dressed, under-dressed or what. I felt and looked like a behenji. The ladies were glancing at me too—I was so obviously an odd visitor.

Where *was* Divya Dhanda?

The sale was picking up. 'Tight-fitting dresses sell most,' said Radhika, a girl in her early twenties who started First Row after finishing her fashion education, the last leg of it in London. Now based in Mumbai she runs a fashion portal and also takes previous season's clothes made by Indian designers to small cities and towns to sell them at slashed prices. In most towns she works in partnership with a local socialite, who chips in by drawing up a dashing guest list. The spoils are shared in proportion of the work the two put in.

In Ludhiana, Radhika Dhawan's partner was her namesake: Radhika Gupta, a 31-year-old mother of two in logo screaming, figure-hugging, Roberto Cavalli jeans with a Cavalli belt, Gucci T-shirt and Coach Shoes.

'Designer' is an infectious word in Ludhiana. In this group, I couldn't spot one person in non-branded clothes. 'Even Mumbai is more conservative when it comes to dressing. So I keep the edgier pieces for Ludhiana,' said Dhawan. Punjab may be the land of the salwar kameez or the 'suit' as it is called here, but designer wear had edged the traditional garment out of wish lists and it now seemed to have second citizen status. The designer boom was also singularly responsible for the kurta being thrown out of favour. It was now the kurti that vowed the older aunties who wore embellished ones with black trousers. Saris attracted a certain clientele but only if they were designer made, in chiffon or crepe, were crystal encrusted, and came with sexy cholis that had plunging necklines. It didn't need a Laila Tyabji to see that the Dastkar society with its consortium of handloom weavers, and craftsmen could never dream of having a Nature Bazaar exhibition in Ludhiana and sell Bhagalpuri silks. This was a different market. As Dhawan pointed out, the fight among the younger crowd was for dresses and gowns.

I noticed a few trays of costume jewellery displayed on a table covered with a white table cloth—cocktail rings, charm bracelets and long, stringy necklaces, but nobody was really interested in buying them. The women picked up the rings like nuts that might taste nice if bitten into, but on second thoughts dropped them back on the trays. These were well to do women dripping with diamonds and faux stuff didn't exactly stoke their desire. They breathlessly asked for big names in Indian labels and Dhawan added that Rohit Bal was the bestselling designer among them. Younger designers whose names had still not been splashed by fashion glossies as must-haves were still to make a debut in the wardrobes of the Ludhiana ladies. Once they were mentioned in magazines or endorsed by Bollywood, their clothes too would start rolling off the hangers, someone explained.

'Hi, where are you from? Are you a designer?' A lady asked me inquisitively.

'Ah, er, no, I am just...'

'Are you from Delhi or Mumbai?'

'I am from...'

'Okay, no problem ji. Listen, can you tell me where I can get the black net and sequins sari with a fuschia border that Katrina Kaif wears in *Singh is King*? The one she wears when she and Akshay Kumar sing "Dil Kho Gaya, Ho Gaya Kisee Ka", that song baba, the one shot around the pyramids in Egypt...'

'Me? But I have no idea...'

'Oho, the sari that looks like a Manish Malhotra. It is Manish Malhotra? I really want to wear that for my sister-in-law's engagement ceremony,' she went on.

'Don't you think that sari will look better than the usual Armani dress? My friends say I should wear Armani with a beret and a pair of nice, lacy gloves like Sonam Kapoor in *Aisha* instead of a sari-shaari, but what do you think, what's good for an engagement party? The bride's family is from Mumbai, I want to make a solid impression,' she hurried on, barely allowing me to get a word out.

An Armani dress was 'usual' for her? I hoped my eyebrows didn't rise involuntarily. Beret and gloves? In Ludhiana?

As I chatted with her at the payment counter, Dhawan excused herself to rush towards the makeshift trial room set inside the banquet hall, her thick black Swarovski wedge slippers making a rubbery sound. A gaggle of giggling ladies was trying on clothes, taking turns to come out and show them to a slender young girl, surely the leader of the chic pack. She also looked the youngest of the lot.

'Yes, no, not sure, can't say,' she went. Right, they chimed.

'See this, see this, I can wear this with the Burberry stole that Biji gave me on Holi,' one young girl said holding up an ochre Shantanu and Nikhil tunic-shirt.

'No, it doesn't suit your skin tone at all, and I think you should buy something more eye-catching if you want to use that dull stole,' said the team leader, diverting her attention to another lady who was holding up a purple dress.

Divya Dhanda, someone alerted me, was finally walking in. She had been declared my Ludhiana minder over the phone by Gita Bector, a popular local socialite. Gita was apparently the symbol of the Ludhiana Ladies club and if I met her, I won't need anyone else or so I was counseled by the representative of an Italian luxury brand.

'Gita sends the best fruits from her farms to all her friends every season. Homemade jams too.'

'Gita goes to Milan twice a year to shop.'

'Babe, you should meet Gita, you have no idea the kind of money these Ludhiana women spend on luxury brands.'

'Gita is the Gauri Khan of Ludhiana.'

Coordinating with Gita Bector was like chasing an investigative story. She was always busy, travelling, or entertaining and asked me to send her an email explaining the purpose of my visit. I did and booked my train tickets after much back and forth, convincing her that I would like to visit Ludhiana while a designer exhibition was on.

But just the day before I boarded the Shatabdi to Ludhiana from Delhi, Gita called me to say that she had to suddenly travel to Mumbai and had worked out a minder for me.

'Meet Divya Dhanda. She will look after you. She is just what you are looking for,' said Gita on the phone.

Wrong. Divya was more. Age: 40. Two children: 17 and 12 years of age. Waist size: 24. Hair colour: Auburn. Bag: Prada. Jeans: Rock & Republic. Belt: Dolce & Gabbana. T-shirt: Monisha Jaisingh with the words Maharani embroidered on it in large crystals. Bracelet: Beaded Venetian glass. Earrings: diamond solitaires but not bullet sized. Face: glossy nude lips, peaches and cream complexion. Demeanour: Thoughtful. Diamond bangles: absent.

Divya Dhanda, a graduate of Chandigarh College of Architecture, is now a much envied social hostess. Married at 20 to a Punjabi businessman from the family who owns Sadem Industries that manufactures and exports bicycle parts, Divya worked for a couple of years as a consulting architect before evolving into the glamorous role of a rich wife. She also worked as director in the exports department of her husband's company looking after communication with all the customers abroad. This meant traveling frequently with her husband all over Europe and to the US. He for business; she for pleasure. She had all the money she could ask for, to indulge and that's how she says she developed an eye for fashion.

Divya had come to pick me up from Maharaja Hotel for lunch. After introductions—me staring at her incredibly small waist and she trying to suppress her surprise at meeting a sari-clad Delhiite—she led me to her self-driven Mercedes. It was to be an Italian lunch and over dainty salad nibbles, Divya became my sutradhar for this story.

Before this visit, a conversation with the managing director of Giorgio Armani India had alerted me to Ludhiana's fashion revelry. He had casually mentioned a trunk show here, the recreation of a Giorgio Armani store ambience in a luxury van and his utter surprise at seeing women in sizes considerably smaller than what they had anticipated. Let's not underestimate the housewife demographic, he had said, when I asked him to describe the potential Armani customer in India.

To sell in the Indian market, which has proved challenging for international brands, most luxury labels have had to shed their hauteur of exclusivity. Now, they seasonally take their wares to the doorsteps of rich customers. Ludhiana is one of the most important destinations on the lists of brands, if not *the* most crucial for assured sales.

When I met Divya, everything the Armani GM had said acquired a form. She could have just walked out of an Armani store. She told me that since 2006, she had begun to organize fund-raising exhibitions in cities across Punjab for Nirdosh, a charitable organization. By bringing in a variety of entrepreneurs to sell lifestyle wares to an exhibition cum sale, she could offer business and an assured footfall to her clients. A year later, she was invited to host a trunk show for Jimmy Choo shoes and bags in Ludhiana. It was a runaway success. Soon, she co-hosted Judith Leiber, De Grisogno, Jimmy Choo, and Bottega Veneta shows. These were followed by Mirari Jewellers, Adarsh Gill and Alpana Gujral. Divya was chosen because of her style, her ease with luxury and her now proven ability to convert new customers to the cause of fashion. These trunk shows evoked a bigger response than what the brands had anticipated. They unleashed a new wave of aspiration that could be instantly addressed in the money-soaked city. The tide turned soon–both for Ludhiana and for the brands. While fashion houses needed divas like Divya to make intimate inroads into traditional societies, the ladies needed the labels to overwrite their lives as wives which had begun boring them.

Girls married into rich families in Ludhiana are all well-educated. Many of them are Welhamites; some have studied abroad. They are aware of designer brands and their different statements, can hold their own on a talk on what to buy in luxury. All they needed was the availability to divert their spending away from Jamavaar shawls, gold jewellery, and 'heavy, kadhai wale suits'.

It is an open secret that it is the wealthy, Punjabi clientele that helped international luxury brands kick off and sustain sales in India. 'Our brand sells forty to fifty percent more in Delhi (at Emporio Mall) because of customers from Punjab—Amritsar, Jalandhar, Chandigarh and Ludhiana,' a brand head said. Everyone I met working with a luxury brand here agreed to this without a moment's doubt. 'We survive because of Punjab,' a Fendi representative added. 'The trunk shows are a complete sellout, we have learnt to take bigger stocks for Ludhiana,' someone added about a luxury watch exhibition where the brand had run out of pieces even before it was early evening.

The Punjabi culture of 'show-sha' or conspicuous consumption that formerly shone in lavish dowries, the size and splendour of weddings, honeymoon destinations (Switzerland then) or the value of gifts exchanged during the first lohri (Makar Sankranti), the first karva chauth or the first Diwali of a married couple, now plays itself out through luxury labels. Strappy gowns have usurped traditional phulkari suits and Kashmiri kaani shawls.

When Divya was a young bride, she says her friends and peers were crazy about salwar kameezes in expensive brocades and silks—Rs 3500 for a metre—accessorized with large diamonds to announce their status. That is passé now. The attention had completely shifted to luxury brands. A newlywed bride would still wear heavy Indian garments in the first few weeks after her wedding but she couldn't possibly be spotted without a luxury bag or branded accessories. The clamour wasn't for distinguished goods here; it was for bigger, better, shinier, and more expensive stuff than what the others had. Everything was evaluated on a comparative scale.

When a newlywed couple was invited to the many dinners hosted by relatives, the bride's brands were firmly assessed from top to toe. Diamonds and Tarun Tahiliani saris would get a nod, but LV bags and Jimmy Choos would fetch more marks.

When I asked someone why all the women wore jeans with the shirt tucked in, the response was that a tucked in shirt makes space for a belt, yet another place to show off a fashion label. The label is important, don't you get it, Radhika Gupta chided me. Fashion may be a big fuss here but it is not the only revelry in a society which also aspires for big cars, farmhouses with rare Persian rugs and wooden floors, super deluxe holidays, and big ticket lifestyle items. 'Some of us have to hire more than one nanny for our babies because others have two or three nannies per child. My mother-in-law doesn't like my son to be handled by a nanny but insists that I have two so that 'society' doesn't look down on us,' a 23-year-old Ludhiana girl told me.

I had also visited Hoshiarpur earlier and had noticed a similar frenzy about labels among families there. Invited by one of the ladies to join her family for breakfast one morning, I noticed a mismatch between this obsession for branded worth and the overall cultural language of the family. Aloo parathas, thick, creamy curd, tall glasses of lassi, tangy mango pickle, children running around, mum-in-chief Biji turning up to say a warm hello and Papaji patting my head. None of them looked like Armani or Tod's customers. Except my hostess, who wore, well, what else, but tight fitting blue jeans with a floral top, high heeled gladiators and Chanel chains first thing in the morning. I was afraid she would slip on the tiled floors. The tiles had geometric designs on them, and combined with rugs in multiple colours and patterns, they looked cluttered, too dressed up. As were the sofas—they wore loud, silken prints.

None of the other ladies in the household except Biji wore a salwar kameez. The domestic help wore a long tunic with tights. The salwar kameez, called the 'Punjabi' in Gujarat as well as in South India is considered a liberating garment there for married women in traditional families who are now 'allowed' to wear it. But back in its motherland in Punjab, the Punjabi is treated as an enslaving garment by wealthy women.

'Save the salwar,' would be a relevant campaign in Punjab I would later tell cultural expert Rajeev Sethi of the Asian Heritage Foundation in Delhi.

Back in Ludhiana, Divya wasn't even keen on discussing handlooms and craft. 'No, no, no, nobody likes all that,' she said.

I had clearly brought up the wrong subject.

'Oh, okay, I did wear Kanjeevarams and all that, when I was newly married but no more even though I love them still,' said Divya, trying to balance her views on second thought. She sounded unconvincing.

I tried to wear a more neutral expression.

Once billed as the Manchester of India and now chided as the Crumbling Manchester by business writers, Ludhiana is home to one of the wealthiest industrialist communities of the country. Named after the Lodi dynasty, the town was a part of Maharaja Ranjit Singh's dynasty in the eighteenth century. In modern India, it is known for hosiery, woollen garments, woollen yarn, acrylic knitwear, readymade garments, cycles, cycle parts, and machine tools. Wool is its biggest industry—with Oswal a familiar name to customers across India.

Now a congested but prospering town, with a population of more than thirty-five lakh, it is strewn, like other towns in the country, with star hotels and malls for the rich—night shelters and hospitals for the poor are conspicuous with their absence.

The wild spending behaviour of its wealthy class is not just a familiar anecdote for Yves Carcelle, CEO and Chairman of Louis Vuitton, but also for Wilfried Aulbur, managing director and CEO of DiamlerChrysler, makers of Mercedes Benz. 'The DNA of Mercedes is very similar to the DNA of people in Ludhiana!' Albur had told a journalist. Ludhiana reportedly has the highest number of Mercs in India with most of them bought in the last five years. In 2007, it had 550 Mercs with the S Class series that cost Rs 10 million and above, the most in demand.

Like cars, the indulgence of its upper crust in international luxury labels is higher than anywhere else, with the Reddys of Hyderabad notching a close second. Label obsession and indulgence has lent the Ludhiana Ladies a distinctive look, easily recognizable because of the number of brands they load on themselves at one go. This is different from other cities, even from Chandigarh, which is right next door, making the job of a social hostess hosting luxury brand sales, exhibitions, or parties enviable in elite circles where married women are discouraged from pursuing careers. Those who do work do so as a part time indulgence in their husband's businesses. No wonder being a social hostess is the most coveted top job.

If you are a social hostess, your worth is incremental, even at a party, the new symbol of ascendance. If the fattened Butter Chicken Punjabi wedding was the theatre of excess in Punjab earlier, now it is the designer kitty party—women's kitties, couple kitties, mother-in-law kitties. Which celebrity came as a guest, who was the MC of the evening, who catered the food and what liquor was served determines the pecking order. Nobody carries a fake label; it would be suicide for their reputations. There is a kitty in town, as I was to later find out, where girls were expected to carry bills with the new bags and luxury items they bought, to show the peer group that their purchases were original. Even men have kitties. The Ludhiana Radhika (Dhawan's local partner for the exhibition) told me that her father-in-law was a member of four kitty groups. Cricket kitties, card kitties, badminton kitties, the list is endless. Added to them are anniversary bashes, biannual get togethers hosted by influential families, kids' birthdays, Diwali parties, and Ludhiana would soon vie for India's party capital.

During a later chat, Gita Bector told me (yes, I did finally meet her) that conspicuous consumption was on a new high in Ludhiana. 'It is all about emulating Delhi and Mumbai society life,' she said. So if one lady invited well-known Delhi nutritionist

Shikha Sharma from Delhi for a kitty, another got a Salsa dancer from Mumbai. 'Now people bring event planners as well as celeb chefs. Flying in a veejay or a deejay is common and don't be surprised if you see Bipasha Basu welcoming you at a party—that's what happened at a wedding party recently. It's all *paise ka khel,*' said Gita.

The two Radhikas could not agree more. 'Ludhiana is Delhi on steroids,' said one. The other said that the rampage of consumption included gymming, swimming, power yoga, and frequent trips to the beauty parlour. 'Professional make up and blow drying of hair before every party is normal,' said Radhika Gupta. 'We dress up at parlours if there is a wedding, a sangeet or a Diwali gathering, especially if we have to wear saris. Most girls now need help with tying saris so better do it at parlours. It's normal,' she repeated.

Remarkably, through a combination of starvation diets and regular workouts, the Ludhiana Ladies have managed to challenge the natural Punjabi body, which is buxom and full-figured. The average female body here is now sculpted, perfectly suited for tight fitting jeans. The salwar kameez body is out. Most women have achieved this with the help of personal trainers who charge upto Rs 25,000 a month, about a hundred percent more than in Delhi.

The Ludhiana wives can afford it. The earnings of a wife here range from Rs 50,000 to Rs 2 lakh per month, and are dependent on her age, social standing, and family wealth. It comes in the form of pocket money doled out by the husband or mother-in-law. Add to that the kitty party fund, Divya reminded me, which is a minimum saving of Rs 5000 per kitty. The average shopping budget for every lady I met was at least Rs 50,000 per month, going up to a couple of lakhs in some cases.

Divya seemed to enjoy her new role of my advisor and by the next day had begun second guessing my questions, giving me just the kind of information I needed.

'If a woman gives birth to a male child, the mother-in-law gifts her two diamond bangles,' she told me.

'What would they cost?' I asked.

'Above eight to ten lakhs—depending on how many pointers they are,' she said assuming I would know the financial politics behind the carats of these bullets. Pointers must be carats I figured.

'Return gift for female child?' I ventured tentatively.

'Diamond gifts too but of lower value.'

Radhika Gupta told me she got Rs 50,000 pocket money every month. Her husband never questioned what she did with it. 'Instead of buying a few things from Indian designers every time I step into a store, I save and buy myself a luxury label every few months. I don't want five kurtis or Kaani shawls, I want a LV wrap,' she said.

Her wardrobe and that of her children spoke for it. She showed me pictures of her kids on the cell phone. Her daughter had been dressed up as a princess for her first birthday party, complete with a customized silk gown and a tiara.

In these circles, fashion is as much about dressing games, as about how much your husband earns, how much pocket money you get, how broadminded your mother-in-law is ('does she allow strapless dresses?'), where your children study (London?), and what their pocket money is. Most adolescents get upto Rs 10,000 per month. Unable to duck the hip wave, Ludhianvi men have turned dandies too and splurge on branded belts, shoes, wallets, ties, and shirts. No wonder, Armani, and Louis Vuitton love Ludhiana.

Late evening on the day that Radhika Dhawan had her exhibition of Indian garments, I was sitting around watching her and her friends pack the leftover things in boxes when one of the clients I had seen in the morning came back with her husband to 'exchange' a purchase.

'My husband doesn't like this colour. It is also a bit transparent; I won't be able to wear it. Can you take it back?' she asked Radhika.

Her husband, a turbaned Sikh stood by glumly in loose blue-grey cargo pants, a pale yellow checked shirt, and Tod's moccasins. He had good taste in clothes alright but was brusque with his wife even in our presence.

'Chalo jaldi karo, just take something else,' he told her glancing at his watch and fiddling with his cellphone, twirling his car keys with his forefinger, ignoring Radhika completely. The man's car keys dangled from a slick key chain in steel in the shape of a nude, female figure.

The couple exchanged murmurs and in the next five minutes, the lady chose another garment.

'It will cost you Rs 2570 more,' said Radhika.

The man pulled out a wad of notes from his wallet, counted them and almost threw them on the table.

'Chalo, chalo,' he said again and walked out before his wife could collect the bag. She accepted the change from Radhika Dhawan, thanked her, and followed Mr Yellow Funk out.

Buying fashion is not enough, buying the latest is important, so wives often zip out to Delhi to shop at the Emporio Mall. For 'exclusives', they wait till their next trip to Europe. Not all husbands though are as nitpicking as Mr Yellow Funk.

I had kept in touch with some of the women I met in Ludhiana. I phoned one of them to ask if she had attended the semi-final ICC Cricket World Cup match between India and Pakistan in Mohali in March 2011. Quite a few photos of beautifully attired Punjabi women in the stands standing next to Bollywood attendees had come my way through the Chandigarh bureau of *The Indian Express* where I now work, and I was keen to find out if K had shopped especially for the match.

She had. K had bought herself 'nothing much, just an Anamika Khanna outfit,' she said. 'I had to wear something terrific but Indian, darling,' she told me over the phone, 'my favourite stars were in Mohali that day.'

K was a Bollywood fan and had told me she did whatever she could to get near a star. 'Please, please, please, can I sit with you in front row at a fashion week once? Just once? I will especially fly to Delhi for it. Please, please, pleassseee, call me when Deepika Padukone walks the ramp. I want to see her. I want to get my photo clicked with her. And with Salman Khan. And with Shah Rukh Khan. And with...'

Then rather abruptly, she cut her own rant to say, 'Achha, by the way, we are coming to Delhi tomorrow, why don't you join us for lunch?

'Won't your husband mind?' I asked.

'Not at all.'

He minded though. They called me to regret the lunch invitation but in less than two hours, I would get another call from K, who asked me if I would like to meet her for a coffee at 360, the restaurant at The Oberoi.

K had just bought herself a scarf from the Hermès store in The Oberoi when I reached that afternoon. She was in white, ankle length trousers and a crisp white shirt (I could bet it was Rajesh Pratap but I thought better than asking her). She had accessorized it with a well-chosen LV belt. Her bag was a red patent LV too. She looked her part opening up the nuances of this story in my head once again.

'Somebody must make a film on the Ladies of Ludhiana—you women look so gorgeous,' I remarked as we shook hands.

'Sorry about calling off lunch. R and I had a fight,' she said, as we chose a table with the swimming pool in view.

'Can you get me butter with some kind of masala bread?' she asked the waiter, snapping her ring-loaded slender fingers in dismissal soon as the order was placed. Nail polish scarlet red. Wow, nice with the white outfit, I said reminding myself that I was once again slipping into observing people's clothes and looks more than their moods.

'He is having an affair with some chick here in Delhi. She is also married,' said K. 'The deal is that I do what I want, buy what I want, go wherever I want, but I shouldn't nag him,' she said.

'Has it been going on for long?'

'For more than a year at least.'

Irony now sat between us on the table with her bread and butter. K had found out about her husband's 'chick', through a note that was delivered with a packed Hugo Boss shirt to their house in Ludhiana.

'Love you in blue. Wear this till you take it off for me.' K's eyes filled with tears as she repeated this to me but she didn't allow them to spill.

Back in Ludhiana, the monthly shopping wishlist is often made by looking at fashion and film glossies. Bollywood has the final say. Divya, too, had told me that every morning, she logged into the Internet to look at the Page 3 in Delhi city supplements of *The Times of India* and *Hindustan Times* to keep herself abreast with new places in Delhi to eat, entertain, shop, and find out about art shows and cultural events. Fashion magazines have an eager audience in Ludhiana; women don't buy one, they buy a few of them.

'Nothing is exclusive anymore, my dear, not even what Tina Ambani has,' chirped Radhika Gupta. 'What money can buy, we can buy too,' she said.

Radhika Gupta who sounds like a material girl in my copy is actually a sweet, warm, down-to-earth person. She did not baulk at my intrusiveness. She offered to take me around in her car to diamond stores so that I could understand who bought what, for how much and for whom in the family. 'Diamond merchants know all the secrets,' she said. She would eventually be the one to drive me through one of the local markets because I insisted on seeing the working class in the city.

'What about women who are not privileged as all of you are?' I asked.

'What about them? Nothing. Just leave it na,' she said.

I liked the way she said it without any trace of arrogance. So I left it.

If Divya Dhanda exposed me to the external worth and social grammar of the socialite wives in Ludhiana, Radhika Gupta gave me a peek into their personalities.

In ways that were expressed differently, both Divya and Radhika who belonged to different generations (one was just 30 plus, the other 40) and different income groups—if I could read them correctly through their labels—were anxious about similar things. The big question remained the same: how to distinguish yourself in a society that was saturated with wealth.

According to cultural anthropologist Prof Shiv Viswananthan 'The elite of Ludhiana do live out a parody of Paris. It is a simplified fashion capital, where playfulness and competitiveness turn into a giant kitty party, a game from which there is no respite. A nanny becomes an accessory. This is a tribe which has worked out a stunning grammar for itself,' said Viswanathan, urging me to look at Ludhiana women as birds of a paradise where every feather was a luxury brand.

It was at Bakes and Beans, a centrally located coffee shop in Ludhiana where Isabelle Jain showed me the reverse side of this fashionable tale. Perky sandwiches, dainty doughnuts, smiling staff, long and short coffees give this place the deceptive look of a coffee bar. It could well be called The Wives Cafe. They all flock here every single afternoon in LBDs or jeans, hair prettily styled, nude lipsticks, Lady Dior bags.

Isabelle carried a black Lady Dior. She came wearing a white shirt with blue jeans, tall black heels, a simple gold chain and golden hoops in her ears, enamel bangles on her arms. Her brunette hair was left loose and soft bangs framed her face. A solitaire sparkled on her ring finger. She said she had dressed up for me.

'I was told that the former editor of *Marie Claire* is writing a book on fashion. Naturally, I dressed up,' she said with disarming candour, admitting that she didn't expect to see me in a sari.

This time my sari was a printed crepe worn with a strappy blouse. It still didn't seem to match the mood of the moment.

I had also spent some time the previous evening after Radhika Dhawan's exhibition to polish my nails in the hotel room.

Thankfully, Isabelle Jain, a flesh and blood combination of a French Ludhianvi was almost relieved upon seeing my clothes. She said it would be easier for her to share her thoughts if I wasn't playing the dress-up game.

After completing an MA in Tourism, Isabelle lived in Dubai, working for the Emirates Airlines as an airhostess followed by a teaching job at the Frankfinn institute. It was in the US that she met her husband, a businessman who manufactures silk scarves. They have now been married for thirteen years and live in Ludhiana since. Isabelle, now thirty-nine, says that from her first day here, she observed that the community judged each other by what they owned and how much it cost.

'But once fashion and luxury brands came to India, the entire grammar of competitiveness changed,' she said.

Born and raised in France, the home of many fashion brands, Isabelle initially found the politics around labels ridiculous. 'I have seen the salwar kameez mutate into a dress. And the brocade clutch become the oversized logo bag,' she said.

Isabelle who teaches French at the Sacred Heart Convent School is one of the few working women in this wealthy class. She hasn't joined a single kitty group in all these years after her marriage; instead she enrolled into a Book Club. 'Young girls who marry into rich families take their easy lives for granted. They do little to earn their privileges, none is truly liberated, and none is even distinct in her fashion consciousness. I find it all very superficial,' she said.

One of Isabelle's most compelling observations hit me as ironical. The Ludhiana women, she said, who looked pretty in traditional clothes ended up looking ordinary and dowdy in Western garments. 'Yes, they do know how to style themselves in Western clothes but they are still learning to handle themselves, behave and carry off these garments,' she said.

Next day, over a coffee at Park Plaza, I asked Divya Dhanda if she agreed with Isabelle's observations.

'What she says is more than true,' Divya said for once dropping her cautionary correctness. She also confirmed my assumption that the divorce rate among the rich class is nil.

'Who will divorce here? These are all carefully considered arranged marriages and attitudes are still conservative. Besides, no one wants to give up these comfortable arrangements,' said Divya. 'But if you think all is hunky dory inside fashionable homes, you may be surprised.' She suggested I meet Dr Vanie Thapar, a respected gynaecologist and the confidante of many rich wives.

A small lift that could fit in two slender Ludhiana Wives takes you up from Dr Vanie's clinic to her residence. The bar was in the drawing room. A bottle of Red Label Whisky with a gilded tap fixed on its head had been hung upside down in a ready-to-pour position. Sofas were upholstered with heavy silks in muted colours. Photographs showed the family smiling together, probably at a foreign holiday.

Dr Vanie came in smiling warmly. Smartly dressed in tapered brown corporate trousers and a chic top, she neither sported any fashion brand, nor diamonds. 'I am a true blooded Ludhianvi,' she said gamely. One among four sisters, three of whom are doctors, Vanie's mother is one of the most respected local doctors, a persuasive, dignified lady. The daughters had been brought up as strong individuals—pro-women, pro-choice. Which is why, said Vanie, she found it disillusioning that a majority of her rich, smart, fashionable patients did not have a voice of their own.

I asked her if young, educated girls too expressed a preference for a male child, repeating what I had learnt from Divya—two diamond bangles for those who gave birth to a baby boy. 'You can't imagine how deep and intense this preference for a male child is in this society,' she replied. 'They are all good looking, trendy women and it is a pleasure to see them so well dressed. But fashion, which is now their common religion, hasn't changed the mindsets. Not at all,' she emphasized.

Regardless of social class, wealth, international travel and brand consciousness, Dr Vanie said she saw very similar problems across social classes in her OPD. Shockingly for her, girls who had studied abroad or lived in hostels didn't behave very differently from the underprivileged ones. Sexual confusions and discord in marriages, fear and doubt about clinical interventions, resistance to vaginal checkups, stress and health issues caused by early pregnancies were all a part, she said, of the lives of the women from the rich set like any other.

'The investments of both husbands and the girls themselves are all neck down,' said Vanie adding that barely five percent girls could stand up for themselves, rebel against mothers-in-law or husbands when it came to gender selection of their unborn child or their own rights. 'The same people who give them diamonds also put a lot of emotional and social pressure on daughters-in-law. The priorities of this new swish class are too skewed at the moment. They have become modern in their wardrobes but remain feudal in their mindsets.'

On the train back to Delhi from Ludhiana, the compartment was littered with brands—some fake some real. Before luxury brands poured into India, even the rich dressed as if they were not wealthy. Now the wealthy dress to announce their economic power. A new lexicon of success has replaced the old vocabulary of self-denial. To consume is to be successful; words such as nouveau riche, conspicuous consumption, or show-off I realized are devoid of negative connotation.

Walk, Don't Talk

'Part of the problem is that people only take models at face value... When you have a very visual job, your appearance is taken to be the most important thing about you. There is no defence.'

—Naomi Campbell

Walk, Don't Talk
Property: Satyendra Sattu, 2002

Written in white on the yellow painted back of a cycle rickshaw, Nagma* read it compulsively for the sixth time. It was 9 am in the morning and she was sitting on another cycle rickshaw right behind Satyendra Sattu's 'property' in the Paharganj traffic on her way to the Delhi Metro station. She had spent the previous night with her 'Boss' at a Paharganj hotel.

It was the first day of a fashion week in the summer of 2011 and Nagma's first runway assignment yet. So far she had modelled 'here and there' and 'oh yeah, at the Jaipur Fashion Week'. This was the time of the summer Navratras and she had vowed to fast for all nine days to appease Navdurga, the nine goddesses. Her appeals were fervent; each had to do with seeking blessings to make it to Bollywood. Ready-to-eat fasting food was available everywhere, but it would mean carrying all that nonsense—kuttu ke atte ki roti, sabudana papad, saltless potato chips—backstage.

'Fuck.'

Nagma, 22, a new model, single if you went by her Facebook status, on the Pill and drugs to keep her awake, on a slimming diet as well as currently on a fast, was sulking because of an unpredictable bout of facial acne. The make up artist would scream as had her Boss.

'Fuck, acne on the first day of fashion week!'

Boss who smelt like Rajnigandha paan masala mixed with vinegar had helped Nagma crack the auditions. He told her that model auditions for big fashion weeks were clean, where talent mattered more than sifarish but he would go with her to lend support. Most new girls from small towns came with their mummies. Mummies were nervous, wiping their made-up faces with tissues. Mummies were also queuing up, filling forms while their betis stood by. After registration, Nagma was told that her weight and height would be measured to check if she met the 'fit and healthy' conditions.

I went to one of the auditions to be a fly on the wall.

'Arre, Mummyji, yeh film ki shooting nahin hai, this is fashion, yahan bust chhota hi chahiye,' an exasperated coordinator told the eager mom of a busty young girl. The girl with boobs that looked barely size 34 B, pushed her mother aside and suggested several desperate solutions. It was agreed that she would tape her boobs back and force them into a tight bustier.

The girl breathed in, showed her boobs their real place in the modelling world, and squeezed into the clothes.

Nagma had a paradoxical problem. She was lighter than the ideal weight prescribed in the form. She weighed 52 kilos at 5'10". If they really followed all rules as they claimed, she would be disqualified.

'Fuck.'

Boss took someone aside and after some whispering and a quick handshake, her weight was recorded as 54 kilos. She was taken in. Height, looks, fitness, vital statistics, attitude are the categories on the form in front of the jury on which models must score marks. Education qualifications are not asked for. 'Dekho ji, we don't need education or intelligence if you have the right attitude,' a coordinator told me. 'Even if a model's elbows and knees are not as scrubbed as they should be, it is okay at this stage of her career. But she should have some attitude.'

Nagma had attitude alright. She said fuck every thirty seconds and kept tossing her hair with effortful nonchalance. She was asked to walk before eight well-known fashion personalities from Delhi, including designer Rohit Bal who had sauntered in, two hours late.

Model auditions for fashion weeks especially those held by the FDCI in Delhi and by IMG for Lakme Fashion Week (LFW) in Mumbai are seen as power platforms. I had heard how organizers went to great lengths to get the combination of 'personalities and realities' right on the jury. Gay, heterosexual—male and female, married, etc. Choreographers, preferably journalists and a couple of current top models were roped in too. 'The fashion bodies invite respected married designers like JJ Valaya and Ashish Soni because they are heterosexual and have clean reputations. These days everyone is very worried about allegations of the casting couch,' someone told me confidentially. Once selected for big fashion properties, all models, including the newbies are given air fare to fly in from their respective towns. Not everyone is provided with accommodation though.

Later that evening after Nagma's first audition, Boss told her to parade up and down in a bikini in front of him—ostensibly to help her perfect her model walk, now that she had been selected. And anyway, as he reminded her, her next goal was the Kingfisher Swimsuit calendar hunt. The 'walk rehearsals' were in a Paharganj hotel with stained curtains but clean bed sheets. He held a glass of pungent Bagpiper whisky on the rocks—in his hand and Nagma could see him undressing her in his head. She was getting used to the fact that he still didn't touch her or force her to do all the casting couch business the world believed models did to get work. Instead, he asked her to rest and left the room only to return after midnight. He quietly slid into bed while she gagged on the vinegar smell that had become stronger than its paan masala foil. Nagma had been prepared to 'sleep around' to become a model but nothing was going straight in this fucking industry. Even Boss did not want to sleep with her.

Fuck, the cycle rickshaw braked abruptly and she fell on the driver, her boxy vanity kit and her large grey-green fake Prada bag tumbling out of her hands. As she pulled her short, blue skirt down, she noticed the waxing rash that she had got on her legs yesterday. Everything was so fucking stressful. Nagma felt intense palpitations in her heart, her hands trembled. She badly needed a smoke.

As props for a fashion story called 'Dark Desire' that appeared in *Elle* magazine some years back, stylist Gautam Kalra had used handcuffs, a line of cocaine, stilettos, a vial of Botox—encased in a glass globe. The model, styled as a puppet was held up by strings, a glazed wistfulness on her face, looking at the globe in a daze.Nagma reminded me of Gautam's story. But I wouldn't know for another few weeks which stage of attachment, detachment, fascination, passion, disgust, despair or despise, she had for her profession.

'A story on models?' asked the man dressed in what looked like a rented suit and tie as he tried to stop me from going backstage at Wills Fashion Week. He was a senior bouncer. 'A model can only be understood after her initial bouts of fatigue and fear stabilize, madam. Their moods are like blood pressure; you cannot make a right diagnosis based on a high reading one day,' he went on.

I showed him my media pass.

Backstage at a fashion week is chaotic and noisy. This is where fashion's wabi-sabi (Japanese for acceptance of imperfection) is most evident. Pots and jars of make up to hide natural anomalies, a perplexingly large array of brushes, wigs and hair extensions, Mickey Contractor, the celebrity make up artist of M.A.C cosmetics holding his tools like the Lieutenant General of make up wars, accessories strewn all over, half-dressed models sitting before mirrors, some smoking in corners, trying to avoid each other, a forgotten panty hose, half-tantrums of assistant stylists, odd job boys dragging in trunks of wondrous clothes, a designer losing his cool, someone tearing out his hair. I had asked one of my designer friends whether there was a lot of politics among top models backstage and she had said yes. 'I know a couple of girls very well personally but they become different kind of people backstage. They turn into aloof and haughty girls instead of the warm women I know them as,' she said.

Once, invited by Sabyasachi, I watched a rehearsal at the Grand Hyatt hotel in Mumbai during the LFW. The models sans make up were in casual wear yet they all looked stylish. A wireless microphone in hand, and a kaani shawl over her peacock blue knee length dress, Harmeet Bajaj, one of the industry's veteran choreographers was directing them how to walk, where to turn, how to do a mock drill of handling the fall and drape of their garments, swirl at the head ramp, then turn back.

Sabyasachi was to present the finale collection called Bridal Sutra that evening. He had wanted the show to be like a baraat; this meant doing fittings with male, female, and child models. Some had to walk out alone, others in groups, a little behind or ahead of each other, like in a wedding procession. This wasn't the usual catwalk.

While the rehearsal continued, Sabyasachi took me backstage. 'You must touch and feel the clothes,' he insisted. Gautam Kalra was there too, to help with the fittings and style the ornate looks. Make up and hair were elaborate and the clothes weighed many kilos. Suddenly, in one corner, a loud argument ensued between an assistant stylist and a model. Sabyasachi left my side. Designers often talk about how they become a bag of nerves before their show and now I could see why. Sabyasachi was furious but he brought quick order to the floor. I was only glad to find my way out.

'Carol, remember you are Number 5. Now come on, get out, babe, out, out, out, I want everyone in the wings NOW,' a stylist–choreographer screamed. Gautam, as one of India's most sought-after stylists was the backstage mentor often enough and I would try to disappear into the woodwork to marvel at the fastidious detailing with which he handled models.

'For those who can resist its fatal attractions, fashion is a fantastic profession. For those who can't, it is a tale of delirious ups and downs,' Gautam told me later.

A Punjabi by birth Gautam looks Turkish with his flawless complexion and round, handsome face. He had promised me a tell-all session on Indian models and fortified himself with cigarettes at his Noida home while I piled cheese on crackers. Deep pink curtains, blue chairs, Andy Warhol cushions and a plus size silver ashtray shaped like a slipper looked at us as we talked.

Gautam is my favourite dresser among all men and women I have met in the industry. As a student of Delhi School of Economics in the late Eighties, he would wear electric blue YSL glasses with thick frames, shorts, colourful, checked kurtas, his hair bleached at the back. Pitched against nerdy boys in khaddar kurtas who had come to Delhi University from Kolkata's Presidency College, he looked like a fun boy. He organized rock concerts and hung around K-Nags (Kamla Nagar), then the ultimate dude hangout. A decade later, when he partied in Bangalore, the local Page 3 got a new hero. That was the frothy fag end of the Nineties and the IT city's parties were riveted by liquor baron Vijay Mallya's Armani jackets, model maker Prasad Bidapa's textile dhotis, and dancer as well as actor Kamal Haasan's first wife Vani Ganapathy's oxidized silver. 'Bangalore then was genuinely cool, parties were not a bad word, raves were about trans music and smoking up,' said Gautam who had moved there to work with Lintas, had shaved his head and sported a goatee. Influenced by Japanese design and Issey Miyake-inspired anti-fit clothes, he would wear kimonos with fuschia sneakers, lungis and kurtas in orange, lime green, and purple. 'Gautam brought style chutzpah to Bangalore,' remembers a journalist who then worked with *Society* magazine.

'You need chutzpah and an I-don't-give-a-damn-attitude, babe,' Nagma had been told on the first day of the modelling course she had enrolled for. The admission had cost her Rs 40,000 and her father, a senior officer in the Indian railways, now posted in Bhopal, had parted with the money without argument but with reluctance, his eyes moist and anxious as if she was going far away, and nobody knew if she would ever return. Her mother was dead against modelling and had lamented Nagma's decision to move into a PG dig in Delhi.

In the capital, Nagma was listed with one of the smaller modelling agencies that offered girls of various skin colours, body types and rates. Fair skinned East European and Russian girls were available for as little as Rs 3000–5000 a day, even less, for commercial shoots. For hand and feet modelling (jewellery or nail polish), you could find a pair of 'gora haath–paer' as they called it for Rs 2000. No contracts were signed here to determine working hours, advance payments, the number of times a photograph can be used, etc. You booked the girls and they just came along.

'Can I meet one of your Indian models?' I had asked.

Nagma was called. It was a first floor office in South Delhi's Malviya Nagar, and she was freely smoking indoors. She stubbed her cigarette before putting out her hand for me.

Our first conversation was awkward.

'Hi, am doing some research, am curious to find out why so many young girls want to become models,' I said.

'I am tall, slim and want to become famous,' she said unhesitatingly. She was a fidgety girl and kept running her hands through her hair. Nagma was not pretty; I wouldn't even call her good-looking but she did have a model-like body. Boyish chest, long slender legs, a small waist, mid-length hair, and a triangular face. She was in a short, polka dotted, green dress gathered at the waist by a slim belt, and badly constructed tall heels. She wore false eyelashes even though it was only 1 pm in the afternoon and looked sullen and bored. Her nails were chipped and when she raised her arms again to tie her hair into a bun, I noticed messy armpits.

'Famous? Models don't become famous; actresses do,' I said.

Nagma had her script ready.

'I want to first become India's next Mehr Jessia, then an

actress. My dream is to act opposite Shah Rukh Khan like Anushka Sharma,' said Nagma. Anushka was a model before she got a break *in Rab Ne Bana Di Jodi*, she reminded me. 'I will do anything for a good role and I mean anything,' she added looking me straight in the eye, as if daring me to ask what 'anything' meant. She had sized me up, I felt and thought if she gave me the 'I will do anything line', I would quickly conclude the interview.

This 'anything' route isn't such a simple shortcut to Bollywood as the modelling myth suggests. There are three categories of models in India and not all of them want to become film heroines. The first is a bunch of senior, assured, successful girls, who have been in the business for long and want to stay right there. Sapna Kumar, Bhavna Sharma, Carol Gracias, Noyonika Chatterjee, Indrani Dasgupta, Joey Matthews, Jesse Randhawa, Lakshmi Rana and some others belong to this category. A couple of them are in their thirties, they work independently like freelancers, choose their shows and only align with agencies for specific events not for all their contracts. They dictate their terms, handle their own finances and are their own agents. Whether they could not make it to Bollywood or did not want to go that way, may not be a very well-kept secret but it's clear that they have stayed on the ramp long enough to be taken seriously. They are the ramp's A-listers. They make between Rs 30,000 to Rs 40,000 per show.

Then there are two other categories. One, as a fashion week source told me, comes all the way from abroad to 'make a name in India as the only route to Hindi films is modelling'. I asked Sunil Sethi the President of FDCI if this was true. He more than agreed. He told me about a girl of Indian origin who worked in the nuclear engineering department of NASA in the US who wanted to model for the WIFW. 'Her mother pleaded with us to give her a chance,' he added, remembering another who would come every year from the UK for five days just to walk the ramp. 'Her name is India,' Sethi told me. This category of models is not the 'I will do anything' type but they brought sifarish from powerful and rich Indians. Many do get to walk on the ramp but then disappear.

The third type is besotted with Bollywood. They suffer from what's called an acute and compulsive 'I-want-to-be-in-Bollywood' disorder. Some of them realize from day one that the only way is to work hard on their walk, grooming, discipline, dancing, attitude, and networking. They do not touch drugs, cigarettes, or alcohol because they want to be here for a long haul. Some among these are the 'I will do anything' types, who strategize their sexual charms and assume that they would sleep their way to Bollywood. Others don't want to do so but are so desperate with ambition that they are often misguided and land up doing 'anything' because they don't know better. 'Once you enter this profession, a number of doors open for you and you have to stop and think about your choices and where you would go from here,' Lakshmi Rana, one of India's A-list ramp models told me. 'Some are so desperate that they get their portfolios shot wearing very little. That then sends out the message that the girl will do whatever it takes to get a break. They don't realize how these messages are read by the industry,' she added. Surprisingly and perhaps unjustifiably, this category of models dominated Madhur Bhandarkar's film *Fashion*. It did offend many real models. Lakshmi Rana was furious. 'What does he think, that guy, I didn't even want to see the film after I heard what all he had portrayed. As if we are a bunch of neurotics,' said Rana in her deep, husky voice.

Lakshmi is a level-headed girl, who graduated in maths and physics, qualified as a flying pilot for the Indian Air Force. She was born and raised in a defence officer's family and has been married to an army officer since she was 23-years-old. Now thirty, she is considered to be one of the best models on the catwalk. I met Lakshmi at her home in Delhi's Cantt area, in an army colony. In a previous interview for *The Indian Express*, she had told me she made good money, was into serious stock trading on the side and had invested well, so I was surprised to see her inconspicuous setting. There was no ostentation of any kind in the drawing cum dining room. Lakshmi, as always, was in great spirits. She was dressed in a hoodie and pyjamas and wore slippers. Through our conversation on modelling, she repeated what Gautam had told me that the desperate girls who get obsessed with modelling as their one and only reality in life get nowhere.

'I always counsel the younger girls to treat modelling as a hobby till it becomes a career for them,' said Lakshmi telling me why she left a pilot's commissioning letter from the Indian Air Force to participate in the Femina Miss India contest in the year 2000. After she won a Navy Queen contest in Dehradun, where her father was then posted, she had begun to get local modelling offers and decided to apply for the Femina Look of the Year contest. She not only got through that but also through the Femina Miss India contest, which in that year had Dia Mirza, Priyanka Chopra, and Lara Dutta as her co-contestants. 'It was a strong batch, but I came out as the third runners up,' she said, after which, a well-known choreographer invited her to walk in the 2001 fashion week in Delhi.

Lakshmi has been walking the ramp now for a decade. She does her bit as an army wife as well as signs up for dozens of ramp shows every year. She has travelled the world, been exposed to hundreds of opportunities. Modelling has worked out very well for her because she made some rules for herself. 'No smoking, no drugs, no excessive partying or cosying up with people in the industry,' she said cryptically.

'Don't you get frustrated, when your brains, which might be as important as your physical attributes are ignored?' I asked. 'Your work has no use for your intelligence?'

'That's only partly true,' she said. 'Of course it is not a profession that makes a difference to anything and if we didn't wear fashion garments, the world is not going to end but the assumption that top models don't need to use their brains to stay where they are is incorrect.' 'I am my own Boss. I choose my shows, read the fine print, and invest my money well.' Lakshmi said. She felt beautiful and powerful.

Carol Gracias was hung-ho too. 'I know I am not saving lives, but it is a profession like any other, and I treat it with discipline and maturity,' she told me for a story for *The Indian Express*, adding that she was her own agent.

These girls frequently travel abroad, some work for international brands and walk for designers in Paris and Milan and most earn more than bankers and IT professionals. The only compromise they must make (if it could be called a compromise at all) is to hobnob with powerful designers and head honchos of fashion brands at parties and events. They accept that their leggy, glamorous looks are the stamp of the industry and they are invited to parties to keep up the image. Designers love and favour some models over others and many have longstanding friendships with some of them. Unlike the prickly relationships between fashion journalists and designers, the friendliness between stylists, models and designers is real. For an edition of *Marie Claire* awards, when we opened an Internet poll for designers to vote for their favourite models, the responses came fast and were clear. Attitude is the single biggest attribute that a model must have, say designers. Noyonika Chatterjee, a product of St Xavier's College Mumbai, is now 40-years-old. She has been walking the ramp for almost two decades, yet instead of getting bored of her designers love her; she is friends with many and her attitude, I hear, is super.

Attitude is what models wear well for parties too. No model arrives in a six-yard sari, a salwar kameez or a Fabindia kurta. They play their roles like actresses, both in the way they dress—smart Western clothes, often short dresses, messy hair, nice make up. Unlike professional socialites, they don't carry branded bags. They descend upon parties thrown by their designer friends like a loyal army happy to be seen and consumed by others like products; and air kiss like it was going out of fashion.

'What does a model want from the world? Has your career made you a narcissist? Are you addicted to glamour?' I asked Lakshmi.

'I would be lying if I said the glamour didn't attract me. After hundreds of fittings, rehearsals, make up, the act of walking on the ramp with the full production in swing, the music, lights, hundreds of cameras taking our pictures is a big high. But I consciously remind myself not to get carried away, I know that will lead to insecurity about the physical self and that it will end soon. It is a career, and there is no room for neuroticism if I have to stay at the top,' she said, admitting that the reason older girls like her were still in demand in India is because the newcomers weren't exciting or tall enough.

'Younger girls don't have the X factor that contemporary Indian fashion now needs, it is rather unfortunate,' she said.

Nagma said she knew she didn't have the X factor. When she didn't get the WIFW contract the following season, she told me she understood why she should have taken the modelling classes seriously and not only because her father had spent Rs 40,000 on it. Other details that she had ignored earlier—shaving armpits, registering with a professional agency, sleeping well, exercising, regular spa treatments and drinking a lot of water (not just alcohol)—meant survival for her now. Drugs, cigarettes and saying 'fuck' in a dozen ways, she realized would not take her to Bollywood, nor would Boss.

I felt Nagma was with a wrong agency. Also, this Boss of hers sounded odd to me but she continued to walk in the nude for him in a stinking hotel room.

Leena of the veteran designer duo Ashima–Leena told me that for their first show in 1992, they had worked with the best models of those days. 'The girls then had pretty faces, were voluptuous, and never looked sick,' she said recounting Aishwarya Rai, Sheetal Malhar, Pooja Batra, Madhu Sapre among others. 'Now it is such a sad scenario, they starve and this craving to be out there and become someone pushes them to the wrong kind of agencies sometimes,' she added.

Starving was unheard of in the time of Meher Castelino who won the Femina Miss India in 1964 and was the first to participate in the Miss Universe contest in Miami. In fact, she was advised to put on weight. Her mother would force 'milk with Complan' to help her add on to her 51 kilos. She wasn't voluptuous enough. A year later, Miss India 1965, Persis Khambatta faced other hurdles. She was brazen in look and body language. She may have worn a Benarasi red gold sari with short, blunt hair for her costume round in the Miss India pageant but India couldn't really consume her sex appeal. She was great for a beauty pageant but too 'forward' for films. In those days, Hindi cinema still loved coy girls who laughed or wept hysterically. The Lux soap model was an exaggerated version of the rich housewife, with bangs falling on the eyes and black eyeliner that winged out. Persis was neither hysterical nor coy. She left for Hollywood to become the bald Lieutenant Ilia in *Star Trek* and became a Revlon model. On the other hand, Zeenat Aman whose bust was her PR agency looked like a sex bomb in the swimsuit round of the Miss Asia contest in Philippines in 1970. Even so, for the obvious India effect, she wore a tiny bindi and jhoomkas with her one piece swimsuit. She won the pageant. This styling wouldn't have worked in 2012. Bindi with swimsuit is now a behenji thing to do; even newlywed brides don't do that on their honeymoons.

Looking sexy became a model's business much after Zeenat Aman. The first Kamasutra condom advertisement shot by photographer Prabuddha Dasgupta in the early Nineties with Pooja Bedi and Marc Robinson paved the way for sexy models. He shot a Tuff shoes commercial with the nude (except for a python wrapped around their waists) Madhu Sapre and Milind Soman, highlighting the idea that Indian models could be sexy too. Prabuddha remembers the commercial he shot for Blue Lagoon jeans—a little before Kamasutra—as the first real fashion shoot he ever did. 'The model had tousled, hair, I borrowed a Volkswagen from a friend, did the hair and the make up, but it was 'fashion,' he says. In an India pre-occupied with moral policing, these were turning points.

Now, girls who want to walk the ramp must be thin, tall and preferably fair, as Lakshmi told me. She is as lean as can be and I find her almost flat-chested but she pointed out that I was wrong and she was, in fact, one of the bigger girls. 'If I would be half an inch more on the bust, I wouldn't get into any clothes,' she said reminding me that designers now made samples for the international market; they catered to fashion buyers from all over the world. Lakshmi often has to squeeze into the garments created by India's top designers. 'I barely manage to get into them,' she said telling me that her height (5'11") cut the effect but she was actually 36 and ½ inches on the hips. She felt strongly about India's unchanging preference for fair skin. 'That's why there are so many Russian and other European girls in the market. They come cheap and now even wear lehgnas and wedding jewellery. We have no modern, national concept of beauty,' she added, as always emphatic.

Gautam had a strong opinion about skin colour too. He talked about India's top model Lakshmi Menon, the first to be featured by American Vogue and model for international luxury brands like Givenchy and Hermès among others, whose beautiful dark skin was appreciated by the West before Indians realized what they had missed out on. 'I do hope things are changing in favour of our natural dark skinned models,' he said.

Dark skin is okay on the ramp but not for print commercials which favour the fair and lovely. Half-Czech, half-Pakistani and a model from America, Nargis Fakhri, last year's most watched debut in *Rockstar* was quickly signed up by some of the bigger brands after the release of her first film. Van Heusen was one of them. Her fair skin helped her score over other fresh girls from India. The game shifts slightly if a model moves to Bollywood to become an actor. A good bust line is welcome in films. I am told that in South Indian films, flat and small boobs mean no work. Sushmita Sen in the Nineties and Kangna Ranaut recently added to this theory. I remember Kangna as a flat chested new actor when we shot for the cover of *Marie Claire* India's January 2007 edition. Five years later on *Simi Selects India's Most Desirable*, her cup was flowing over.

Actresses may diet but models starve.

'Why do you make such a big deal about starving, what is a girl supposed to do if she has to stay awake and thin?' said Nagma, defending her diet and drugs. 'I am a liberated girl, I know what I am doing,' she said.

Models were female embodiments of urban liberation long before stylists gave them silicone pads and photo retouch artists shrunk their blemishes. Bold, outspoken girls even in the late Eighties, they defied conventions about passivity and domesticity. The country was unprepared for young girls storming social barriers through unconventional looks and clothes. They were clubbed with air hostesses and private secretaries and called 'forward'; certainly not the kind men would take back to their moms. They were the spectacle on Indian ramps long before fashion became one. Nafisa Ali, Anna Bredemeyer, Nandini Sen, Rhca Pillai and Queenie Singh followed by Sangeeta Bijlani, Mehr Jessia, Lubna Adams, Feroze Gujral, Shyamoli Varma and Noyonika Chatterjee defined feminine consumerism in the Eighties and Nineties before global brands stormed in. They sold Cherry Blossom shoe polish, Garden Varelli saris, Lakme lipsticks, Khatau fabrics, Keo Carpin hair oil, and Usha sewing machines to us. Women wanted Libertina bras and Nivea creams because these girls made fashion look like a guiltless trip.

If masculinity was a hunky hero in VIP underwear rescuing a woman from a villain, femininity was a Liril soap advertisement. A bubbly young girl frolicking in water wearing a bikini—imagined and created by Alyque Padamsee—was how we wanted to be.

Those days, only mills like Garden Varelli, Bombay Dyeing, Khatau, and Mafatal had fashion shows. Hindi film music played in the background, there were no designers or stylists and models were expected to be the show as well as the showstopper.

'We walked the talk. People came to see us. Now, ramp models are like mannequins in a funeral march despite an army of stylists, choreographers, make up artists and fawning designers,' says former supermodel, the statuesque Anna Bredemeyer of her three decades in Indian fashion from 1973 till early 2000.

Mannequin is how a model was known as in the early nineteen hundreds. The first person to be called that was Marie Worth, a shop model, wife of English designer Charles Worth. Swedish girl Lisa Fonssagrives one of the first 'fashion models' of the world, told *Time* magazine in 1949 that the fuss was all about the clothes, never about the girl. Designers were ambivalent about them including the radical French designer Coco Chanel. 'They're beautiful, that's why they can get these jobs. If they were intelligent, they'd give them up,' she said.

In the West, doubts over modelling as a decent profession continued even till the late Fifties, when British *Vogue* ran its first modelling competition. 'You can reassure your father, your husband, your son on one point: modelling is terribly respectable,' said the announcement.

'Terribly respectable?' laughs Anna.

That's not how people looked at models in India.

Miss India 1975, Anna was one of three gorgeous sisters—Adrianne, Indra, Utrike—nicknamed the Bredemeyer Trinity of the Seventies. She had a show stopper personality.

Next to the bell that tolls inside Anna's Perry Road apartment in Bandra, Mumbai, is a black and white photograph from her days of glory. 'I won't allow anyone to forget who I was,' she said in her resounding voice, as she answered the doorbell and caught me staring. She was in a white Fred Perry T-shirt, white shorts and sneakers, hair pulled back in a thick pony tail. Anna who was the face of Mont Blanc for some years after she stopped walking the ramp, now works with the Bada Saab group that retails Brioni in India. In the past, she had also started the Anna B grooming school for models.

At home, the former supermodel is a hygiene freak. You could eat off the floors in her white, painted flat which shines with spotless surfaces. 'I prefer scrubbing floors to partying,' said Anna.

Modelling was no party in the Seventies. The girls styled their own looks, did their make up, and used personal charisma to substitute for the grooming courses they never attended. Shyamoli Varma, the face of Lakme and the Garden Varelli girl who now lives in Pune told me how they had to perform on the ramp in those days; act, dance, and mime to songs that played in the background. 'We were mimicry artists and it took many years of arguing to be compensated well,' she had told me for a story. Money was meagre. 'I was given Rs 30,000 for the Lakme campaign for three years and thought I had hit a jackpot,' she said.

Things changed when India's first real designer Rohit Khosla came along. A Doon school product who went to study fashion in Europe, he was the country's first brilliant stylist. His 'styling' of Garden Varelli fabrics shot by photographer Ritu Nanda were among the first fashionised garment commercials. He made supermodels out of middle class girls like Nafisa Ali, Mehr Jessia, and Shyamoli Varma.

'A supermodel is born when she knows how to convey on the ramp that she is a special person and feels worth a million bucks,' said Anna who said she lived for her profession; it gave her the biggest adrenaline rush in her hey days and nothing has been able to replace it.

Nagma was in a hurry to feel like a million bucks. So when her agency informed her that her first assignment had been signed, she quickly encashed that wish into a feeling. She was one of the five girls who would model for a premium, ready-to-wear fashion brand. It was an outdoors shoot in Jaipur and she would have to travel by road with the crew. She would earn Rs 6000 for the entire commercial after her agency's commission.

In the very first hour of the shoot, she had a rude awakening. Nobody even looked at her. The vibe among the crew was bitchy. The creative director of the brand they were shooting for treated everyone like minions. The photographer was aloof; he fiddled with his laptop and camera while his assistants fussed with the lights. A senior Delhi model who had arrived more than an hour late and in a separate luxury car, took one look at Nagma and decided she would shoot only in the clothes listed for Nagma and threatened a walk out if her wish was not granted.

The art director agreed and Nagma was told to hand over her clothes and find others from the heap lying on the sofa in the make up room. She was clearly an extra here. Her turn for make up was last and the make up guy refused to clean the brushes or use fresh ones for her. She wanted to puke with the odour that hit her when he wetted the make up sponge to apply the cake. It was past 2:30 pm already and all that the cast and crew had been offered so far were Marie biscuits with machine tea or coffee. She had risen early for the 8:00 am call time after the bumpy ride from Delhi the previous night and was hungry and angry.

Not one shot had been canned yet. Her stomach groaned; she lit a cigarette. Fucking crew, she told me, adding that she popped a pill to keep awake, now and then. These tablets were easily available off-the-counter at pharmacies in Delhi and had been suggested by a colleague at her former agency to survive long working hours. Those who do drugs are seldom on just one substance. They drink, smoke, smoke up, also try Ecstasy and other heady stuff. Nagma had tried Ketamine and other easily accessible anaesthetic drugs too. These were to sleep after she had tried to keep herself awake for long hours.

But not all shoots are as unprofessional as the one Nagma described to me, nor are all professional models coked-out zombies. The image created by Madhur Bhandarkar's 2008 film *Fashion* that focussed on the dark side of modelling did not reflect as intensely in my research. I had been to many shoots over the years and found that model coordinators, stylists, hair and make up artists, models and photographers work diligently and professionally. The exceptions were few.

Behind-the-scenes at a fashion shoot is different from backstage at a fashion week. Air-conditioned studios (unless it is outdoors), stimulating background music, endless cups of coffee or Diet Coke served by shoot assistants, usable loos and a well-organized fashion rack is a rule not an exception. Catering is ordered according to shoot budgets; some brands have accounts lavish enough to order from posh restaurants. Others rely on caterers who supply only food for 'shooting'—and take care of the entire day from the first coffee at call time to all meals.

Clothes are put out by the stylist on a rack, accessories laid out in rows on tables, ditto for shoes and bags. If the stylist and his assistants have done their homework well, they would have photographs from the previous day's fittings, with the looks completely styled from head to toe in advance. Such shoots are rapid and successful. The photographer knows exactly what a client wants, whether it is for a fashion magazine, a commercial brand or with a Bollywood star. Make up usually takes more than an hour per face, not including hair. Sometimes, the look is same for all shots but often the make up and hair artists have to change the look completely or deepen the intensity of a lipstick or an eye shadow to go with the change of clothes.

Such shoots are fun for models. Stylists worry about masking the soles of shoes borrowed from global luxury brands to prevent dirty marks; clothes need to be protected from make up marks or tea-coffee stains. The photographer has no choice but to be nice to the model while assistants of all kinds run around, straightening a crinkle here and there, and the make up person or hairstylist intervenes with that extreme last minute dab of lipstick or to tick off an errant hair from the face. It results in a big fuss around the model who is the goddess of the moment. I noticed that when a fan would be put on to get the hair of a model blowing for a shot, the act lent the girl some kind of glamourous power. She would straighten her back, pull in her tummy, arch her eyebrows and go for the kill. The power of being sought after and making a picture that millions might love added a tremendous boost to a model's confidence.

Good modelling agencies protect working rights of their models. Contracts are signed, and the shifts are fixed; food and beverage choices of the girls and boys are conveyed clearly before a shoot. Sometimes, a person from an agency accompanies a new model to the shoot. Modelling contracts are legal documents now. 'We not only ensure that models are cast appropriately, we also look after their professional rights, safety and comforts and counsel them about the realities of a competitive market,' Sushma Puri, CEO of Elite Modelling Management told me when I went to meet her after Kamasutra model Viveka Babajee committed suicide in July 2010.

An investment banker from New York, she had worked in an event management company before taking over Elite Modelling Management. Now her life is busier than ever with admissions multiplying by hundreds. The hyperbolic society exclamation: 'everyone wants to become a model' is true, says Sushma, who leads an all-female team. 'Modelling has become a respectable profession even among well-to-do families,' she told me. Medical students, sound engineers, lawyers, and call centre employees—Elite gets admission requests from people of all backgrounds including from some with already established careers.

As we talked, a girl whose father is a farmer in a Haryana village walked in with her parents. When Sushma had first met the 21-year-old dark skinned, 5'10" tall girl, she spotted potential and was confident that the three-month course, would kit her out for the modelling world. Elite gave the girl a scholarship because her farmer father couldn't afford the fees. 'My only insistence is that the girls must complete their formal education and get a basic degree before getting absorbed into full-time modelling,' says Sushma.

A professional, three-month modelling course costs Rs 60,000 at a good school. Students are taught for four hours a day, five days a week and the curriculum includes personality development, ramp walk, fitness, hair and make up, dancing, posing for photographs, wardrobe management and social etiquette. Training dwells on details: how to enter and exit an event, the use of mouth fresheners and deodorants for fittings and why female models must always carry their own underwear, paddings, and stockings. A model's portfolio is made for each student towards the conclusion of a course. Editorial, ramp and modelling for commercials (TV or print) are the main job categories.

Debutant models make Rs 8,000 to Rs 10,000 per ramp show. Fees and contracts depend upon the charisma and abilities of the girl. Many new girls get up to six shows a month on average. Even smaller cities like Chandigarh, Bhopal, Kochi and Guwahati now host fashion events while booze companies sponsor the travelling shows. Almost every day there is some fashion event happening somewhere or the other in the country and the moneyed fashion market has inflated catwalk opportunities. On the other hand, the highly paying commercials fetch between Rs 1 to Rs 2 lakh per assignment. Agencies send a bunch of suitable girls after seeing the script of a commercial and the final call is that of the creative director of the client company. While it lasts, modelling is a very lucrative career and many girls can support entire families with their incomes.

Not male models. Unfortunately, they do not have it as easy in the industry. Thousands of boys 'float around', I was told. Eager to be the next Arjun Rampal, they go on crash diets without medical guidance, exercise like maniacs, consume high, unmonitored doses of steroids to build muscles and stand in model hunt queues for days, forming a desperate club. Many young boys accept assignments for Rs 2000 or even for free. The casting couch, allegedly, helps cast more boys than girls, say insiders. 'They are unrealistic about their looks. There aren't enough opportunities for even a quarter of them. We firmly counsel them to have secondary careers and a Plan B, lest they need an emergency landing,' says Sushma.

'Plan B is important for girls too,' said Lakshmi telling me about girls in her peer group who had worked for years but had no savings. They had spent too much on the good life in their best years and needed to model to sustain that standard of living. 'These are the kind of girls who end up committing suicide; they either need regular work or need a rich boyfriend to keep them going,' she explained.

Amit Ranjan arrived in the industry without a Plan B. We had chatted on the phone after his agency introduced us and he wanted an assurance that I would not write about him scandalously.

How will I know it is you? I asked him when we fixed a time to meet at a Barista.

'Don't worry, you will recognize me,' he said over the phone with a self-conscious laugh.

Next afternoon, when this tall, lean man with long, jet black hair dressed in a white shirt, black leather jacket and blue jeans tucked into ankle length sneakers walked into Barista, the coffees froze on all tables. He was right. He was no supermodel but nobody missed his fantastic entry into Barista. He looked like Jesus Christ painted by Michelangelo. He brought his own bottle of mineral water and kept sipping from it. He refused to eat or drink anything. 'I am very conscious of my diet; I don't eat between measured meals and I don't even touch coffee,' he told me.

'How long do you exercise every day?'

'One and a half to two hours, six days a week,' he said.

'Even during fashion weeks and events?' I asked.

'I try to do some form of exercise every day, come what may. If I can't go to the gym, I do yoga at home, or in a hotel room,' he said.

Amit told me that the current trend for male models is to look lean, not bulky. They were encouraged to have triangular backs that tapered into a slender waist.

'No bulging biceps anymore,' he said.

'It must have thrown all your hunky colleagues into a tizzy. It isn't easy losing so much muscle. And what about the steroids you all take?' I asked.

He smiled. Amit was a cautious guy and not for one moment did he forget that he was chatting with a journalist. He wasn't about to make the mistake of admitting anything. If he took steroids, I had to read it through that killer smile of his. What he did tell me however was about the 50–60 friend requests he got on Facebook everyday—all from girls.

Unable to concentrate on Premchand and Harivansh Rai Bachchan, Amit, a student of Hindi literature at Delhi University found himself in a queue of a few thousand boys for the Gladrags Mr India contest one day. Three hundred odd were asked to stay and he was one of them. He didn't become Mr India but soon won the walk-in Model Hunt contest by Elite Modelling Management.

Today, the 25-year-old opens some of the most important menswear shows. 'I am the sexiest man alive—that's what I tell myself when I walk the ramp. There is no one like me.' Amit told me. With that conviction in his mind, Amit said he was working his way towards (where else?) Bollywood.

A feeling shared by Hari Rathod and Anil Vats.

Rail Trek to *Star Trek*: Known as Surat's Bobby Deol, Hari Rathod, a coolie at Surat railway station—Billa number 858—dreams of becoming a fashion model. (TOI, Ahmedabad, October 18, 2010).

'The glamour world and the railway platform are the same, as both depend on hard work and long hours,' the 6' plus tall coolie told the newspaper. After two bit roles in Gujarati films, Rathod was biding his time, earning his daily wages as a coolie before he could walk the fashion ramp in Delhi.

Even as Rajasthan boy Anil Vats waited to do the same.

hi i m anil vats from rajastan. i have done graduation from delhi university and i am an artist in moorti kala in like a god krishna, shiva, ganesha, i want to be a model i hv a good personality and good health. i am a perfect boy plz tell me how I become model? i don't know from where i start... i have no money. but i am a honest and hard working boy. i will struggle in my life contact: anilvats.com

Vats posted this on the Net as a response to Wills Lifestyle India Fashion Week's call for 'New Faces Going Places' an audition for new models in 2010. He did not make it. But he wanted to be an Arjun Rampal and said he would work his butt off for it.

John Abraham to get his butt insured for 10 crores. Hindustan Times, August 4, 2010

Many years before John Abraham filed for butt insurance, Arjun Rampal set Rohit Bal shows on fire with his sexy swagger and SRK soaked himself in rose petals for Lux soaps, it was Milind Soman in Thackersay fabrics who disrobed the male body in India. That was the memorable commercial of Tuff shoes for which Milind wore his girlfriend Madhu Sapre on his arm and a python on his crotch.

Designers like JJ Valaya, Tarun Tahiliani, Abu Jani–Sandeep Khosla designed for men but the men's retail market was small for many years and the male model only an aside.Till Rohit Bal exploded violently into the scene, with a sexually charged portrayal of his models. He often mocked at convention and ushered a sexual movement on the ramp by reversing heterosexuality as the only determinant of a model's body language. He gave expression to the undercurrent of homosexual liberation by bringing beautiful as well as hunky male models to the ramp. They combined machismo with bashfulness, symbolizing the coming out of gays. It was to Rohit Bal's credit that fashion welcomed homosexuality long before the rest of Indian society did.

Bal, who is gay himself, once urged his male models to wear sindoor and nathnis (large nose rings with chains across the cheek). They kissed and embraced on the ramp and winked naughtily at the audience. Female models picked up cues of bold sensuality from the way their male counterparts ignited the ramp. Unafraid that his clothes would get sidelined by the spectacle he mounted each time, Bal turned the page for male modelling. He made men like Arjun Rampal and John Abraham objects of desire. 'Made by Bal,' was not just a line used for his garments. He made models too. One of the more recognised male models in the late 2000s—Lalit Tehlan—was allegedly Bal's boyfriend till he shocked everyone by marrying Mandy an Iranian female model.

Was Tehlan bisexual?

Had Bal broken up with him?

Will Tehlan now get work in the industry?

Do you have to sleep with Rohit Bal before walking in a Bal show?—all this and more was the gossip floating around when Tehlan and Mandy got married in 2011.

'Nonsense,' said Amit Ranjan, telling me it was preposterous to assume that everyone who walked for Rohit Bal had to sleep with him first. Before he himself became an object of desire, Amit was forced to sell burgers at McDonald's. He was sandwiched between his ambition and the wishes of his family, who wanted him to pursue academics or become an engineer. As soon as they heard about his Model Hunt victory, they stopped his allowance and turned him out of the house. He went into a downward spiral but was determined to survive. He would spend the money he made at McDonald's to scout for modelling jobs. Girls chased him relentlessly; he stopped counting the tissues that would be sneakily left on McDonald's trays with phone numbers written on them.

Many girls to flirt with, but very little work. That's how the cookie crumbles for most boys. Rajat Awasthi, a 23-year-old struggler who had also passed out from Elite in 2010, told me that a Delhi photographer had asked him to 'compromise' in exchange of a modelling break, but he refused. Rajat, whose parents lived in Panipat while he managed in a PG dig in Delhi before moving to Mumbai to work in TV serials, added rather matter-of-factly that if it were the campaign of a lifetime, he would simply shut his eyes and do it.

Not Amit Ranjan. 'I don't want a shortcut. The casting couch exists for those who want to climb the ladder fast but there is nothing anyone can do if you say no. I firmly refuse. Earlier I was nervous about it all but nobody assaults you. I like girls and sex. Can't you see it on my face?' he asked me with a smile.

I could see and he knew how to convince me.

'I thought you'd be a fat aunty. Isn't that how all senior journalists look?' he said when we first shook hands. I was pleased and thought this was one person to whom I didn't want to reveal my age.

Though we got along warmly, Amit remained elegantly guarded in his manner. I loved the way he subtly confessed to his admiration for his looks. He smiled like a God anyway and I found myself bantering easily with him. He was right, heterosexuality spilled out of his personality. So when he insisted that the casting couch would disturb his craving for straight sex, I agreed without much questioning.

'You are hinting that all casting couch suggestions come from gay designers,' I pointed out.

Amit shrugged, insisting that life was sexually charged in the industry and sexual escapades were common, but it was also a question of what models wanted for themselves. He admitted that it could be very tempting at their age. But of the many bits of good advice given to him, the best was that designers may like to take pretty boys to bed or to the bathroom, but gave consistent business only to those who were well-behaved; not coked out or undisciplined. Amit gave me a list of shows he had done with all big designers and told me to verify his behaviour and commitment with some of my designer friends. It was important to him that I checked out his credentials, he didn't want to be listed as a cokehead.

Meanwhile, Nagma, too, was trying to discipline herself and focus on her career. She had changed her agency but had kept in touch with Boss for reasons I couldn't fathom. She had posted her picture and vital statistics on adult friendship sites on the Net and unlike Amit, who wanted to make it big by hard work and strategy, Nagma was open to experiences. She worked long and partied hard; really hard.

'I never pass up an opportunity to party. I love the smell of booze, cigarettes, expensive perfumes all rolled into one. There is music, good food and I get to hobnob with so many designers and powerful people who may give me work someday. What is modelling without partying?' she said. The addiction to parties had started at the finale party of a fashion week she had attended as a wannabe. She had no modelling contract then. A male model whose name she did not know had held her by the waist and tried to slip his hand under her dress while she sat near the bar. They had then kissed outside the loo. 'Lot of hot kissing and rubbing thighs but he was too sloshed to take it further,' she laughed.

'Would you consider being an escort for money on the side?'

'Why not? I don't want to miss out on anything,' she said and added that she was signing more contracts and wasn't short of work even otherwise. Free and frequent sex was just the bonus. 'Arre yaar, who doesn't exploit someone or the other?' she asked me. 'Tum ko mauka milega, tum nahin karoge? (Won't you do it if you got the chance?)' she asked me. The only downside she admitted was she felt fatigued all the time and lost her cool frequently.

'Bigger models get VIP treatments backstage and on the ramp; they get the best outfits and the first turn on the make up chair, they are pampered by everyone. But I am going to fuck the dumb bitches one day,' she said haughtily.

The 'big models' are not always as arrogant as Nagma pointed out. Nor are they dumb. In fact, if you did an industry average, male models are dumber compared to the girls who are audacious and bright. The older ones are mature and intelligent. They defy the mythical construct of the dumb model. Whenever I got a chance, I would ask them if they were frustrated by the zero utilization of their brains.

'This profession is only our bread and butter, not our intellectual or emotional nourishment,' one of them told me. She had been arguing at length with me about a political subject at a dinner hosted by a designer at The Oberoi in Delhi and I had to rest my case; she won hands down. Had I not seen her face in advertisements and on the ramp for years, I would have never guessed that she was a model. She was intelligent and wanted to show it.

Not all models are interested in showing off their brains. A number of the older girls come across as aloof and their rigid looks are difficult to miss. Was this cynicism for real, I wondered, or was it a part of the cake they wore to work? Was it the first coat of the 'dead man walking' demeanour that Anna had talked about?

'Are you South Indian?' a model once asked me in the lift of a hotel lobby where a fashion week was on. She was staring at the Coorgi thali I wore in my neck, a sign of marriage worn in some parts of the South.

'No,' I replied.

'I am. My mangalsutra is a thali too,' she said, adding that she never got to wear it. 'Today is Karva Chauth, I should have worn it today at least,' she said sighing. Adrak chai at work, missed Karva Chauth fasts, acne, bad skin, diets gone wrong, having to wear thongs during periods, sleepless nights, bags under eyes, family concerns, the mangalsutras that the married ones never get to wear—all this knitted a tapestry of backstage baubles. Little everyday concerns in the lives of female models that must morph into faultless poise on the runway.

Their working lives are so cramped with accessories, clothes, and jewellery that their personal style gets buried under the burden of glamour dictated by the designer, the product, and the client.

And yet, when you see models anywhere, at formal events, having a quick coffee at a fashion week café or at a party, they are the best dressed people in the room. They are so exposed to the best of clothes, accessories, make up tricks and the talent of the stylists they work with every day, that they learn to wear and pair well. Fashion's core talent—experimentation—doesn't frighten them. 'Lakshmi Menon even allowed me to stuff socks in her panties for an androgyny theme shoot,' Gautam had told me. 'A good stylist is one who understands brands and a good model is one who listens,' says Gautam. 'To be edgy, you must be unafraid.' By listening to fearless stylists, models learn to take the fear out of fashion. They can wear anti-fit garments and crazy shapes with as much ease as a nine yard sari. Surely, the attitude they learn helps, which is their biggest qualification. 'I can wear a sari faster and better than women who wear saris every day,' Lakshmi Rana told me, adding that a model's carriage is her biggest distinction.

'When you go to public places, bars, pubs, nightclubs or parties, the gaze that follows you is a male gaze, does it bother you?' I asked.

'It did earlier, but over the years you get used to the idea that a model interacts with others only through her physical attributes,' she said.

Being friends with designers has its advantages. Models do have access to the best clothes, can buy what they want; many of the garments they own are gifts from the designer who might personally be advising them. They also become make up pros, having gone through hundreds of make up and hair sessions. Make up artists are the best gossips in the industry and models learn more than make up tricks from them; they know what their rivals wore and which designer favoured who.

It isn't a coincidence that so many of them turn choreographers and stylists later or run grooming and modelling agencies after their ramp and print modelling careers wind up. Anna Bredemeyer did it, so did Noyonika Chatterjee. Shyamoli Varma now does freelance choreography as do many others.

There are many perks of the industry: power, money and glory but each model knows she has to make friends with insecurity. Work depends on good looks, which has a short life. Standing at the edge of the precipice, despite good money and years of success leaves many of them cynical. 'Thick skin is the best undergarment for models,' someone had told me and as I reported this story, the phrase picked momentum.

It was Mehr Jessia's brief modelling career that struck me as the most intelligent choice made by an Indian model in a long time. Tarun Tahiliani's muse and showstopper for the longest time,

Mehr, the unblemished face of classicism in fashion is a perennial favourite with fashion photographers of different decades. 'We have made lives too easy for models now and sometimes I get the impression that the girls are doing us a favour by walking the ramp,' she told me.

Miss India 1986, supermodel Mehr Jessia understood the short life of a model. A model at seventeen, she retired at twenty-three, for a life of domestic bliss.

I met Mehr, now a ravishing Bollywood wife in her super-sized, airy, modern apartment in Bandra that overlooks the sea. A part of the drawing room is built like an open terrace and the sea shore with lapping waves traps your gaze every time your eyes dart towards the horizon. A mother of two girls, she looked as slender as she has always been; elegant in her blue jeans and navy blue cotton top, her hair in a ponytail. Her husband Arjun Rampal, also a former model, sat in a corner towards the French windows wearing a red bandana and talking into his phone. The voice that bounded back to us was guttural and resonant, like in his films.

'I am a Parsi. I eat rice all the time. It was only after I gave birth to my second daughter that I stepped inside a gym,' said Mehr. Her face, scrubbed clean seemed that it would wrinkle before its time but clearly the laugh lines around the eyes would precede other concessions to age.

Mehr went to the Miss Universe pageant by preparing for it with Rs 5000 given to her for three costumes. She was dismayed when she found that other contestants had dozens of dresses and matching shoes with all of them. She told me that her way of staying on top of pressures was to try and remain happy. Besides as she emphasized, the industry was not so bitchy and crazily competitive then. 'We did things for each other, jumped in to a flight to go and walk for a designer friend in another city,' she said adding that there was comfort in familiarity. To her the current crop of models looked like assembly line products. And as she emphasized, nobody could tempt her with a Bollywood offer.

Nagma who had hero worshipped Mehr though lived for the day that she would go to Bollywood. She told me that Lisa Hayden, the younger sister of Miss World Diana Hayden had got the film *Aisha* through Elite Modelling Management and asked if she should try and register herself there. Kangna Ranaut and Anushka Sharma too were Elite models. Nagma was trying to find out how Monikangna Dutta, one of the Indian ramp's top young models had landed a role in Sanjay Leela Bhansali's film *Guzaarish*. What she didn't notice was that Moni as Dutta had a minor role in the movie and disappeared from the audience's recall in a flash. Lisa, too, failed to make a mark. Both looked like easily dispensable faces in films.

I noticed how Nagma diligently followed such stories. She was earning better now and exercised three times a week at a gym. She was still on the Pill as well as the keep-awake pills. 'I am not worried about kicking these little golis, I will do that when I have to, what I am getting more used to is the white wine that I can't seem to stop drinking at parties,' she said. She dated different boys and told me with a giggle that she enjoyed herself. She also warned me that all the interviews the bigger models had given me were bullshit. 'Everyone fucks around, they have drugs, booze, boys, phir doosron ke samne sharif bante hain (they try to look innocent before others)'. But I wasn't convinced that Nagma's was the only kind of story.

Her boyfriend of three weeks, also a model she had met at a shoot for a magazine, had once taken her home. He was a rich industrialist's son, drove around in a big car and brought her lilies on Valentine's Day. He flirted with all the girls at the shoots and was known to be a Casanova; he changed girls every week. Even so, she hung around with him. At his house in South Delhi, when he introduced her to his mom and dad, the dad looked away in resentment and the mother spat venom. 'Model ko ghar mein le aiye ho; en ladkiyon ka kya hai, yeh toh paise ke liye kahin bhi chali jayengi,' (You have brought a model home! These girls will go anywhere for money) she had said.

Nagma cried herself to sleep that night. She and the 'boyfriend' (saala kutta, she said), had left his house immediately after his mother's outburst and he had dropped her at her PG. 'Don't cry, baby, my mom does this to all my girlfriends. She just can't accept anyone in my life, it is not about you,' he told her.

'Kutta saala, he is worse than Boss,' Nagma told me. Boss would only make her walk in a bikini in a room but never touched or tortured her in any way.

The surface of a model's life had begun to crack in the late Eighties. For the girls, cigarettes were torches of liberation and for the press, every smoke was fire; a tabloid headline too. The casting couch became a moral debate as the media played moral police. Newspapers highlighted smoking, drugs, parties, suicides as sins committed by the fashion industry in the main sections but relegated achievements of the girls to society supplements. Society magazines made celebrities out of models, news magazines made them vamps.

Over the years, the word play was delirious. Sample this series of bad news.

Persis Khambatta died in 1998, of a premature heart attack.

Zeenat Aman, who became Bollywood's Zeenie baby, had a series of failed relationships and was subsequently bashed up by her husband Mazhar Khan. Till today, her damaged eye reminds every one of the life she led.

Miss India 1982 Pamela Singh Bordes was accused of being a VIP escort. Her relationship with dealer Adnan Khashoggi and marriage with another arms dealer Henri Bordes broke down.

Nafisa Joseph killed herself in 2004.

Gitanjali Nagpal slipped into severe clinical depression. She was found wandering on Delhi streets in 2008.

Jessica Lal was killed in a fashion party at Bina Ramani's restaurant Tamarind Court in Delhi by the reckless son of a politician.

Ujjwala Raut became the face of a messy public divorce in 2009.

Viveka Babajee committed suicide in 2010.

Madhur Bhandarkar, a co-panelist with me on an *NDTV* talk show after model Viveka Babajee's suicide in 2010, told the anchor that he had withheld many realities that he unearthed about the fashion industry and that the truth was murkier than what his film suggested.

Swimsuits, suicides, cigarettes, and the tragic murder of Jessica Lal. It was this cocktail of headlines that reverberated in the mind of Vipasha Agarwal's father. The Marwari sari merchant from Benares reacted strongly when his daughter told him she wanted to become a model. Raised in a family of traders, Vipasha came to Sushma Puri at Elite modelling agency for a personality development course in 2004 attracted by its advertisement. She was pursuing an MBA at Amity University in Delhi at that time. 'Later, when she walked the ramp for the graduation ceremony, we were all stunned. The girl was born to be a model,' says Sushma.

But Vipasha's father remained cynical for months before he could be convinced that his daughter had the makings of a top model. Even after he did, he would donate her earnings, unable to digest that a family where women had never worked, had a daughter making a living as a model. Wherever Vipasha would go for a shoot, a family member would escort her till her father learnt to suspend his suspicions. Once allowed to take on more assignments, the petite, olive skinned girl with fiery 'Indian' looks was everywhere: magazine covers and commercials—Fair & Lovely, Garnier, Lakme, Tanishq, to name a few. Vipasha signified docility and a simmering sensuality in her manner; a fragile, dark beauty, who could make sticker bindis look like a million bucks and green eye liner an emerald dream. A girl you could take home to your father in Hazoorilal jewellery.

Nagma's father did not accompany her mother and younger sister on their Delhi visit, to see the success of their daughter as a B-grade model. There had been some emotionally tough phone conversations but that had only led to a facade of a patch-up. Her mother, who had been dead against modelling was fascinated by Nagma's pictures from the fashion week, and now admired her new wardrobe and her 'attitude'. She no longer scolded her for saying 'fuck' and enrolled into a parallel, dream journey of her own where all roads led to beti's stardom in Bollywood.

Nagma's younger sister remained aloof on the first day of the Delhi visit, but soon warmed up and wanted to become like didi. Nagma would gulp down her pills in the loo, smoke up and emerge bright eyed but bored all the time, ready to take on the world and her mum. She wore a bra at home with a pair of shorts and her mother soon learnt to accept it.

'The bikini walk that she had been doing for Boss will finally come in handy,' she told me, trying to sound macho about her exploitation.

'How?' I asked.

'I am going to participate in the Kingfisher swimsuit calendar model hunt. Now it comes on Imagine TV. Once I bag the swimsuit calendar contract, and am on TV, there will be no looking back,' she said.

Glamour photographer Atul Kasbekar, who is behind Vijay Mallya's Kingfisher Swimsuit calendar, told me that the maximum number of girls who queued up for the bikini model hunt were from small towns. 'They are really perseverant. You ask them to stand with their hands on their hips for the whole night with their feet in sand and water and they will do it,' said Atul, adding how the Swimsuit Calendar had changed how India looked at women, and how models and Bollywood heroines looked at their bodies.

If Prabuddha Dasgupta's Tuff shoes commercial with Madhu

Sapre and Milind Soman had been the first turning point, the Kingfisher Swimsuit Calendar was another milestone for modelling in India.

'The big difference is that Indian girls are now at ease being exhibitionists about their bodies. It is no longer the bad girl who wears the swimsuit and models are the front runners of this change,' said Atul.

Hot-headed, fanciful and friends with anyone you can name in the glamour industry, Atul has been a photographer for twenty years and still attracts female models and film actresses to himself like bees to a honeycomb. He not only runs Bling! a celebrity management agency but is a brand ambassador himself for Carl F. Bucherer watches. Atul told me that both fashion photography and modelling were in a constant flux as a new page was turned every day. The supermodel has been killed and the bikini model had been born, he said adding that tearing the mystique from the model and leaving her shivering in the cold was media's doing. 'Mehr Jessia used to sign more autographs in her day than a Bollywood star does today,' he said.

Elite Model Management which now has a film casting unit in Mumbai for girls who want to make a Bollywood debut has proved that by grooming models especially for the film industry, they can crack success. Kasbekar's Bling! on the other hand only signed up with those with clear star potential. He has a team of nine people taking business and finance decisions for these girls. He had formerly worked with Matrix, one of Mumbai's top Bollywood agency and pointed out that the X factor that interested him in investing in girls was what Deepika Padukone and Katrina Kaif both had (they were Matrix models). Padukone had been minted by Wendell Rodricks who had spotted her at a Ganjam jewellery class he taught on how to match clothes with jewels but she had come to Mumbai later and signed up with Matrix.

Agencies now work hard to make celebrities out of models. 'Both sides should start making money in three years,' says Atul Kasbekar, 'if that doesn't happen, I'd rather bid a cordial goodbye than continue,' he added.

Sushma Puri of Elite agreed. 'It is not like Paris that you go to a mall at any given time and find 200 girls ready for modelling. Here, it takes time to work on them and get them ready for ramp or print. And it takes ever so much more to make them a star.'

Perhaps this is why Lakshmi Rana said that it is hassling to see the industry make way so easily for fair skinned models. 'It is not easy for us to break into contracts in Europe. They take only two or three foreigners at a time, but here we hire them by the dozen,' she said.

Pressures on models are severe. The biggest reason is the raging war with Bollywood divas for endorsements, magazine covers, and showstopper appearances on the ramp. Girls like Priyanka Chopra, Katrina Kaif, Bipasha Basu, Lara Dutta, Anushka Sharma who were all models and had contested for Miss India now stop a show while their colleagues like Lakshmi Rana have to walk as part of the herd. The stress to maintain super fit and slim bodies, with a now fixed Western ideal of feminine beauty—tall, thin, leggy, small busted—has only increased. The body, the site, cause and reason behind all success and failure in modelling is a big bone of contention. Yet as Prasad Bidapa says, 'Everything can be fixed. Bring me anything, anyone, I can fix and alter it and make a model, except height, which I can't manufacture.'

Once 'fixing' is done, they all look the same.

'Shut up and walk' is the unspoken code, as Nagma told me. 'And network hard,' she added. Models must get their networking and PR right to keep getting contracts, agencies notwithstanding. Not everyone becomes a Miss India.

Even those who do, find that the crown can be thorny. They have mentors to tell them how to walk and talk, dieticians and fitness experts to worry about their already thin figures yet, it is 'an intimidating and sometimes frightful journey,' a Femina insider told me. She had seen girls slip into sullenness from the time they entered the contest, to when they became winners (or losers). 'They forget to laugh except giggle on cue and lose the spontaneity they had as free spirited girls who had come to win the pageant,' she said. Some have nervous breakdowns, crack under pressures of surgeries for face, nose or chin, articulation in speech and manner, punishing fitness regimes, starvation diets and recovery from it all before they leave for the international beauty contests.

It reflected in the breakdown of Miss India first runner up 2009 Pooja Chopra had on the Miss World stage in South Africa. The girl who had broken her ankle days before the contest was disallowed from using a wheelchair and broke down on the stage in the final round, sobbing till she was ushered away.

Gautam who has worked with all models and often styles the tall, dark and handsome Lakshmi Menon, also the only model whose name has a recall value in Europe now, says she is the story of the New Indian Female Model. Lakshmi is the only model who was invited by the American *Vogue* to feature in their pages for a solitary fashion editorial. She was also the only Indian model whose photograph was displayed as part of 'Beauty Culture', an exhibition in Los Angeles that ran till November 2011. It focussed on female beauty and its evolution through the twentieth and twenty first centuries and was seen through the work of globally acclaimed photographers. Among photographs and digital images, classified under labels like 'The Hollywood Glamour Machine', 'The Marilyn Syndrome', 'Barbie Doll' or the modelling industry, was a photograph of the tall, dark, and distinctly androgynous Lakshmi Menon. She was among girls from different ethnicities like German Claudia Schiffer, American Cindy Crawford, British Naomi Campbell, Canadian Linda Evangelista, Brazilian Gisele Bundchen, British Kate Moss, American Megan Fox and Sudanese-British Alek Wek.

Lakshmi, said Gautam, is underwhelmed with fashion's snobbery and doesn't give a damn. 'She has a quality of intelligent arrogance which no one else has. That makes her the current top model,' he said.

Nagma New, as I would learn to later call her (shaven armpits, fewer F words) agreed with Gautam. Emotional distance, she said, helped her deal with the demanding clauses on their contracts, and post-show partying as non-negotiable for the IPL Season 2 last year. The noose has become tighter for models as a maniacal media chases them 24x7. On the one hand, it wields the Photoshop, quick to airbrush reality. One the other, it zooms in on slender limbs, shrieking about starvation, and gleefully flashes every fashion malfunction.

They all come with good intentions from good families, who don't want them to enter the profession. But once they are in, they are surrounded by parties, drugs, egocentrics, long hours of work, putting on and peeling away of make up, false lashes, false boobs, clamps and have to master the art of expressionless talent, a model coordinator told me. The smaller ones start doing escort services and sex work on the side. It is not rampant, and boys do it too, but if you looked hard enough, you will find enough cases, he said.

Amit Ranjan came up with an important argument. Models no longer just compete with Bollywood, he said. Now a designer is free to bring a transgender person, a Kathak dancer, a ghazal singer, or a nautanki artist on the ramp to rustle up a 'spectacle' giving even the best model competition from unknown and unpredictable quarters.

Rajesh Pratap Singh brought musicians from rock bands like Parikrama to walk his ramp among professional models for his show at Men's Fashion Week in 2010. Designer duo Lecoanet Hemant brought Queen Harish, a drag queen on their ramp.

Nagma New was trying hard to be a bit removed from it all. It worked well for her, even though she is a nobody in the industry. She made good money, smoked, did some drugs and booze, bought a lot of designer clothes, sometimes flew abroad for magazine shoots and lived the fast life. She couldn't break into the league of A-lister models till the end of 2011 when I concluded this story. She was nowhere near becoming India's next Mehr Jessia and there was no sign of 'Bollywood' happening to her. 'If I can't become Mehr Jessia, I will marry Boss,' she said when I prodded her about her frustration.

To Boss? Vinegar with Rajnigandha paan masala and no sex?

She laughed nervously. She stumped me. I thought she liked to go out with different boys every week and here she was suggesting marriage with someone who had never touched her. What was going on?

I'd never find out.

Vipasha Agarwal of Benares, who is now married to a fashion photographer, says she prefers her life as a homemaker to the modelling assignments she now selectively accepts. 'I am at peace at home. I love it this way, even if I have to pick up the broom and sweep the floors. Otherwise modelling can become an addiction,' she says wisely. Lakshmi Rana had told me many times over that she had a life beyond modelling and was comforted by it.

Models are fashion accessories in India now, not embodiments of women's liberation as they were forty years back. In the last shot of Gautam's shoot Dark Desire, the model is shown trying to cut the strings with a pair of scissors.

'I now have four pairs of scissors in my styling kit,' he whispered into my ears. 'Who knows when I will need them?'

*Name changed

Boy, Interrupted

'I am free and that's why I am lost.'
—Franz Kafka

Imcha smiled. Only with his eyes. His lips refused to oblige. He had lost many kilos since I had seen him in Nagaland a year ago. He was 29-years-old but looked like a college student. He wore blue jeans, a white T shirt and funky emerald green suede shoes. His hair was sticky like I remembered it but the spectacles had been replaced by contact lenses. His most noticeable accessory was a certain shade of ease that he didn't have in our former meetings. A National Institute of Design (NID) student who had debuted as a designer in Lakme Fashion Week's GenNext show some years ago, he sat across me in my office at *The Indian Express* last October describing The Episodes.

'My friends thought I would jump from the college building and kill myself,' said Imcha Imchen.

Killing himself was certainly the last thing on his mind when he had packed his bags in his Mokokchung village house to leave Nagaland for further studies in the 'mainland'. He had completed junior college in Kohima and wanted to enroll for a degree in Environmental Sciences in Bangalore.

That was the summer of 2001. Mornings in Nagaland were lambent, and sunsets a tapestry of ochre weaves with trees swishing restlessly under the spell of temperamental winds. As he looked out from the window of the bus which drove him to Dimapur airport to leave for college, he knew he would miss the pongsen fish his mum cooked in bamboos, the cognac evenings when he walked by himself, humming a song, greeting vendors who sold pineapples by the roadside and Naga women who ran rice hotels (sic).

Imcha Imchen belonged to the Ao tribe and was the youngest of five siblings. They are a very progressive family. When Imcha was a child, his father was an office clerk who would go on to become one of the most recognized university professors in Nagaland. Before that, they had very limited means and Imcha with his other siblings would distribute milk in the neighbourhood. Since pigs are reared in most households in Naga villages, his mother would make sure the pigs were taken care of, as piglets sold for a decent amount. His mother, a school teacher would also weave mekhlas on the side and sell them to cachet extra earnings. That was not all. 'My mother makes excellent homemade jams and juices and she would conduct training classes for the women's department in the Church to generate additional income,' he recalled.

With five children to be raised, the Imchen family had to stretch to make ends meet, but Imcha says that things improved when his father was transferred to Medziphema. 'My father was the first in the town to buy a television set in the late Eighties. I remember watching Aamir Khan's *Qayamat Se Qayamat Tak* shown on Doordarshan with the entire colony cramped in our drawing room,' he recalls. 'The womenfolk wept as they watched the film, also because Khan fetching wood in the movie to keep his home fire burning was something we all related to.'

Imcha's father played the saxophone in The Living Gospel Band, and with his sister Achi, also as naturally inclined to music as himself, the siblings would accompany their father to villages and sing with the band during church seminars and village celebrations. Achi and Imcha even recorded an album when he was thirteen and the album was a local sellout. Their mother, who would go on to become the principal of a government school also sang Alto in a women's church group. Till today, the father plays happy birthday for his five children on the mouth organ whether on the phone if they are away or in person if they are with him at the family home.

Given the warmth of the cocoon, going to 'India' to study was a leap of faith for Imcha. Who knew, certainly not him that the next time he would return to Nagaland, there would be an insurgency in his mind.

Imcha tried to keep his head down at St Joseph's College in Bangalore to study Zoology and Chemistry. But he couldn't keep his mind down. It would wander too much. He was a restive young man, either excessively fidgety and impatient or prone to depressive spells that would be like dungeons of deep, scary, self-questioning moments. 'Mostly self-esteem issues riddled with doubts about my identity, purpose in life, religion, roots,' he would say later.

Creative arts stirred his imagination more than Zoology and soon after his graduation in 2003, even before his final year results were announced; he applied to NID in Ahmedabad, where he felt he would be closer to the artist in him. He managed a seat for a diploma course in Apparel Design and Merchandizing.

Initially, Imcha warmed up to the NID campus. It was just his kind of place—meaningful and inclusive. It invited him to discover India through design and textiles, life through freedom of inquiry. He would play Frisbee with friends, and eat batata vada with packed Amul lassi in the outdoor canteen in the evenings, assimilating his surroundings closer to his sense of self. The quiet, grey carpeted library became his mentor, the course his design studio.

Till, the First Episode happened.

Imcha would have fallen off the building that day, barely a few months after starting the course, had one of his classmates not noticed that he was leaning dangerously over the balcony railing.

'I have no idea where I was, except that it felt like a heavenly, dreamy place. Though if you ask me what heaven looks like, I wouldn't know what to say. I felt nauseous and lightheaded, not in control of myself at all. I don't even know how to explain it...'

His small eyes crinkled even more and he attempted a laugh. This time, his lips tried to support him.

Soon after that precarious moment, he found himself sitting before a psychiatrist, who wanted to know everything about this young, suicidal boy from Nagaland.

The First Episode was like a free fall for him. 'I remember sitting in the basketball court at NID with my head in my hands and then just lost it,' he said. It was all catching up. Turbulence in the mind, restlessness, agitation, severe mood swings, dreaminess, insomnia, anger, followed by long, visceral bouts of depression. Imcha had swung between acute depression to hyper agitation, all symptoms of bipolar disorder.

'I neither smoked, nor had alcohol or any kind of drugs but felt that I was out of my body and zombie-like,' he said.

His friends assumed the obvious. They thought that either it was a case of severe drug addiction or he was suicidal.

The psychiatrist at the Ahmedabad hospital he was taken to by his friends diagnosed him with bipolar disorder after a series of tests and queries about his past history and sent him back to Nagaland to 'recover'.

I saw Imcha for the first time in 2008 at Lakme Fashion Week's (LFW) GenNext show. He was one among the ten designers chosen to debut on the platform, which has been flush with media attention. His small collection (each debutant is invited to show a few garments each) was called Mangkoakir. Inspired by a headhunting Naga tribe, it was dominated by blazing red and black colours. The music was Echoes of Alleluia by Nise Meruno, a Naga musician. Nobody in the audience could have guessed that the short, sweet Naga boy taking a bow that day was battling with bipolar disorder.

Imcha's next collection, also at LFW had Naga musician Senti Toy's track Kohima roll in the background. From a GenNext debutant, Imcha had become an emerging designer and his clothes once again got him thunderous applause on the LFW stage. The collection was named How Many Stories Can You Read on My Face.

But no one in the audience could read Imcha's face.

It was the opaque quality of his face and the reluctance with which he sometimes wore his identity as a fashion designer that drew me to Imcha. In an industry full of self-obsessed people, his words 'fashion's bottomless disenchantment', were an unforgettable headline.

It was only later when he explained the shattering intensity of his Episodes that I realized that his bipolarity would push his likings and disliking to extreme edges, sometimes opening up a war between his own multiple talents. His creative pursuits were defined by music, fashion and photography, but there would be phases when he would feel acutely polarized against fashion and couldn't understand why. When the Episode would ebb, fashion would again beckon and music would recede to become a background score instead of a live performance in his mind.

'Do you remember the hospital you were treated at?' I asked him as we chatted in Delhi five years after his diagnosis.

'Yes, of course,' he said.

'Tell me its name,' I asked.

He couldn't recall it.

'Do you remember the doctor?'

'Of course,' he laughed a big laugh this time.

'Tell me the name.'

He couldn't recall.

'Male or female?'

'Male.'

After a year of being nursed and cared for by anxious parents and concerned siblings, Imcha had returned to NID to finish his course, having fallen a year behind.

'Talking about my problems is like therapy,' he said. His sincerity would bob up repeatedly in his eyes as if the opaque features were cracking in places to allow transparent pools for his soul to peep out.

I also noticed that the zillion little insights that his illness had thrown up about himself were adding to the complexity with which he now interpreted life. When he would tell me his story, it was like he was reading out from a book from which some pages had been ripped out; his narrative was broken, jagged. I tried to piece together his story after repeatedly interrupting him with questions.

Some of his comments would be absolutely unexceptional but they would be punctuated with searing philosophic observations coming as if from a compelling intellectual. Conversations with him were an exploration of the inexplicable connects between mental illness and raw intelligence that modern psychological thought has engaged with. Imcha represented that dichotomy.

His cryptic, unfinished thoughts and sentences weren't new. We had been communicating off and on for a few years now, ever since his LFW debut. His inconsistent communication, befuddling phone smses, sending of photographs instead of writing email notes had indicated that all was not well.

Dear Imcha, (I remember writing in one of my emails to him) I want to come to Nagaland and see you in your hometown. I want to write about you and about Naga fashion through your eyes. When will you go home? Can I join you?

No response for weeks.

Then one day, I got a photograph from him of what seemed to be a building under construction. He had captioned it as the office of his Heritage Foundation Project in his village Mokokchung. He added that he was in Ahmedabad, assisting a designer. Then what was this photograph about, I wondered. And why was he sending me something completely unconnected?

'Aren't you doing fashion anymore?' I wrote back.

No response.

I wrote again asking him when I could meet him in Nagaland.

'Dear Shefalee,' popped up an email one day, many weeks after I had given up on Imcha. 'I will be going home for the Hornbill Festival; do you want to come at that time?'

I visited Nagaland during the Hornbill festival in December 2010. Imcha came to receive me at the airport with his elder sister Achi who had also flown in from Bangalore, for the festival. Achi is a pretty, petite Naga girl with impeccable manners who works as a human resource trainer in Bangalore. She is urbane with an enviable lightness of being and yet has a maturity about her that makes you take her seriously from the first instant. She smiles a lot. But I could barely recognize Imcha. He had put on weight, wore specs, his face looked greasy and exhausted. The opaqueness of his expression had only intensified. He was now like smiling wood.

He told me he was in the throes of the Second Episode. Though by now, he was under the care of a psychiatrist at Nimhans in Bangalore and on daily medication. Achi took me aside at the house of one of their sisters in Dimapur and told me that Imcha wasn't well.

'He didn't want to tell you over email or phone,' she said. 'I suggested that you do not visit us while he is unwell, but he wasn't sure about what to say to you,' she added.

Imcha was pacing the corridor outside the house while Achi told me about his bipolar disorder, his inability to take his medicines regularly and how he had been drifting aimlessly.

As a result of these confessional exchanges, our conversations became easier and friendliness seeped in. The baggage was out of the closet and it was as if we had jointly opened and rummaged through it. Imcha was clearly distressed but the fold of his warm and caring family was a nurturing influence. His older siblings—I would meet all of them including a dentist sister—were protective of him. He was the kid brother and they had agreeably agreed to indulge him.

This was also the time when the viral connect Imcha had earlier felt with fashion hung like a fragile thread in his head. 'The bipolarity puts a complete block and a shutter on everything; it distances me from everyone. Every belief and strength that I own goes down the drain,' he would tell me later. We would be wrong to assume that he had parachuted out of the fashion world, but he just couldn't help drifting away from it when possessed by an Episode. The burden on his head had descended to his heart. During an intense phase of bipolarity, fashion didn't seem to be the charming world of vanities and wonderment it was when all was well. During an Episode, everything was like a visceral vacuum, which led Imcha to find solace in contemporary pop and soul, his favourite music genre and his childhood love.

Imcha was confused and unsure; fatally attracted to the

deep reds and burning blacks of Naga textiles but momentarily disillusioned with the way urban India treated fashion. If cling and bling, parties and Page 3, narcissism and creative compromises were what the industry impelled, he wondered what he was seeking there. Very odd, till his therapist helped him understand that such disillusionments were temporary and wouldn't necessarily last once his medication and therapy began to work. Till he could learn to decode the patterns of his illness, he tried to make sense of the noise in his head through music.

The rock bands that played on the fourth day of the week-long annual Hornbill festival were deafening and unmelodious. The music, said Imcha, was screaming anger. 'They aren't singing, just ranting against the system,' he said when Faded Black, a Naga band, roared into the cold night.

His female friends however didn't agree. The girls were enjoying the medley and the backslapping camaraderie with pals they hadn't met in months. They chatted excitedly in Nagamese and hugged each other warmly even as the chilly Kohima evening held everyone in its unrelenting embrace. Dressed in slick western garments, mostly in blue jeans, Ugg boots with faux fur trimmings and stylishly layered tops, long belted jackets, knitted mufflers, berets or woollen caps, the girls looked like they had taken fashion lessons from magazines. Poker straight hair, soft, nicely applied make up with blue and silver eye shadows, an occasional well-chosen piece of costume jewellery—their style was admirable.

The bright, cold amethyst winter evening was accessorized by emerald bushes around us, a gem of an evening you could say, but Imcha's restlessness was palpable. He wrapped a knitted stole in natural coloured nettle plant thread on his head like a Gujarati villager's turban, something only a fashion designer would do.

He looked different from the other boys of his age who wore sweatshirts and thick boots. He also stood a few feet away from his friends, arms folded, thoughtfully gazing at the clear night sky and pointed out to me the design alliance formed by the constellations of stars.

After the performance of the band Faded Black, Imcha's older brother dove us to an open air food court in Kohima. Over bonfire smoke, pork chowmein, beef chutney (sic), sticky rice and snail masala, Imcha told me that every time he came back home, the disconnect between his state and the mainland made him wince. This time the cultural nostalgia churned by the Hornbill festival only added to his disturbed mental state.

The wedge between mainland and Nagaland had a cultural texture to it and my first rapid fire round with a group of girls and boys having rice beer around a bonfire inside the Pochury tribe hut would reveal it more.

Preferred fashion style?

Korean or Hollywood red carpet.

Hair?

Ironed like Jennifer Aniston.

Bollywood influence on Nagas?

Zero.

Bling?

We hate it.

Aishwarya Rai?

Like her at Cannes but haven't seen her films.

Priyanka Chopra?

Uh, ummm... not sure.

Kareena perhaps?

Glamorous and stupid.

Twinkle Khanna?

Who's she?

Shilpa Shetty's body?

What do we care? Naga girls have 20-inch waists.

Why isn't there a local Page 3?

Facebook is our Page 3.

Kurtas and leggings?

Thank you, but no thank you.

'*Aisha*, the Sonam Kapoor starrer was successful in making Naga youth take notice of a Bollywood movie for its clothes. Pernia Qureshi, the stylist of the film had fans in Nagaland I was told and that's testimony to the wardrobe hype the film created.

Imcha told me to take this swagger about not being crazy about Bollywood and Hindi serials with a pinch of salt. This was an exaggerated front to be used for 'outsiders'. 'There is a big segment of Nagas who are crazy about Bollywood and saas-bahu serials,' he said recalling an incident when, during a prayer meeting in his town, a cluster of women discussed why they didn't want the protagonist from a Hindi serial to die!

Not that anyone would own up to this.

Rozelle Mero's outburst would explain why. 'Fashion, décor and lifestyle magazines ignore us, nobody writes articles on our cuisine, reality TV in mainland has no place for us, our clothes are considered unwearable, North Eastern girls are raped and molested in metros.'

'If I go to a party in Delhi and introduce myself, people start looking away as if they don't want to waste their time,' said Rozelle breathlessly, fusing the strands of her frustration.

Persuasive and persistent, she stood out in this otherwise PR unfriendly society. The full-figured and trendily dressed Rozelle had walked up to Imcha and me as we sat in the Kisama open air amphitheatre watching tribal dances at the Hornbill venue. A 41-year-old single mother, with a Punjabi father and Naga mother, she was an information directory. Vocal, vociferous, former hostess of the Miss Nagaland contest, jury member at the first ever fashion Naga week of 2010, a consulting vendor for Kingfisher air hostesses and five star hospitality executives and an interior designer by training, Rozelle, was a Jill of All Trades. She was also the publicist for Imcha Imchen during his fashion week debut in Mumbai. 'It's time India helped us realize our dreams. Visiting us during the Hornbill festival is a token but it is not enough,' declared Rozelle.

The Hornbill festival that derives its name from a native bird with white and black feathers extolled in folk tales, completed its ten years in 2010. Bound by Arunachal Pradesh in the north, Assam in the west, Manipur in the south and Myanmar in the east with an area of 16,579 sq km and population of 19.81 lakhs by the 2011 Census, Nagaland is a jungle-clad isolated region. The Hornbill Festival is a cultural regalia set in the Heritage Village in the hills of Kisama, beyond Kohima, it is about 87 km from Dimapur which has the nearest airport. Kisama—acronym for Kigwena and Phesama—both Angami villages has been developed as a permanent venue to showcase the Naga way of life. The seven-day fest overflows with pungent rice beer, the ambrosia of all moments of fun and celebration in an otherwise dry state where alcohol is prohibited (though easily available). Rice beer is served in bamboo mugs or recycled bottles of mineral water. These bottles are beheaded to let the fermented brew bubble without restraint. It's a local favourite as is zarda paan. Throw in a few smokes and you have a languid crowd. No flighty laughs or piercing laughter, no blaring Hindi music, just drum beats with groups dancing around a fire or sitting by without any fuss, a trifle high on beer, and chewing paan as the day unhurriedly clambers on.

Dances performed by the sixteen headhunting Naga tribes, narrating stories of victory over man and beast entertain tourists; morungs showcase the lifestyle and cooking spaces of ethnic tribes. Alongside, there are stalls that sell traditional textiles, beaded jewellery in orange, black and white beads, totemic masks, pendants made from bone and wood, long red earrings from dyed yam hair, bracelets of piped metal. Alongside many stalls sold indigenous food items like cakes of sticky rice wrapped in leaves, dried wild apple, gooseberry, pickled beef and pork, spiced soya bean seeds and the deadly Naga red chilli—pickled, fried or raw—the hottest chilli of the world, an angry red in colour, deservingly called Rajah.

'I like red,' says Imcha holding a red beaded necklace with little metal pendants on it.

'Is that why you used a lot of red in your first fashion collection?'

'It is not only a tribal colour but look around, even the turbans of the Sikh jawaans posted in the army all over Nagaland are red,' he said. Red made Imcha feel cheerful, it was also the predominant colour of the textiles of his homeland.

Mangoakir, the name of Imcha's first collection meant Head Taker or Headhunter—a common reference in their society, but he told mc that thc younger generation didn't want to be referred to as a warrior tribe all the time. They believe that there is more to Nagas. Imcha agreed that the common perception that Nagas are obsessed with the motif of war is probably because of the striking parallels between the textiles and crafts of Nagaland with the head hunting rituals and ancient practices and customs.

'Is that misleading?' I asked.

'Of course. We are a warrior tribe but we are not at war. War remains in our consciences as a bookmark. Given the historical background of Nagaland, the war cemeteries around us and the insurgency that has stabbed our state, it can't be deleted,' he said.

During Imcha's many conversations at his mother's village with elders about mekhlas, the traditional garment for women, he learnt how women started wearing jeans and layers of trousers underneath the mekhlas to protect themselves from the Army during the late Sixties. 'It made it a lot easier for them to run,' says Imcha. Once his mother with her best friend, had run away scared by a group of jawaans marching towards them. Only later they realized the soldiers were marching past the area.

The Naga problem is the epicentre of all North-Eastern insurgencies, provoking almost all ethnic groups in the region to push for secessionist demands and a separate statehood within the Indian Union. Ironically, the Kohima World War II Cemetery is now an important tourist site in Kohima. I was told it had more graves of British soldiers than Naga nationals.

What certainly stood out was a distrust for outsiders among the locals even the younger generation. One of the girls at the stall from where Imcha bought the necklace was an MBBS graduate who had studied in Orissa and was back home to look for a job. 'I feel unsafe in other cities,' she said. She and her mum sold hornbill feathers and wooden pendants including some with ghoulish faces. I resisted one with an angry, sullen expression saying it may bring me bad karma. The doctor–salesgirl smiled wanly. 'Nobody takes bad luck from Nagaland, but sometimes it does find its way in from other parts of the country.'

Nagas believe in destiny and luck. Before their conversion to Christianity in early twentieth century, they were Animists, with faith in spirit or soul of everything including inanimate objects, plants, animals or geographical entities like storms and earthquakes. Animism is a primitive belief held by indigenous tribes in the world and those who are followers of neo-paganism or totemism. An open talk on animism with contemporary Naga Christians is difficult unless they trust you. Innately, they veil these leanings, if there are any traces. 'If you guys wear a mask as a pendant it looks very nice, if we wear it, people stare at us in the mainland thinking we are wearing an ominous totem,' Imcha's sister said.

The conversion of Nagas to Christianity, seen initially as a controlling tool by the British, eventually did bring a change in their primitive temperament. The influence of the missionaries paved the way towards the Westernization of Naga lifestyle. This Westernization is more than obvious. The local girls we met at Hornbill were dressed like those at the rock concert the previous day. Boots, jeans, caps, scarves, long jackets. Very few wore woven, tribal mekhlas which are tied like sarongs around the waist. Those who had, paired them with short silk tops accessorized with sling bags and kitten heels. They seemed to possess a talent for well-coordinated dressing with an eye for proportions in colour and shape. No sequins, no Swarovskis, no embroideries. Except on wives of military jawaans who came wearing patiala salwars, multi-coloured kurtas, toe rings, bangles, red and white wedding choodas, a bold line of vermillion in their hair, flashy jewellery and sandals with golden buckles on them. The difference between the North Indians and Nagas was stark, in-your-face.

Kohima is a scenic but dumpy little town, with congested traffic and dismal tourism facilities. After sunset at around 4:30

pm in winters, the streets are desolate without street lights. It was Christmas season when I was visiting and stray sparks of light scattered from the decorations lit up a corner here, a speck there.

Yet, at any moment if the gaze moves from the town to the people who walk by, it is as if the town has shifted in its boots. In stark contrast to the surroundings, the people are a delight to watch. Even village girls wear neon nail polish with long striped T-shirts, legging and shoes, multiple piercings on their ears (none on the nose) and have tattoos. School girls are allowed to wear blue eye liner or purple mascara to school with funky hair accessories and ribbed black stockings under school frocks. Everyone speaks English.

Yet, the definition of fashion and culture is Korean—in posters, clothing, music and Naga youth speaking Korean language. When he was still young, Imcha's father had worked on a cross border trading project. That's when Imcha had first found out that second-hand clothes were brought into Nagaland from other neighbouring countries. Now, a large number of older people in Nagaland, like any other community in the country lament about youth vs tradition, holding Koreanization responsible for the degeneration of Naga culture. Imcha who often wears textile kurtas was once told by a shopkeeper not to wear them as they would make him one from the 'mainland'.

The Nagas are a fashionable people but there is no tangible market for fashion in Nagaland. There is no Westside, Pantaloons, Shopper's Stop, Lifestyle, or Big Bazaar in Nagaland. Not Fabindia or Khadi Bhandar either. Contemporary Naga fashion is at best a smart amalgamation of second-hand clothes consumed by richer countries brought here through porous borders, even from the US via the Spice Route. It was only in late 2011 that a fashion store opened in Dimpaur and Kohima to stock designer wear from all over India.

The Koreanization of the people realized ironically through American brands in dressing is fuelled by the street shops of Dimapur and Kohima called Hongkong and Shangri-La markets. They are flush with goods from China, Thailand, Myanmar, and Hongkong. Here, shutters go up as early as eight in the morning during Christmas as residents of towns and villagers come shopping in droves. At the Hongkong market in Dimapur, sneakers in vibrant colours, ballet flats in suede, wedge-heeled slippers with stripes, checks, and flowers, T-shirts and tops in a hundred different varieties, dresses, vests, skirts, and jeans were all over. An odd sling bag with an Andy Warhol sketch too. Made in China knock offs of Western luxury brands were aplenty as were T-shirts with I Love New York or Chicago on them. This is why, most North-Eastern girls, found themselves compulsively drawn to high street shops in Indian cities, a Naga designer would later tell me.

Interestingly, the Chanel logo with its two intertwining Cs is a common sight in the street markets. It is pasted on everything from ankle boots to caps, handbags to sweatshirts, even on goods that Chanel doesn't make as a brand. In this grey market, Chanel had overtaken LV fakes. But when you look around, there is nothing remotely French about the fashion language of Naga girls, even when they wear a fake Chanel bag. Not one girl wore a Little Black Dress with black stockings, two-toned shoes with strings of pearls, embodying the Chanel sensibility. Japanese Harakuju in dressing, yes; French chic and Indicoolness no.

'It is not a coincidence that the most popular bloggers in India are from the North East, particularly Nagaland,' Imcha pointed out. Their do-it-yourself fashion is laced with romantic angst, both common afflictions among the Naga youth. 20-year-old Al Walling who started writing a blog to 'get the attention of publications' is a premature victim of this disease. His mental brewery fantastically titled iknowwhokilledmonsieurpromiscous.blogspot.com is a furnace where a promiscuous fire keeps both hope and disillusionment burning.

Sample one of his Tweets.

AIDS. An Isolated Dirty Secret or, Another Island Defying Scorn. I choose the latter. It's a fight and what's a virus against hope and love?

'The name of my blog is a word play on self-love and suicide,' Walling wrote to me on email. He is the eldest of three brothers who grew up in Kohima, schooled in Dimapur and enrolled in a college in Shillong only to drop out to find work in Mumbai.

Fashion influences Al as it does many other young Nagas. 'It inspires me. Don't ask me what kind of fashion. It would be like dissecting a body,' he said. Lahlahishere@blogspot.com and lazymanxcat@blogspot.com both blogs of Naga girls more than validate Walling's statement. Leslie Lobeni, the blogger of lazymanxcat is now a fashion week regular. These blogs reflect the democracy of dressing that Naga girls and boys associate with fashion.

Dream Café in Kohima is a popular local hangout where people can sit and chat for hours. Its large, wide windows look out at the tropical, evergreen forests on the hills of Kohima, dense with Pine and Alder trees, as clouds waltz by. They serve chicken chowmein for Rs 70 only and a cappuccino is priced at Rs 30.

This is where I waited for two Naga designers. Roshu Ri and Keds Krome, as different as chalk and cheese.

The bespectacled, plump, Roshu came across as earnest and tentative, a Simple Simon. Raised in a rural family in the Chakhesang tribe of Zhavame village, he started hand sewing and modifying his own clothes on his sister's old hand machine when he was in Class 4. By the time he was in the Class 10 he would stitch clothes and sell an odd one to his classmates for pocket money. This continued during his years in college as by then he had lost his father and badly needed the money to sustain himself. Roshu who could not afford the fashion course at NID, settled for a polytechnic degree in fashion and apparel design. Now he makes bridal gowns from a small house in Kohima. Since travelling to Thailand to buy materials to make corset bones or get fancy fabrics is not within his means, he cuts plastic files and bolsters his corsets with it.

'I deliberately make unwearable garments to display my creativity,' said Roshu Rhi. For his Hornbill Contest collection titled Reverie, he had showcased everything he knew about making clothes. Fabric flowers on gowns, corsets with appliquéd motifs, laces, frills, flounces, sheathing, chiffon trains... Whatever it takes, Roshu wants to be in fashion.

Like Keds Krome but for entirely different reasons. Unusually tall for a Naga, Keds strutted down like a model in her high heeled red boots, spine pulled back, her slim body taut and purposeful in its walk. She wore camouflage jeggings, a long white T-shirt with digital black printing on it, a long Japanese style sleeveless hosiery jacket, leather earrings, black nail polish, black eyeshadow and bright red streaks in her short punk hair. Her eyebrow had been pierced with a tiny gold ring with a blue stone. I stared unapologetically, afraid that I would miss some detail. Keds was effusive in her manner and her dressing combined military and rock chic—two dominant realities of her life as a Naga.

Keds turned out to be a former model and now runs a boutique from her Kohima home supplementing it with a fitness centre. She went to NIFT Bangalore for a post graduate course in fashion designing. Even before she graduated in 2003, she started an eponymous label. She came back home because she saw sense in consolidating a local clientele. She now specializes in Western garments with 'Indian embroidery', bridal gowns and, the rare dhoti salwars.

'Indian embroidery?' I asked. 'There are hundreds—which one do you do?

'Maybe zardozi,' she said, trailing off and unsure but quickly pulled out some clothes she had made from bamboo fabric with subtle chain and satin stitch embroidery.

'Most of us work from home and we are dependent on bridal gowns for business. There is nothing like a shelf of ready-to-wear, nor do we have walk-in customers,' she said explaining how the social unrest in the state had been detrimental for business. With camouflage as her central theme, one of Keds's favourite collections was called Alternative Destiny. She admitted she was deeply influenced by the insurgency and the military deployment in her state.

'What do people do in the evenings; they are so long and stretched?' I asked Keds. I didn't want to confess that I had felt claustrophobic in my hotel room on evenings when I didn't join friends for hangout-and-do-nothing parties.

'A lot of young people now throw private parties and their friends as well as friends of friends get lured to revelry. There are many rich Naga families, some people throw a party every day,' said Keds.

Bridal designer wear is the only consistently selling category and to make ends meet, everyone makes bridal gowns, which cost between Rs 10,000 to Rs 60,000. Naga brides who would earlier wear traditional mekhlas for weddings with silk or satin tops and white, lacy beaded veils now wear strapless gowns with long trains and corseted waists accessorized by designer veils and pointy Bangkok shoes. The mekhla is very much around but more as a ceremonial garment like a kimono. Curiously, most Naga mekhlas, symbols of tradition and identity, are made from an acrylic fabric called Thai, imported from Thailand. Only a select few are woven in pure cotton or silk by the village artisans. Imcha told me that since synthetic colours are now available in Kohima and are also brought in from Assam, the use of natural dyes for mekhlas has diminished. Natural dyes are now considered inferior to synthetically coloured garments. 'If it rains, folks wearing Indigo-dyed garments would find their bodies soaked in blue,' said Imcha. Not much textile innovation has been done to revive mekhlas in natural dyes which don't fade.

Local textiles and colours are used as symbols. Naga designers had used trimmings from tribal textiles to embellish gowns copied from Valentino and Roberto Cavalli. Others had converted green and red checked textiles into short, cinched dresses, sent down the ramp with high-heeled boots.

Yet, without stylists, the interpretation of fashion is so wide and scattered that it translates into a fancy dress parade at fashion shows. After seeing the Hornbill Designers' Contest, I could understand why Al Walling called it an entertainment filler.

That's why local designers feel no obligation to follow international or Indian fashion trends, seasonal distinctions in collections nor do they conform to quality control standards of the industry. They look at fashion magazines like *Vogue*, *Harper's Bazaar*, and *Marie Claire* sometimes, but more for amusement. Unlike the North Indians, they are not logo-obsessed. They are as happy carrying fakes. It's a free-for-all scenario and process management is always a hiccup. To be selected for a fashion show, a collection need not even be suitable to the theme announced by the organizers.

The Miss Nagaland beauty contest represented a similar absence of frenzy for grooming. Imcha is a fairly well-known name in Kohima as a Lakme Fashion Week emerging designer and had been invited to be on the jury of the Miss Nagaland contest. He didn't accept; he said he was not up to taking any kind of pressure or expectation but he went with me to watch the rehearsals. 'Do these girls really stand a chance to become mainstream models?' I asked him, as we sat through the rehearsals and giggled when the girls practised the catwalk.

Most don't. Not just because they are shorter than mainstream models but because there is no one to train them in styling, grooming, articulation, catwalk, or professional make up. There are a couple of modelling agencies in Nagaland now, as well as in other North Eastern states as many local beauty contests have sprung up. Each state has its own beauty pageant as do different districts. These contests and the agencies are conduits for job placements inside the seven states or for girls to land contracts for local product endorsements. Contestants who participate in district pageants usually go on to enter the Miss North East contest, this side of the country's answer to Miss India. 'Even if some girls are keen on modelling, parents are reluctant to send them to the mainland given the way we are treated there. Everyone finds us pretty, humble, adaptable, and easy prey. It is only in the mainland where "chinky" is a ridicule instead of a compliment,' said Rozelle. Something about me was clearly provoking her rant against 'mainland India'.

But Monikangana Dutta from Assam and Esther Jamir from Nagaland proved the grand aunties wrong. Moni (as the industry calls Monikangana), now one of the hottest models on the Indian ramp, has been on umpteen fashion magazine covers including some of the top ad campaigns. Designers and fashion photographers love her. Enchanted by her dark, tall, sinewy looks, director Sanjay Leela Bhansali gave her a break to act with Bollywood dreamboat Hrithik Roshan in *Guzaarish*, his film on a magician who turns paraplegic due to an accident.

Esther Jamir, too, is a Naga model who debuted at the Wills Fashion Week in Delhi five years back. The tall, skinny, light skinned Esther landed plum modelling assignments. Her pictures now sit on Naga pride websites and for many aspirants back home, she is a poster girl.

'Esther made it because she stopped behaving like a Naga,' a girl told me over red tea at the Hornbill venue. She had worked with an *India Today* lifestyle publication in Delhi and knew what it took to survive in the mainland. 'You have to be aggressive, market yourself without worries of being exploited and make friends with everyone around instead of clinging to your sisterhood.'

Like the choices Naga designer Atsu Sekhose, now based in Delhi, made. He carries his Naga identity lightly on his shoulders and doesn't wear it as a badge. 34-year-old Atsu studied at Delhi's

NIFT and went on to work under Tarun Tahiliani. Since he started his own label, his ramp shows have won applause, his clothes have been on covers of almost all fashion magazines published in India and he has fans among fashion stylists and editors. He makes contemporary Western garments, subtly embellished with sequins. 'A little of what Delhi wants and a little of want Mumbai wants,' he told me when, adding how he has been able to pin down a market for himself without becoming oblivious to Indian crafts or the karigars.

When I queried the mainstream designers in Delhi or Mumbai, very few had anything to say about Naga fashion. Most of them drew a blank. Many didn't even have a visual reference in their minds for it. Maybe they would recognize a Naga shawl when they see one, but Naga fashion?

Back in Naga villages, the mekhla or a tribal shawl is a part of ritualistic life. What you wear and how you wear it, is bound by tribal rules. When I was about to try a black and red shawl with thick patches of white embroidered animal motifs, an Ao tribe creation, Imcha's sisters discouraged me. 'That's for men; in our village, a tribal chieftain can fine women who wear men's garments. Try the blue one for women,' said Achi.

Imcha's relationship with fashion again became passionate and all-consuming once his bipolarity loosened its claws on the insides of his brain. He has also learnt the importance of being earnest the hard way and now goes through fashion experiences with the curiosity of a student–learner instead of trying to be smug about them. 'I want to see myself as progressive and fashion is a means of my expression. You don't know what it feels like to be that kid by the corner, with a load of turmoil in the head and the chants of violence and turbulence,' he said.

He is also keen to start a creative, learning centre for adolescents in Mokokchung to bring back positive change. The Heritage Foundation Project, a name Imcha has registered for his future organization, is his dream. It is a part of the family house in the village but he wants to 'go back home one day'. He wants to initiate a library to lend free books to teenagers and students and through his textile expertise and the little understanding he has of the fashion industry, make use of his Naga heritage. The photograph he had sent me two years back now makes full sense.

'I don't know why I got bipolar disorder but I am sure it has something to do with my childhood,' he told me during our freewheeling chat about The Episodes. 'A lot of my childhood memories are about being bullied and I lived in a shell most of the time and remember hating school,' he confessed, adding that he can't remember playing in the fields, or even the faces of most of his school friends.

Imcha's sentences were fragmented as always and though he wasn't trying to hide anything from me, he couldn't describe what was going on in his mind.

'Do you take your medicine regularly now?' I asked.

'Yes, yes, if I don't, I start feeling very unwell and lost and am very scared of another episode,' he said.

'Do you have a girlfriend or a boyfriend?' I asked, perhaps out of turn.

He didn't respond, so we left it at that.

During our last meeting in October 2011, I could see Imcha still struggling with his mental state. While he was recovering from the shattering Episodes at home, he travelled to the villages and worked with craftsmen in Dimapur, training them to orient their work towards a contemporary approach. He now lives in Ahmedabad and is working on his new collection and signed up as the costume designer for a Hindi feature film to be directed by a former student of NID. Creating fashion is restoring his faith in himself.

A sense of contemplative awareness now wafts around Imcha—both about the severity of his bipolar disorder if left unattended and of the need to do something meaningful. He has been visiting fashion weeks every season to assist Aneeth Arora, the designer behind the label Pero. One of the industry's most talented young designers who had been lucky to get commercial breaks, Aneeth was Imcha's classmate at NID who supported him unconditionally through his First Episode.

Through Imcha's depressive and manic states photography and music remained his constant companions. Music, as he says, keeps him umblically connected to life.

It reminded me of December 2010 in Nagaland during the Hornbill festival. Imcha and his siblings were all singing in the car, drowning out the numbers playing on the stereo, when we drove up from Dimapur to Kohima, but I had no idea that Achi could sing a Mariah Carey song as well as the original. I was dumbfounded.

The Home Minister of Nagaland who was at the Karaoke club that evening sang too. As did a 17-year-old boy who looked barely thirteen but had the deep, guttural voice fit for the angst of an opera singer.

And then 'Umbrella' by Rihanna opened. Imcha pulled his headgear off, twirled one side of his block print cotton kurta into a stylish knot and went on the floor. Loud, clear, sonorous, he sang the song in Sonu Nigam's layered voice. He then sung an

Eric Clapton song. And another and another, and another joined by Achi, they sang their hearts out.

It was the only time that transparency had seeped into Imcha's face. He laughed, his eyes crinkling and disappearing behind his scant lashes as he told me that Rufus Wrainright, Amos Lee, Sam Cooke and Amy Grant were his current favourites. Lucky Ali too.

'I am an Indian first, Naga later,' he had told me then, seconds after he stopped singing.

The Raja and the Yuvraj

'Where's the man that could ease a heart like a satin gown?'

—Dorothy Parker

The Raja

'How can anyone not love the lotus?' asked Rohit Bal. It wasn't a question. He said it like a quiet prayer, meditative in its strength, powerful in its belief like something one would say the first thing in the morning, within moments of opening their eyes to a new dawn.

'It emerges out of dirt, from the murkiest of waters and becomes an object of eternal beauty. The form of the lotus and its humility hypnotize me,' he added.

We were not in the land of lotus-eaters. We were in Toyland. What else could you call the personal space of Rohit Bal, the Indian fashion industry's Pied Piper and its Gudda?

Gudda. That's his pet name, that's what the industry calls him. What an indulgent little tag. Gudda. Why had he allowed it to swamp him and define him? Later, I realized that Rohit Bal with his Kashmiri looks, crinkly grey-green eyes and thin well-woven wrinkles around them, fair skin, long, wavy, blond hair, carved little nose, cheer and chutzpah, bizarre bravado, medium height, acquired cynicism (which he keeps swallowing back like a bitter pill) and nice, whimsical dressing doesn't look 'Rohit'. He does look like a Gudda. Rohit Bal is fine. Isn't that what they call him at Cannes, Kolhapur, and all over the world? But just Rohit? No. Rohit Gudda Bal. Bcttcr.

Haylo, hi, hey, hiya, Gudda, say his friends, visibly excited when they spot him sauntering into a party.

Where *is* Gudda? whisper fashion week organizers, perturbed (no, really), if he doesn't turn up.

He is the foremost crowd puller in Indian fashion and also a spectator who troops in after the lights have dimmed for shows to start, to clap for his peers and juniors. Designer ego? He doesn't carry it around like his mobile phone. This is one 'big designer' who makes it a point to cheer for everyone and anyone in the industry.

Duffy was waiting behind the door when it opened after Gudda rang the bell to his home in Defence Colony in South Delhi. Duffy and family actually. Despite the natural petulance of a Boxer's face, Duffy—short for Duffer—grinned uncontrollably when he saw his master.

'Why Duffy, why not Duffer, it is such an original name,' I muttered, drawn towards Duffy's baby doll Boxer granddaughter.

'It's embarrassing,' said Gudda.

He asked me to make myself comfortable while he got back in a minute. I secretly hoped he would take longer as I wanted to look around. The number of books that lined this room had left me overwhelmed. They were everywhere and yet the room didn't look like a study.

Wood, art, brass, books, lamps, textile pieces, tall stems of Rajnigandha flowers, cream-coloured sofas with tasteful, floral upholstery, more books. Lotus patterns on cushions and curtains. Cream everywhere. Many lotuses. Even more books. Warmth. Thought. Intelligence. Pride in surroundings. A flair for tasteful design.

Gudda had suggested we drive together in his luxury car from Noida where his factory is, so that we could chat on the way. He had sat in the front seat with the driver while I sat at the back. This was the first time I ever had a real conversation with the king of Indian fashion. That's how I labelled him in my head. It is easy to demarcate spaces through hierarchies. Desperate clichés like 'king' help. Then, as a small town girl, I had grown up to believe that Rohit Bal was a fashion celebrity like none other. Just because I would go on to write on fashion didn't mean his image in my mind had changed.

Everyone, just everyone I interviewed from any town, about anything, including Vishakha Dave*, the tailor from Nadiad, one of my favourite subjects (Ladies Tailor Chapter 7) knew who Rohit Bal was. Affluent families swear by his clothes; rich housewives tolerate their husbands better if the men buy them Rohit Bal garments; girls wait to get married so that they can wear a Rohit Bal lehnga; his revival of Kashmiri embroidery is breathtaking; his use of the meditative lotus on mulmul garments sometimes leads to entire collections selling off to foreign buyers; his khadi ensembles give the freedom fabric an enticing swagger; his men's jackets would make *Men in Black* look humble; his heart attack in early 2010 was front page news. People in the fashion industry prayed for Gudda. Not everyone may love him, but few people hate him.

If there was one designer who I felt mildly tongue-tied before in the fashion industry it was Rohit Bal. Also, because I have always been clueless about him. Like most others around, I am familiar with his persona but who is he as a person? I have seen and touched his clothes in stores and I do this routinely even now, but I have never been able to afford a Rohit Bal choli, let alone an Anarkali that women say makes them momentarily erase their tragedies and is more uplifting than time with a therapist.

Guddaji jaisi Anarkali koi nahin banata, say the karigars.

A Rohit Bal phone chase is a tedious project. Like playing a musical instrument that you haven't learnt and like a novice feel that if you struck a higher note, someone would pay attention. Many former attempts to reach him as a journalist had gone in vain. He just doesn't respond easily to messages or phone calls. He is better on email, his responses are more regular. He writes back in all caps. I remember how he had won an award each year at the *Marie Claire* Fashion Awards with unanimous jury voting, and upon being invited by me over the phone, would come happily to receive his trophies. At those times, he would finally pick up the phone after a dozen text messages had been sent out, each more frantic in tone than the previous. Gudda does eventually respond, if you are persistent enough.

At the award functions, we would greet each other warmly but that would be all. Not being the party type, I hadn't partied with him either. He was known for easily getting drunk and getting photographed with pretty boys. But I wasn't even a pretty boy.

Since I knew little about Gudda, except what others had to say about him, I had relied so far on the zillion little snippets that appear in the press about him. All that gossip about his live-in partner and model Lalit Tehlan who would eventually go on to marry Mandy Karimi, an Iranian model was what I found from the papers like others. Then, confounding enough, Lalit, Mandy, and Rohit Bal would pose for the cameras together giving a damn to the lamenters.

Gudda's fashion shows are legendary and hypnotic in their effect—this much I can vouch for. The spectacle he mounts with his stunning clothes is almost tactile because of the erotic energy seeping out of them. Siyahi, Shararat, Shanti... notice the Ses.

Before we reached the home he shared with Duffy and family, I had spent some time earlier that evening, observing him working in his office at his Noida factory. I was quite happy not to start the much-awaited 'interview'. You know how it is when you have never done something you have always wanted to do, and when it is actually time, you want to push it away, dreading that it would fall from the pride of place it has in your head. I found it easier to count the books (yes, there were hundreds in his office too), gaze at an odd red wall offset by a mud-coloured one in his studio. The moment I had entered the Noida studio and workshop, I stumbled into what appeared like hundreds of yards of cream coloured fabric that seemed to flow out like a stream of water from a sculptured gown worn by a female mannequin. Wont to observe the expressions and body language of mannequins, I noticed the lady didn't have an Indian demeanour. She was not too fidgety in manner and didn't have an 'I want a Rohit Bal at any cost for my wedding' tantrum rolling out on her forehead.

Silly details these, but my head was beginning to feel crowded even before Gudda Bal came to say hello, sit down, will you have a glass of water, coffee, I will just take fifteen minutes, just some last minute work for men's fashion week (this was 2010, mind you).

So while he was at work, I quickly flipped through some Italian magazines, quietly and hurriedly noting down words that would later help me write about men's fashion better and asked him if I could touch the fabric that another of his mannequins was dressed in. Another extremely sculpted gown, hundreds of metres of fabric again. There was a muchness about his clothes. They were larger than life. Gudda indeed was very generous with cloth.

For now let's get back to Gudda's Defence Colony drawing room. He poured for me a rare, 18-year-old whisky, out of what seemed like a Venetian cut glass container, an enlarged version of a decadent ittar bottle. For himself, he poured a glass of red wine. Post his heart attack, he wasn't drinking alcohol and wine was all his doctor had allowed him. We talked about ailing hearts, his and mine, high cholesterol, the miracle pill called

Sorbitrate—it had saved Gudda's life till he could be rushed to the hospital, the imminent dangers of excessive passion, the Ayurveda he wanted to try, the dawai made from resin. He had been to hell and back, his face mourned that return trip so clearly. He was gaunt, tired, had lost what seemed like twenty odd kilos and looked much older than his forty-four years. Before this conversation, I had seen him at a Mercedes Benz fashion show in Delhi, his come out show after his heart attack. He had looked terribly beaten even then. But he hadn't lost any of his verve. Or nerve.

Rohit Bal is a philosophic, reflective man. After a glass or two of wine, relaxed but not yet drunk, he is like a deeply thoughtful commentator on life—wise and ironically funny. He spoke to me about the fake and shallow nature of the fashion industry, the megalomaniac beliefs of designers who are barely mediocre, those who had sold out their souls to cheap, Western aspirations, and the poverty of commitment, ideas, and thought in the fashion media. 'People forget who they are, they try to change their personalities and forget their values. Designers think they are the nouveau celebrities of the present.'

This was not the Gudda the press painted so dearly. This was another man, lost in his musings, momentarily forgetting someone was sitting in front of him. 'I seldom give interviews to newspaper reporters. Yet they concoct and print stories without any verification. Headlines carry my name as some wannabe journalist wants the proverbial fifteen minutes of fame at my expense. Our so-called Page 3 journalists are cheap, publicity seeking snakes with too much power in their acrid, blood-filled quills,' he told me. That was the only time I felt his heart beat quicken. A nerve throbbed in one of his temples. 'Positive energy is my protective shield,' he said, calming down almost instantly.

Rohit Bal has found himself at the centre of so much attention—both good and bad—in the Indian press that he is perhaps the sharpest critic of the media in the industry. Bubbly, brazen and boisterous, he is also the fashion press's Pied Piper. His love–hate relationship with fashion journalists is legendary. Some say it is a case of sour grapes. In the late Nineties and 2000s, Bal made friends with the media, indulging some journalists lavishly, giving some of them intimate access to his home and heart. His later fall outs with those 'who will do anything for a free drink' is meat for a novella waiting to be written. 'That's the toilet where a couple of your colleagues have been sick, while I have held their hand and nursed them back,' he said pointing to a door adjacent to his drawing room in the house.

We were jumping topics as we chatted but you may not blame me for that. I wanted to squeeze two decades of questions into this one meeting because I knew there would be no other interview after this. 'Humility' and 'purity'—these two words spill out easily from Gudda's fashion consciousness. Like the lotus, he is also enamoured with the champa flower. 'It is the gentlest flower that comes out from the good earth,' he said.

Those who wear Rohit Bal know how he can make magic out of mulmul. His Anarkalis (yes, again), are made from 50 to 60 metres of crinkled mulmul in fascinating colours with finishing as luxurious inside as it is outside. 'It is the purity and humility of mulmul and khadi that attracts me,' he said. 'The purest form of textile outside khadi is mulmul,' he explained.

'Why are you besotted with cream as a colour?' I asked.

'Cream is unbelievably untouched; it has an intrinsic sense of purity. It has the innocence of a blank canvas, a blank slate. It is

Tabula Rasa,' he said. His metaphors and reflections suggested intense reading. These books then were not a part of influential décor, he actually read them.

Plagiarism, derivative design, me-too spending, the noisy, obtrusive clutter and clucking of families when they come with brides and grooms to order bridal wear, fashion week politics, he spoke about it all. 'I no longer consult brides if they come with their maasis, mummies, and chachis,' he said. 'I just get up and leave the room. Enough. I am not going to be a part of a group that behaves like it is preparing to send a lamb to slaughter,' he added, explaining that customer behaviour during bridal shopping in his studio had begun to tell upon his nerves.

'Bridal wear is big business; the only business. Without bridal wear, many Indian designers would be dead. How much does it contribute to your earnings?' I had asked earlier in the car.

'Fifty percent work is bridal wear but today if every single bridal order dried out, I would survive. There are facets to a fashion business and I haven't been oblivious to them,' he said.

As a businessman Rohit Bal is more than successful. As an artist and creator he is loved. He is original and passionate. As a mentor and boss, he may be overrated because while he gives all the freedom and more to those who work under him, he may not go all out to invest in their growth and individual flowering. 'You waste hundreds of metres of cloth but Gudda never thinks it is a waste. He wants you to experiment and learn and he respects mistakes,' a designer who had worked under him for many years told me.

Gudda has erratic work schedules, he is undisciplined say his current and former colleagues, he doesn't come to work at designated hours, nor does he keep a hawk's eye on who is doing what at his studio-factory. But everyone says that what he manages to do in two hours many other designers take a full day to finish. His trainees and apprentices don't get much time with him but he influences them with his mastery. 'Gudda sahib se poochhlo,' insist the masterjis hinting that the final word is his.

He is not a laborious mentor, and 'for some inexplicable reason, despite the exposure he allows, you can't grow out of his fold or out of his influence to make an individual statement while you are with him,' said one of his former designers. Gudda not only conceives, creates and implements his own ideas for each collection and each fashion show staging, but directs all details himself. So if you see his male models kissing each other on the ramp or his sensuous female models taking a dip in the pool for the final bow with him, it's all his idea. That's hardly odd. Most senior designers and directors of fashion houses work in a similar way. Yet, even though the designers argue that they would have benefitted had Bal given them more training and personal time, they swear by his evolving ideas. 'He is never static, has something new to do and offer every season, even if it is bridal wear,' I was told by a junior designer who recently branched out after working with Bal.

'You survive if you have a product to back you, without a good product you are a joker, the bubble bursts sooner than later,' he would tell me at his home.

It is easy to write a Rohit Bal resume but his profile will remain elusive. He comes from a well to do Kashmiri family who inculcated traditional Indian values in him. He has a sister. He went to St Stephen's College in Delhi and then in 1986 was one of the first batch of students (with JJ Valaya, Rina Dhaka, and others) to enroll for a six-month diploma course, when NIFT opened in Delhi. He became successful almost immediately. Popular and famous too, both for his clothes and as the bad boy of Indian fashion.

Rohit wore parrot green trousers to college, drank too much, loved too much, danced like mad (he still does), was sexy, funny and unapologetic about his sexuality. If he had any demons, he wrestled with them regularly at home but locked them in the closet before coming to work or to parties. And oh, did he party.

When I prodded, he agreed. 'I fit the image of the designer. In the Eighties, I more than fit the bill of Indian fashion's poster boy. I had the look, knew how to dress, spoke well, I was forward, crazy, loved, unloved, open to experience, visible, intelligent. I had the courage to be gay and tell the world about it. They needed me there. I filled all the gaps. There was nobody else around. There was an effortless absorption of me,' he added. He surprised me by the near-total absence of snobbishness when he said this.

What could clearly come across was that Rohit Bal is unafraid. To create originally, you have to drive away your fears. That is why Indian fashion has needed him and will continue to depend on his legacy, his design, his thoughts, and his boisterousness. His Anarkalis will outlive him not because the cream-coloured mulmul is like a baby's wrap, but because they breathe independence. India wants to wear that now more than anything else. There is so much colour about him, all dyed in white.

In many ways, Rohit Bal is also one of the most passionate ambassadors of the gay community in India. His male models openly love each other on the ramp. They wear sindoor and nathnis and smooch with abandon. These actions may have been scoffed at by society and debated by the media but they cannot be dismissed. Bal isn't like the late and equally, if not more talented, designer Rohit Khosla who kept his personal life veiled from the world and died prematurely at the age of thirty-five on February 16, 1994.

When I was researching this book, many people told me that unless I contextualized nostalgia about Indian fashion, I wouldn't know where it is heading. They were right.

'You can't write a book around the Indian fashion industry until you understand who Rohit Khosla was and what he stood for,' someone said.

'You can't write a book till you speak to Bina Ramani, model choreographer Vidyun Singh... and people from those days,' said others.

I could not nail down every interview. But Rohit Bal singularly provoked both the nostalgia and the futurism that Indian fashion has in its warp and weft. He is not the Manish Arora of Space Age kitsch, nor is he is the Wendell Rodricks of research, reasonability, and resort wear ease. Rohit Khosla has long been dead but Rohit Bal stands for the Indian fashion industry as it is today—its triumphs and quirks, its failings, vulnerabilities, and resilience. A psychoanalyst also one of his admirers, rightly says, 'There is something about Bal's imagination which translates into his couture, which is restless, fresh, deeply Indian, yet universal.'

Rohit Gudda Bal doesn't do drugs. The Raja doesn't need the Powder Room.

The Yuvraj

'I don't want to do fashion, I want to make clothes,' said Sabyasachi Mukherjee, in a warily sweet manner but a bit on the defensive should a rebuttal come his way. He is one of the very few designers Rohit Bal admires for originality. Clothes vs fashion once again was the theme of the day when Sabyasachi showed Peeli Kothi, a couture line in November, 2011. The only rituals of excess in his spectacle were sound and smell, the voice of classical vocalist and musician Shubha Mudgal and the fragrant mogra flowers that were infused into the air conditioners of the hall since the morning of the show. Mudgal's performance, also the first time an artiste of her stature had performed live during a fashion show, gave the Indian fashion spectacle an altered dimension. No press photographers were allowed. Sabyasachi hadn't agreed to get any sponsors for his show and was not obliged to anyone for 'coverage'.

The designer's guests also make his shows distinctive. A certain sub-culture is visible at these gatherings, culturally directed by his aesthetic. For Peeli Kothi, the women in his work team wore white, woven saris with black ornate blouses. Men wore white khadi karats and churidars with black Sabyasachi shawls. The guests came wearing his intricately embroidered garments, layers of stunning salwars, Pharsi pyjamas and kurtas, or his famous saris with multi-coloured borders (these must become his Election symbol if he ever fights one).

37-year-old Sabyasachi was born in Kolkata in a middle class family from Ballygunge. He was not raised to be a celebrity or a social do-gooder. He went to study at Sri Aurobindo Vidya Mandir, out of the city. Then he attended junior college at St Xavier's before enrolling at NIFT Kolkata, where his graduation collection in 1999 won him three big awards.

Sabyasachi did not suddenly bulldoze his way into the fashion industry. Even before his debut, he had won a British Council award to work under a Salisbury designer and had gone to show by invite at Milan Fashion Week as well as at a Singapore fashion event. A business and trade magazine from Singapore listed him as one of the most influential, young Asian designers; long before he would go on to employ 800 people to work in his company, including karigars skilled at dyeing crafts and weaves.

Sabyasachi may have known his mind even before he debuted on the Indian ramp, but was tentative about dealing with the media. This is what Varun Rana who worked with him in 2004, a crucial time in the designer's career, remembers. Rana who then went on to work as fashion features editor of *Harper's Bazaar* and is currently with myntra.com managed Sabyasachi's embroidery unit and remembers him as someone who would go out of his way to make an outsider to Kolkata feel at home. 'He would take me home and make me eat food cooked by his mother and make sure I felt at ease,' says Rana.

As a child, he would make clothes for his younger sister Singini's (nicknamed Payal) dolls long before he could make them for her. After his Delhi couture week show, his father who retired as a chemical engineer and now manages all his finances, hinted at the complexities of having a genius son. Sabyasachi wasn't a cute child; he was precocious.

His sister Payal, also a NIFT Kolkata graduate, and now the head of management and infrastructure in her brother's enterprise is his muse. One of his early collections The Frog Princess was inspired by Payal. He seldom ever replicates clothes that he makes for his sister. He wants her to look distinctive and stand out in the crowd. Payal is a lovely girl but doesn't care much for trends. Styled by Sabyasachi, she does stand out. You would see her wearing a long, khadi top with the Communist party's election symbol with loose trousers, incredibly high heels and a tiny purse. When he dressed her for a photoshoot in a fashion magazine, she wore a white and gold traditional Kerala sari holding a classic, quilted Chanel bag. The photograph, directed by Sabyasachi showed just the string of the Chanel purse slung on Payal's shoulder and the hint of a black, Sabyasachi choli with his signature tassels.

He would indulge his mother and sister with rare jewellery, vintage mostly, that he would bring back from his travels all over India or the world. Once in the US, he took Payal shopping asking her to buy whatever she wished. Payal refused, nothing tempted her. When he insisted, telling her he had to treat her from the money he had made after his show at New York Fashion Week, she picked up a classic, black quilted Chanel bag. This is the nonchalance that Sabyasachi loves.

At the Peeli Kothi show Sabyasachi himself looked different from the way I remembered him from our last meeting. His hair was now long and he was dressed in a cream-coloured churidar kurta, with a black bandhgala that had gold buttons (delicately embossed with the S of Sabyasachi) and an antique shawl. He looked like a Shanti Niketan artist visiting Delhi for an art summit, not one of India's top designers. His body language was warmer, easier, his characteristic restlessness suspended. There were no last minute jitters; he seemed to instinctively know that his collection would be more than just applauded.

Little though had changed about his thoughts on fashion.

Sabyasachi has hope and vanity that one day India will dress differently. 'My work is not fashion. I want to change the way India dresses,' he said. He has been reiterating this for the last couple of years and especially after his previous outing at the Delhi Couture Week of 2010. Unlike Peeli Kothi, that show was the inaugural show of the couture week, and had to appease the sponsors and the media. It was populist to the brim, packed with guests of various persuasions in style and fashion. There were textile experts as well as Delhi's fashionistas, the latter wearing a look-at-me urgency. It was opened by the designer's two favourite ladies from Hindi cinema: Rani Mukherjee and Vidya Balan. Rani wore a black jump suit and carried a Bottega Veneta clutch while Vidya, was draped in a red-orange Sabyasachi sari. *No One Killed Jessica* was readying for release and its leading ladies, both personal friends of the designer, seemed happy to embellish the front row together. He walked between the two on the ramp, smiling self-consciously. All three knew that it would be the lead picture in coloured supplements of newspapers the next day and played to the gallery.

After Vidya and Rani were escorted to their seats, the audience was asked to rise for Tamil Carnatic singer, D.K. Pattamal's rendering of the 'Jana Gana Mana'. A rose pink vintage finish tin had been placed on front row seats. It had 'Save The Sari; Hand-Woven and Hand Dyed' printed on it. Beneath, it said: Curated by Sabyasachi, 30, Green Row, Calcutta. The black and white image on the tin had a Bengali woman in the traditional drape and a blouse with puffed Charulata sleeves. Inside were rolled handloom saris, striped, cotton Maheshwaris intended as gifts for front row guests. This was the trailer of Sabyasachi by Sabyasachi, a line he was to launch soon. He curates these saris from weavers all over the country and sells them at affordable prices from his flagship stores in Delhi, Mumbai, and Kolkata. 'This line is to rescue myself from the commercial emphasis of my brand,' he said.

If commerce drives Sabyasachi's vision, art anchors it. The set of his 2010 couture show looked like a heritage bungalow with antique clocks, forgotten wall-hangings, rusty trunks and wooden cupboards with enamel chips on them. A deliberate walk into an era gone by. Authentic enough to tempt the ghost of Satyajit Ray to fade in and say hello to Vidya-Parineeta-Balan. A short, black and white film was screened before the show began, acknowledging the contribution of weavers and karigars from Behrozegar Mahila Samiti in West Bengal and khadi spinners in Andhra Pradesh.

The clothes that walked the ramp had the designer's unmistakable signature. Textiles, weaves, and embroideries fused in uncanny partnerships to remind us of India's craft and art supremacy. Inside Sabyasachi's mind, India is perhaps called Mother India. Here, women dress beautifully but conservatively; men look dutiful; they walk holding hands of innocent little children towards happily ever-after tomorrows. This was also evident at Bridal Sutra, 2008, in Mumbai, one of the most important collections the designer had mounted. Clusters of models walked like families as if in a wedding procession. Such narratives of community fashion keep getting repeated in Sabyasachi shows. Ankle-length khadi skirts with dense Parsi Gara embroidery, Benarasi brocades, embroidered net saris, and embellished angarkhas. The colours belie an artist's palette or a dyer's shade card. They are pulled out as if from a Shaman's schizophrenic imagination. Female models wear their hair in loosely knotted braids, their make up sparse; garments are over-layered to obliterate any hint of deliberate sexiness. No jewellery. 'I look at my female clients when they attend my events. That's when I realize I like women wearing cholis held together with tassels at the back, high necks, long sleeves, with heavy drapes as saris and layered garments. I don't like plunging necklines or revealing clothes. My woman is a conservative one,' Sabyasachi confessed.

His male models, too, are overdressed. They look like Bengali bhadralok in delicate gold-rimmed glasses and impeccably groomed moustaches. But neck down, the Bagru-printed or embroidered brocade angarkhas, worn with silken churidars would give even traditional women a complex.

'I don't want to do anything new,' said Sabyasachi defiantly, his wariness as a defence mechanism back. 'Repetitiveness does not bother me. Chanel has done black and white forever. Who defines edgy for us after all?' he asked.

We were standing in the lobby of the Grand Hyatt in Delhi, the venue of the Couture Week. His emphasis dipped for a moment and he suggested we talk over coffee. 'The girls and boys are there packing in my room, so don't mind the mess,' he said.

'What's the feedback to the collection?' I asked rhetorically. I had heard the applause and seen people rushing to hug him. But the fashion industry can be deceptive in its applause and I wanted to hear more from Sabyasachi himself. There weren't many well-known Indian designers in the audience.

'I don't care about feedback,' he said. 'Certainly not from the media. Who can critique fashion?' he said, mixing sugar into his coffee.

Pregnant pause. He sat on the floor, leaning against the sofa. The room was indeed messy, strewn with clothes that leave women gasping in his stores. A captivating choli in maroon-red with twisted gold thread and copper embroidery that would send a bride blushing with desire lay on the sofa next to me.

Sabyasachi's eyes followed mine. He didn't say anything. Usually, whenever he sees a person eyeing a garment, he explains its embroidery, textile, origin. All his garments have stories and he likes to tell them.

'Touch and feel it, turn it upside down. Fashion is tangible; it can't be understood just by looking at it,' he would say admonishingly, pulling off a sari from here, a saafa from there and turning them around to show their undersides.

Not this time. He was in no mood for a fashion lesson.

His clothes for Couture Week were beautiful as always but they looked like museum pieces part of an India exhibition. He had deglamourized his models, covering them up like sacks and I said so. They looked unsexy, instead of desirable contemporary women.

More silence.

And his male models. 'Why obsess with spectacles and moustaches, giving a momentary illusion of bhadralok to only turn them into androgynous boys below the necks?' I asked.

'Yes it was conscious. I almost didn't dress them up like that,' he responded, his defence crumbling a bit.

'In my homosexual mind, there is obviously some battle with heterosexuality,' he said, trying to explain why his male models wore opulent garments.

We spent the next hour arguing over fashion versus clothes, cinema versus the Indian fashion industry, Mani Ratnam's *Raavan* versus R. Balki's *Paa*, Rani Mukherjee vs Vidya Balan. He had been the costume director for *Raavan, Guzaarish,* and *Paa*. In all these films, not one garment was blingy or chiffonesque. Balan wore Kalamkari blouses with woven cotton saris in *Paa*.

In some ways, Sabyasachi has been unable to resist Bollywood. Yet he didn't want to be a part of it like everyone else but rather wanted to 'change it'. When he was working with Mani Ratnam on *Raavan*, he got obsessed with Kerala style houses. He decorated his new home in Kolkata with Kerala-inspired decor. His friends would get delicious, homemade Bengali food in a Kerala home.

'You wouldn't believe the way the scenes have come out, I had gooseflesh when I saw the rushes,' he said, excitedly on the phone while shooting for *Raavan*. As the costume director of the film, he wasn't just dressing up Aishwarya and Abhishek for the film, but the entire cast. He had curated saris and blouses from different states of India and styled them. Lampooned by the critics, *Raavan* got washed away. Sabyasachi who must have been hit by its failure didn't express it. He respects mass opinion and while he would surely work with 'Mani Sir' again any day, he didn't defend the film.

But he went all out to defend Sanjay Leela Bhansali after *Guzaarish* was declared a flop. Thirty-seven long frocks, some dumpy shoes, a shawl or two with owls and talking parrots embroidered in bronzed thread, red lipstick, Goth Chanel nail paint, dull vintage jewellery and Nana Mouskouri glasses. That was the wardrobe of Bhansali's Sofia, a neurotic nurse played by Aishwarya Rai Bachchan in the film. Her Spanish ghaghras didn't find favour with the critics who felt that she was too overdressed around a patient with a death wish (a paraplegic who seeks mercy killing played by Hrithik Roshan).

Sabyasachi was livid. 'To hell with fashion and leather, feather, fuchsia, gold, silver and neon,' he said. 'When you cover up women, people don't like it,' he said, accusing the film industry of being obsessed with sexiness and bling. 'I interpreted Sofia as a borderline depressed woman who had a Seventies hangover from her growing-up years,' he yelled emphatically on the phone. 'She is stuck in a time warp, has a miserable personal life, and work is her only redemption. She is friendless and melancholic. For her, elaborate dresses, whimsical hairdos and red lipstick are weapons of defiance. Her clothes disrobe her character,' he said explaining that he went with Bhansali's interpretation of the character.

But when all such distractions abate in his mind, the 'sari' stays. It is the abiding motif in all his conversations.

'I want to go to the villages and bring back India's most ignored weaves, bought directly from the weavers. I will sell them for Rs 300 each. I have kept Rs 20 lakh aside for weaver support work. I don't want to see the face of a middleman. I give them advance money. I want to engage in corporate social responsibility,' he said.

Weavers are criminally exploited by middlemen especially in off-season when they would be forced to accept lower labour charges. In the peak season, a weaver gets Rs 1800 for a completely hand-woven sari. In the off-season it is Rs 800.

Saving weavers is not the only reason that gave Sabyasachi a sari obsession. It is the symbol of the noise 'India' makes in his mind. 'I care for the cultural stories embedded into the sari's warp and weft,' he asserts. The sari being the most meaningful garment of Indian cultural history, he wants to revive it for contemporary relevance, sometimes at the cost of other things he does.

He may say he only wants to make clothes. But he is no longer just doing that. He has a TV show called *Band Bajaa Bride* on *NDTV Good Times* for which, once every week, he dresses up what he calls 'regular' (non-celebrity) brides from different parts of the country. Oprah Winfrey couldn't stop shopping for his clothes at his Kala Ghoda store in Mumbai, during her recent visit to India. Sotheby's in London had a selling exhibition in May this year titled 'Inspired by India' with Sabyasachi's wedding saris, jutis, shawls, stoles, hair bands. It was curated by Janice Blackburn. Earlier this year, he agreed to direct the set design of Shubha Mudgal's annual music festival Bajaa Gajaa in Pune. For a percussion event which was the finale, he dressed up the stage in deep red khadi and gold Benarasi fabrics. 'The sound of the percussion is primitive, and I connect it to the red colour mixed with the gold of Benares,' he said. Now there is talk in the industry that L Capital, the investment and real estate fund of LVMH is currently evaluating his company to invest in it.

Whatever he does, Sabyasachi tries to sign it off with the arts and crafts of West Bengal, the land of his birth. 'He is the only designer who goes all out to revive, sustain, and contemporarize the traditional crafts of his state. We can't name even one other designer in India who does the same for his region,' says Sunil Sethi, the President of the Fashion Design Council of India.

That's only half the story, so it can never be the headline of an interpretative piece on Sabyasachi. If West Bengal is his signature, at the core of his stories are textiles from across India: Ajrak from Gujarat on the one hand and Kanjeevaram from the South on the other. If West Bengal has the importance of janmabhoomi in his creative mind, Benares is the karmabhoomi. The rest fall somewhere in between. Kanjeevaram became a full-fledged project when Sabyasachi worked with weavers in the small town of Kancheepuram to revive some of the oldest weaving patterns of the sari. To stamp them as Sabyasachi saris, he had put a border each, even three on some saris for a travelling exhibition.

I had heard that his clients queued up long before the shutters went up for a special display but I wanted to see it for myself. At Aza, a fashion store in Mumbai, where one of Sabyasachi's bridal collections was to be shown and sold, I saw his upper class, female clientele standing in small groups since 9:30 am in the morning for the 11 am showing. By 1 pm, every single piece had been sold out. Despite the all-pervasive myth that sexy, short, tight fitting clothes define modern Indian fashion and this is an era of Swarovski embedded garments, his layered and 'unsexy' pieces attract customers in droves. Even though he refuses to pay heed to seasonal fashion trends, his business soars each year.

At these exhibitions, Sabyasachi offers breathless consultations to his clients on what to wear and how. If the mind boggling sales give him a swagger, he consciously tries to temper it down. 'Such experiences can make one arrogant about oneself. Once I know I can put out my kind of sari and people will pay a lakh rupees for it, I can become lazy,' he says.

I noticed a similarly crazy turnout at his Delhi store Sabyasachi@Carma when he showed his revived Kanjeevarams. His customers, he admitted, came lured by his sari borders that had become the Sabyasachi hallmark. I found his revived Kanjeevarams saris cluttered, if beautiful. But customers continued to troop in. Here, too, by lunch time, a sale of Rs 10 lakh and more had been made. Sabyasachi stood around smiling thoughtfully, jubilant yet trying hard to look matter of fact. His customers no longer cared what he made. They weren't buying revived Kanjeevarams; they were buying a Sabyasachi, an arrival statement like a painting by one of the masters.

'Your bill is Rs 4,48,000,' the sales in charge said at Carma to a lady. She was a Punjabi from Jalandhar, with large diamond bangles on her arms and carried a Burberry bag. Not a Satyajit Ray woman with long, messy tresses that Sabyasachi romanticized about. She dished out the cash, thick wads from her handbag, and happily accepted the parcel.

'She's chosen all the wrong saris,' said Sabyasachi observing from a distance, as the lady walked away. 'That's one of the reasons I make khadi saris now, I want to teach taste to my rich clients,' he added.

'Do your customers know what revived Kanjeevarams mean?' I asked him.

'I am not sure if everyone does,' he agreed, but emphasized that as long as they bought them, whatever their reasons, a revival piece had been sold to an urban Indian woman. Yet I never saw male customers queue up for his garments and had always suspected if his menswear sold at all, except perhaps in the bridal market. He insisted it did.

Non-conformists appeal to Sabyasachi. Perhaps that's why he chose to debut on the Indian fashion ramp underlining his own non-conformism. Inspired by his mother's look, an art teacher, his first collection was called Kashgar Bazaar and was shown at Lakme Fashion Week in Mumbai in 2002. The models wore large-framed spectacles and carried books in their arms. The story of the three Nair sisters on the ramp, as he would later tell journalists, was borrowed from the lives of three sisters in his own neighbourhood. They often wore their father's shirts, rejecting submissive femininity for a nuanced statement.

'Intelligent fashion' the obvious interpretation derived from the presence of books and spectacles on the ramp thus arrived in

India. This was at a time when fashion was reeling under excessive embellishment and tight, Western (not global) garments. It was urban, it was rich. It was sexy without being edgy. Sabyasachi swum against the tide, bringing in admiration for the rough-hewn. He sent models on the ramp wearing dishevelled clothes in muted colours and block prints. He had a story to tell and the narrative didn't conform to the way the fashion world had interpreted new India, so far. If other designers had assumed that we as customers wanted to look like damsels in distress, Sabyasachi assumed that we wanted to rescue ourselves from fashion enslavement. That was the first time, say some fashion writers that they got a proper fashion story that had nothing to do with designers on drugs, alcohol, or raves. Sabyasachi found willing converts to his cause as people could suspend fashion's capriciousness (at least in their minds) and yet be 'fashionable'.

Sabyasachi has always been embarrassed by fashion's association with flippancy in India. He wants to be taken seriously, not just as a tailor of beautiful clothes for rich women buying trousseaus, but as an artist. This label of 'intelligent fashion' stuck to him and continues to dot the vocabulary whenever anyone attempts to deconstruct the designer's fashion sensibility.

For all his artistic bent of mind, everyone who has known and tried to understand Sabyasachi's success insists that his business acumen competes with and wins over his artistic gene. He may be a designer-artist, crazy and committed to reviving textiles, passionate about Khadi and about the India story but it is all governed and choreographed by an aggressive business instinct.

Sharp and intelligent to the point of being bookish in his arguments, Sabyasachi is also restive, frenzied, idealistic, easily frustrated, intolerant of mediocrity, warm and generous with friends, and a calculative business strategist. Giving his clothes an intelligent label isn't just a philosophic pursuit. He has been able to understand the pulse of the Indian market quickly, while other veteran designers, also front runners in bridal wear took years to disrobe India's wishlist. Sabyasachi doesn't have the draping talent of Tarun Tahiliani or the ebullient personality of Rohit Bal but he has a story to sell and it is called Vintage fashion. He genuinely believes that people are most comfortable when they are rooted to tradition and it is easy to convert them to the cause of India than to tell them how to carry off Dior gowns. 'A property, a piece of jewellery, a fast car, and an Indian garment. These are things people invest in. The rest is complicated. As the West gets more and more demystified, prioritizing the gown over anything else, why must we trade Indianness for global fads?' he asks. The value-seeking Indian's craze for 'heavy, ornate, vintage' garments is spiced by him with intelligent marketing lines on 'khadi, hand-woven, hand-dyed and traditional'. This has created and strengthened the Sabyasachi brand. At a superficial level, Sabyasachi's fashion appears simple, since it deals with saris, salwar kameezes, wide pyjamas, anti-fit tops and layered jackets in weaves and embroideries. But there is nothing humorous or light-headed about it.

This truth reveals the designer's Cinderella Complex. He wants to give the glass slipper to ordinary women so that they become princesses. But there is a catch here. And it has nothing to do with the stroke of midnight. Sabyasachi's Cinderella is one who is unafraid to wear ethnic, even regressive garments while standing in an ocean of bling and Western luxury brands. Every collection of his has the stamp of individuality. It may be easy to look distinctive in a Sabyasachi garment but to 'feel' distinctive his customers need to get into his mind. Take for instance a prêt line he showed in Delhi in 2011. He focussed on the underwear of the 1950s. 'It's a spoofy take on crystals. But even my corsets are hand-woven. It is like Bhagalpur Woodstock going sexy,' he said.

He is a businessman at heart but when he speaks, it is like a professor of fashion sociology. That's why fashion writers hang on to his words; they know he will give them good copy. He knows that too now, the fact that they need him because without his articulate contentions, they wouldn't know what to make of his clothes.

Sabyasachi doesn't just sell clothes, he hands out a way of life. It's an empowering vocabulary exhorting customers to invest in celebrating who they are. It is as if he has gone inside the mental breweries of his competitors in the Indian market and come out fuming but clear about what he doesn't want to do. Yet, whatever he creates or curates, he likes to direct the way the clothes look when worn. He always gives styling tips to his customers. 'You just need a large man's watch with my sari,' he would say. Or, 'nothing but antique earrings, not even a bracelet.' His marketing genius pulsates with the anxiety to bring about distinction.

I bumped into him once at the All India Weaver's Exhibition organized in Delhi by the Crafts Council of India and saw him buy 80 saris from a couple of weavers. Almost everything a weaver group from Andhra Pradesh had was bought by him. 'It's for my next collection,' he said when he saw me staring.

He 'seriously' believes that the country's nouveau riche as well as Bollywood divas need lessons in taste. 'The pink and bling of Bollywood disturbs me. It's as crass as their crotch-thrusting dances,' he would say. 'How can anyone wear pink as pink?'

Colour in Sabyasachi's clothes comes from a maniacal, fearless pursuit of combinations. That's what all those sari borders stand for. His riotous colour combinations leave people gob smacked because they stem from boiling rebellion and afflictive nostalgia.

I had seen him at work with a dyer near his workshop in Kolkata where he spent a few hours trying to attain a particular shade of aubergine that lived in his mind. He would pair it with dhaniya green. Not the dhaniya you see every day, but the fresh, out of farm dhaniya available in vegetable markets before the sun rises and starts killing its colour.

While no one, not even his worst critics doubt his marketing brilliance, there are quite a few who say he is overrated as a designer. He creates easily replicable fashion. Sabyasachi is indeed the most plagiarized designer in India. Man Mandir in Chennai, Sushma Saris in Juhu, Mumbai, Chhabra 555 in Chandni Chowk Delhi, or Geeta Circle in Kolkata, you will find copies of Sabyasachi's designs in every market. He nailed down many, went after some, and then gave up exhausted. 'I don't even want to look at my own clothes, there are so many copies around,' he said. He would sneak into markets, ask for 'Sabyasachi' garments like a jealous spouse spying upon an adulterous partner and then fly into a rage when he saw the way his designs were being mutilated and sold.

Funnily, the designer was a mediocre dresser himself till recently. He seldom wore anything exceptional, not even when he went to influential forums to receive the many awards the industry has decorated him with. Only recently he dresses up like the man he really is—a Bengali artist. He has begun shunning western garments for churidar kurtas worn jackets and shawls. This happened only after a correction phase. Once, for the *Marie Claire* Fashion awards, he came wearing a maroon velvet jacket with a pair of black trousers. It was a forgettable choice, as one of his friends remarked. He took the jibe well and laughed a big laugh. Unlike his clothes, his footwear has always been given good thought. His shoes are impeccably chosen—a leather pair by Tom Ford, a pair of Prada chappals, Tods' moccasins in pure leather or suede.

It surprises me that there is no particular dressing vanity about Sabyasachi. Unlike many of his colleagues, who give free vent to their sexuality through quirky dressing, Sabyasachi doesn't describe himself through his clothes.

One of my former female colleagues fell head over heels in love with him. He was oblivious to her fascination, polite but distracted and she was heart-broken. Attracted to his brains, she thought he would be a dream boyfriend to have. 'Just imagine, if I can be Sabyasachi's girlfriend!' she had said looking like a besotted adolescent.

Inside Sabyasachi's creative mind, there is a deep cleavage. I assume it is between commerce and art. But you can see a dimly-lit tunnel connecting the two.

The designer is no infantile strategist. He accepts, with a quiet arrogance, that many of his senior colleagues despise him. He has made an acquaintance with some younger designers who he goes all out to promote and support. But among the older generation of designers, he has neither fans nor friends. Seldom do designers worth their name come for his shows except textile conservationist Neeru Kumar and Rohit Bal. Bal is an unflinching supporter of the industry, he comes to applaud everyone. Designers like Rajesh Pratap Singh and Neeru Kumar are equally committed to the cause of khadi that Sabyasachi has turned it into a marketing line. The Ministry of Textiles loves him, as do various state governments and their craft revival project managers. He is the guy they are all looking for. Fashion Week bodies love him too; his show spells clout, promises a large, appreciative audience, good media and sales. In 2010, he was signed up by the Textile Board of Tamil Nadu to do a Kanjeevaram show in Chennai. He doesn't just understand Khadi and Benarasi weaves but cares for them. 'Khadi requires privatization of ownership. Its biggest problem is that a political intent dominates its inherent beauty,' he says. Some of his competitors accuse him of over-embellishing it and using it to differentiate himself through a patriotic identity in times where buyers count crystals.

'He is India's highest selling wedding designer,' say industry insiders. In a country where wedding wear defines both fashion and couture and is the number one selling category, competition with Sabyasachi is almost unavoidable for anyone who plays the game.

'He will never compromise a design, never change the length of a sleeve or a hemline for a customer or change colour combinations,' says Tina Malhotra, the owner and curator of Chennai's most prominent multi-designer fashion store. She is also his only representative in Bangalore and Chennai as the designer now likes to sell only from his own flagship stores. 'Chennai is a tricky market given its Kanjeevaram culture but Sabyasachi is an instant sell out,' affirms Tina. She told me about bank employees who save for months to afford one Sabyasachi garment. 'Even those who won't be seen dead in a salwar kameez buy them from him because they feel it is like an investment into a garment that has so much craft infusion. Once you get inside a Sabyasachi garment, you understand why you will never buy a copy.' If Sabyasachi had to be described in one word, I would choose 'nostalgia' of a deep and intense kind. It works as his ally as well as his saboteur. His clothes, decisions, friendships and choices, are carved out of nostalgia. Since his designs originate from periods of reverie, some look like lemons on the ramp. The chhotu saris he showed in 2008, versions of half saris worn with heavy Amprapalli silver jewellery and incredibly tall stilettos were of that stock.

He belongs to an era that is unable to hold us in its embrace and is always harking back to old times, seeking idealism, trying to restore order as he believes little exists. Some say he is India's Dries Van Noten, who engages with craft and detailing to the point of madness. The industry talks of his first big international deal with Browns in early 2000s right after his debut. But Sunil Sethi who was then a Selfridges buyer and had little to do with Indian fashion weeks says that Selfridges bought huge consignments from a young Sabyasachi and the clothes flew off the shelves. The designer could have continued that happy dalliance between Indian and international markets. But the business wizard in him spoke louder than the dreamy artist. He stopped participating in New York fashion week and focussed his attention towards the Indian retail business. He believes that the land behind his ideas is also the best business hub for his designs. A very risky business decision but one that seems to paying off.

I would observe Sabyasachi as a co-member of the selection board at the Lakme Fashion Week and noticed that he didn't think twice before giving a big thumbs down to designers who plagiarized, those who corrupted the media and fashion week bodies or succumbed to under the table dealings with sponsors. He would stand up, often for the underdog.

Books calm down the designer's fervent, restive temperament. Especially biographies of freedom fighters. 'Every business model I have tried has come from someone's biography,' he told me. 'I want to be true to my roots. I love Bongo bhasha.'

Once, for an interview for *Outlook* magazine's Independence Day special, I asked him if he was playing the game both ways. Rich,

Marwari clientele and Bollywood on the one hand and the revivalist argument on the other. How was he different from anyone else? At least other designers didn't lay ownership on revival work.

'I draw an analogy between Khadi and Aishwarya Rai,' he told me. 'The problem with khadi is that the fabric was used as a political tool. Now, people can't see beyond it. Just like they can't see beyond Aishwarya's beauty. When I dress up someone in khadi without telling them what it is, they feel it is one of the most beautiful weaves. Its simplicity is its cachet. The nouveau riche needs Khadi to understand that the most embellished Swarovski garment will not give them an individuality.'

He did take khadi to Bollywood and to Hollywood. Not only would he dress Aishwarya for an episode on Oprah Winfrey's talk show in an embroidered dress, but during the days when *Raavan* was being promoted, she wore a Sabyasachi sari for Filmfare awards as well as for the preview of the film in London. Aishwarya even chose a starry sari by Sabyasachi at Cannes in 2010 and turned up looking as frumpy as she does sometimes. Sabyasachi's saris did little to raise Aishwarya's fashion quotient. But it allowed Kalki Koechlin to take her boho snobbishness a notch higher.

The same saris made another person out of Vidya Balan. During her alleged and messy relationship with Shahid Kapur and soon after the breakup, Vidya was a fashion disaster. She had given up her Parineeta image and her natural liking for Indian garments to 'please someone'. She told me this in an interview admitting that she was being judged as a frump for wearing Indian clothes both by her boyfriend (didn't name him) and by the film industry. Indian clothes don't get actresses sexy roles, she had thought.

Sabyasachi took it upon himself to approach and reproach her. He suggested a makeover and she agreed. She would only wear

Sabyasachi garments and dress the way he guided her. Vidya, who had also hired a personal trainer to lose flab in those days, generously accepted later that Sabyasachi helped her reclaim her fondness for Indian garments. Damn the film industry, she said.

The two became thick friends. He would give her saris; she would give him books. The arrangement didn't end there. They rooted for each other. When I phoned Sabyasachi suggesting he style a wedding cover for *Marie Claire*'s October 2009 Bridal special, he said we should consider Vidya as a cover girl. In those days Vidya was only known for her disastrous dressing and was like a pariah to fashion stylists. But Sabyasachi was confident that it would work. He said he would dress her in a khadi lehnga for the cover and for the rest of the photoshoot to be featured inside the magazine; we would put up a set that looked like an antique durbar.

It was a gamble. I agreed to play it. An ornate, expensive set costing a few lakhs, sponsored by Gaja jewellers of Kolkata, for whom Sabyasachi designs a special line of jewellery, was set up in Mumbai's Mehboob studio. Vidya wore Gaja earrings for the cover and the brand's jewellery inside. The pictures were breathtakingly beautiful and Vidya looked more than a ravishing Indian bride. Quite a few designers, rather honestly told me that the cover didn't work even if the stunning photographs inside did. Also because a LV clutch had been given to the cover girl, convoluting the khadi statement.

A few birds were killed with that shot. Vidya gave me an exclusive interview confessing about her damaging personal relationship that made her a wreck. Sabyasachi could style Vidya for a cover, drawing attention to a statement he wanted to make. Gaja jewellers got their earrings on the cover. And, LV wasn't complaining even if our readers were.

The Vidya Balan–Sabyasachi fashion partnership, which first got played out in *Marie Claire* would further cement in the days to come. He dressed her for R. Balki's film *Paa*, in well-chosen handloom saris and Kalamkari blouses with three-quarter sleeves. For her public appearances, she continued to wear his more ornate stuff with 'just a man's watch and one piece of jewellery'.

What stands up for him is that he doesn't forget that girls riding bikes in small towns and women making two ends meet don't need fashion. But they need clothing solutions. 'I am still regarded as Rani Mukherji's tailor,' he said at *The Indian Express* Idea Exchange last year. That quote became the headline.

Gripped by nostalgia, he resists change. No one knows if he is religious, he has never made it obvious, and refuses to answer when I ask. But he is an observer, a mind.

Just before Peeli Kothi, his November 2011 couture show in Delhi, he told me about his museum store in Mumbai; it was then work-in-progress. 'People will be welcome to walk in and choose what they want to buy but they can't take anything away. The display will not change. I will make whatever my clients want by order,' he said, not forgetting to add that he doesn't want Mumbai's predictable fashionistas for the store launch.

Peeli Kothi, the name of his last textile show in Delhi was borrowed from a lane in Benares where sari weavers would come together to hawk their wares. Nostalgia again. But like the Yuvraj of Indian fashion, the garments were powerful enough to convert the rebels to his cause.

*Name changed.

Ladies Tailor

'A tailor makes what his clients want to wear; a designer makes what he wants his clients to wear.'

—Manish Arora

'When I broke up with my first husband, I was also going through a tough time in my business, but I would often see the masterji in my dreams, not my husband,' said Sheena* laughing.

This was at her tiny boutique, an almost hidden corner shop, in a sidelined market in Delhi's Sarita Vihar. Before we could resume the masterji's husband loyalty conversation, two young girls burst into Sheena's shop, frenzied with excitement. They were students of Class 12 and were preparing for a 'Conti' (Continuation) party. Black and Bling was the theme of their event. They had come to Sheena for their 'party wardrobe'.

'Aunty, the dress should be at least three inches above the knee,' said the taller and prettier of the two. She looked barely seventeen but her hair was professionally blow dried, her Mango dress well-chosen, her lip gloss a nice, fresh orange. A big bag was slung on her shoulder and she wore her adolescent-adult persona quite well.

'Aunty, it should be strappy,' she went on.

'And, aunty, make it tight. Okay? You just copy this Zara dress, put six gold buttons in the front but only for embellishment and give me a zip on the side.The fitting will be better, okay, Aunty?' She said pulling out a Zara dress from a polythene bag as a sample.

Short, strappy, tight with gold buttons, and a zip. Sheena continued to nod, noting it all down in her large, ruled file.

Aunty, I want it tomorrow, the party is tomorrow, please, please, aunty, it will be ready na?

This pretty much sums up Sheena's life. She is a Ladies Tailor. Her career can be boiled down to three stark words: Copy, Masterji, Urgent.

Given the context, these three get juggled around in order of priority. Masterji, the co-conspirator of her career is Chief of Staff but even he is frequently riddled by the challenges that 'fashion' has brought into their lives.

Between the two of them—Sheena and the Masterji—they work out a strategic management of cutting, stitching, embellishing, and delivering quickly.

Moti, kapda aur dukaan, as a designer had remarked once sizing up the business of Ladies Tailors in India.

Sheena wouldn't have liked it. 'It is about passion, ambition, and recognition of the fact that no one can really manage even a half decent wardrobe without a darzi,' she said. She told me she worked out of a tiny shop that was barely noticeable because of the messy divorce case that was like a noose around her neck. But despite what she called some restrictions in her freedom as a single woman, till the divorce came through, she looks cheerfully adapted to her life. Cuttings of models in trend reports from fashion magazines are pasted on the wall behind her chair. She is always surrounded by half-cut fabrics, a measuring tape slung around her shoulders, a notebook open in front of her. Masterji takes the measurements while Sheena jots it all down, reading glasses perched on her cute nose. A trouser and kurti woman, Sheena is short—just about 5'2" tall and slightly overweight. But she is always well turned out; her skin is smooth and well-nourished and there is a warm Punjabi wholesomeness in her manner. She told me she picked up her trousers from Marks & Spencer ('Zara is too expensive, baba') and made the kurtis herself. The bronze lipstick she often wears suits her. Her eyes are always sparkling and it is easy to assume that she believes in positive thinking as her daily exercise. From the first time I met her in 2006, I found her to be a smart, with-it ladies tailor.

Kapda is the buzziest word in 53-year-old, twice divorced Sheena Sachdev's life. The very smell of kapda, she insists, intoxicates her. That's how she felt as a 16-year-old student of Sacred Heart Convent standing outside the Tata Textiles showroom in Jamshedpur. 'If you haven't smelt cloth fresh out of a mill, you have no idea what fabric is,' she announced. She closed her eyes at that minute; her nostalgia had made her go red in the face.

While I find Sheena talented at making well fitted and sexy sari blouses, that's not why I had continued to go back to her. Her turn of phrase interested me more than her thoughts on plunging backs of blouses. Later she would tell me that she didn't waste time counselling clients like me who knew their mind and didn't bother to listen to the tailor's advice. She had sized me up in various ways and would take notes while I ranted and raved, sometimes arguing with her about why she and her karigars should know better than to hang five kinds of stones and buttons on one tassel for a blouse. 'One story is enough in fashion, why do you tailors tell four stories in one piece?' I would ask livid. She knew how to handle criticism and would thank me for the 'feedback'. She was never short of expressive words.

Sheena considers herself a sibling of *Femina*, the first and for years the only women's magazine in India. Both were born in 1959 and Sheena's growing up years are one of the reasons she is a ladies tailor today.

Tailor is a soulful word in Sheena's life and not only because she is one herself. It strings the narrative of her life's experiences, underlines her childhood memories and explains her calling.

Born in Hoshiarpur, Punjab, in the family of Lala Mukhiram, a well-known cloth merchant of the city, Sheena suffered from a kapda craze from her infancy. Lalaji was her maternal grandfather and she would be most happy sitting on his 'gaddi' in the shop, surrounded by hundreds of rolls of fabrics (thaans) around her. 'All new prints and materials would first be cut for the ladies of the family, before they hit the store,' she said, explaining that wearing the most unusual print in town was back then the way to be fashionable.

Before Sheena's first birthday, her father, an engineer, was posted to work in TISCO in Jamshedpur. The frock for her first birthday was made by Ms Martrice, now remembered as a buxom seamstress in Jamshedpur. That was when little Sheena's tailoring sensibilities began to be sewn. Later, before she turned sixteen, Sheena would take her first cutting and stitching lessons from Ms Martrice.

Sheena's mother, the only female graduate among ten siblings, would often read women's magazines. They were a source of solace and delight for Sheena who at the age of ten, had lost her 7-year-old sister and would feel distraught from time to time. '*Femina*, Stitchcraft books that I would buy for Rs 6 each, Mrs Weaver the wife of an English colleague of my father, and a stylish aunt who had come from Lahore first moulded my fashion sensibilities,' said Sheena. As she spoke, tears welled up in her eyes.

'We were never allowed to sit idle as children.When I was in Class 4, we were taught knitting in the winters and needle embroidery in the summers,' she remembers. She regaled me with tales of how she put real fruits on a hat she had sewn for herself for a school function, how she would design school bags for herself, to be made from casement cloth and mark the pockets and zips for the family tailor.

When Sheena was in high school, one of her neighbours got married in Delhi and brought back to Jamshedpur a bride who had a BSc Home Science degree from Lady Irwin College. 'Everything that the new bride did was fascinating for me. Her crisp organdy saris, her laces handmade with a shuttle, the appliqué on her kurtas, the manner in which she would cook and present her food—her table always an aesthetic delight. That's when I decided that whatever happens, I will do a BSc in Home Science and that too from Delhi,' says Sheena.

She began to understand fashion's hierarchies early enough. 'There were two clubs in Jamshedpur that distinguished the elite from the commoners. The Beldih Club was for the elite. You could wear bikinis around the swimming pool there. The upper storeys of the Loyola convent would overlook the pool area of Beldih Club and we would crane to see the posh ladies in their swimsuits,' she said. 'The other was the United Club, for the commoners, no bikinis there,' she said.

She dreamt big but sadly could never manage to establish a flourishing business. She blames it on her failed marriages. 'I dreamt of a large tailoring consultancy, with cubicles like they have in international banks, where every customer is given a token for his turn and gets personalized attention. But my two divorces and the perpetual problems with karigars and masterjis didn't make life easy for me,' she told me.

'Do you get offended when you are called a tailor especially now that there is such a craze for designers?' I asked Sheena.

'Not at all. I set out to be a tailor and am proud and happy to be one,' she said, telling me that the sewing machine her mother gave her for her first dowry is one of her proud possessions. 'How many people can afford designer wear in any case?' she went on.

'I have so many clients who go to designer boutiques, take clothes inside trial rooms, sneakily click photographs on their mobile phones, then come back to me and ask me to copy. So much for designer wear,' she said.

'Isn't it plagiarism? If the copyright laws were in place in India, designers can sue you,' I said.

'It is not plagiarism really. Look at the work we invest,' she told me, explaining how after she was shown a design, she went to shop for fabrics for many of her clients, mixed and matched buttons, zips, pipings, underlinings. She even hunted for zany blouse pieces for her clients, before carefully creating what she now calls 'couture'.

Sheena believes that darzis are also couturiers in the way they create personalized wardrobes.

Darzi is a leviathan word in the lives of Indians as our first garments are often homemade, or darzi-made langots (cotton diapers) the moment we are born. In that sense of completely personalized and handmade clothing, darzi-made clothes are couture alright.

If you took away the hype, Page 3 photographs, the party culture, fashion magazine spreads and which designer dressed which Bollywood star for a red carpet event, there are a spate of similarities between good designers and good darzis. Both will give you good finish and good fitting. However, if you see an original piece of design or a textile innovation, then in all likelihood it has come from a designer's stable, not from a masterji and tailor—Aunty team. The latter are excellent replicators. But they are replicators nevertheless, not creators. So when a person like Sheena says they can do everything and designers just charge 200 percent more for similar stuff, I strongly and consistently disagree.

The darzi tribe is an intensely hierarchical one. There are those like Sheena who run boutiques and charge upto Rs 1500 for one blouse and then there are those we find in every nook and corner of every small and big market in India—outside grocery shops, near chemists, cheek by jowl with plagiarized DVD sellers and magazine vendors. Not everyone clearly is a couturier in the way Sheena implies. There are tailors in lower middle class residential apartments too who stitch a blouse for Rs 40 and a salwar kameez for Rs 80. My housekeeper Laxmi, who owns more than 50 odd sets of salwar kameez, spends every single penny of her pocket money on clothes and keeps using the word 'fitting'.

'Can I go early today? I want to go for fittings,' she would say.

'Models go for fittings, where are you going?' I would ask laughing. 'To my tailor for fittings,' she would say, offended. Laxmi is diminutive in size, everything is big for her. She can't survive without this fitting tailor of hers. She tried very hard to become a tailor, and would go to a 'shaala' (tailoring classes) regularly but it didn't last long.

Then there is Akhtar bhai, a tailor who works from the small but busy Sector 21 market of Noida. He told me that he runs a fairly successful enterprise by investing in just one sewing machine, a large assortment of threads, needles, buttons, zips and such, and one large trunk in which he would dump, like the cobbler who sat and worked next to him, the bags with people's clothes. Unlike Sheena, Akhtar bhai had no illusions about being a designer to whom life had been unfair. He earned square meals for himself and his family by stitching curtains, doing alterations for the clientele of the sector and making TV blouses for the domestic helps who worked in the same sector.

'Our money primarily comes from alterations and repairs,' he told me. Cutting pairs of jeans to size, loosening blouses of women who perennially put on weight, stitching back missing buttons, repairing zips, opening the hems of school uniforms that had become too short for growing children formed the bulk of the work. Women in the locality would also bring leftover fabric for him to create table linen, kitchen cloths, cushion covers. He was always busy and, like Sheena, would never deliver according to the promised deadlines.

The cultural personality of the Indian tailor demands that they delay delivery. The chase is a reality for everyone who has a tailor in their lives.

'But what would you do without a tailor? There is a tailor inside every Indian woman and she feels restless until she finds that kind of relationship with someone.'

These were Vishakha Dave's wise words. When I spotted her first, she didn't look fash-friendly. Round-faced, slightly plump, thirty-something, she wore a printed salwar kameez in mauve. I saw her in the waiting room at Ahmedabad railway station one late evening as I waited for a midnight train to Gandhidham. Feet curled up on a bench, she was trying to set up a hand mirror against a suitcase. For 23-minutes, by my watch, she did her face, slowly and lovingly applying an impenetrable layer of powder followed by lipstick, kajal, bindi, rouge (blush-on), and a spot of Vaseline on the chin—for 'shine' as she told me later. Then she did her hair, as carefully, sticking colourful clips into it. Two little girls were fast asleep next to her, and the husband, a bespectacled, dark-skinned, portly gentleman completely ignored her vanities.

As a hanger-on in that crowded waiting lounge where people stretched, ate and snored, even I got impatient with the time she took to doll up; but not her husband.

Shringar done, she got up and patted her salwar kameez, trying to catch the full effect in that little mirror. That's when I walked up to her. While we waited for our respective trains, the next few hours with Vishakha Dave, a homemaker-cum-tailor-cum-beautician from Nadiad, a 'fashion-crazy aurat' (in her own words) helped me cut my darzi story better.

Vishakha chatted with me in Gujarati. A set of new clothes, a lipstick or a bag thrilled her more than anything else. 'Whenever possible, I wear new garments when I go to pick up my kids from the bus stop,' she dimpled. She was the small town Babli of *Bunty aur Babli*, who cut up old saris to make kurtis and then would turn into Ms Confidence to counsel her neighbours who were also her clients. Educated in an English-medium school, she had graduated in history through a correspondence course. Now, as the eager fashion counsellor of her neighbourhood, she sought no help from history. It was English and a crash course at a Shahnaz Beauty parlour that came to her aid. It made her 'fashionable'.

She told me she had converted the puja room in their small house in Nadiad into a beauty parlour with only two chairs, one big wall-to-wall mirror, two white painted chests with drawers and a large cupboard for jars of creams, scrubs and gels. The garage outside had been turned into a tailoring unit and she employed one masterji.

'In my beauty parlour, I don't do much, only threading, waxing, bleaching, and mini facials,' she told me rather candidly.

'What's a mini facial?' I asked.

'Oh, a 10-minute face massage with one pack. No scrub, no

steam, no black head removal,' she said. 'Mini facials sold fast and frequently, they cost only Rs 80 and she had a steady and regular mini facial clientele.

'I don't have the time with two small kids, nor can I afford to hire helpers,' she said. So Vishakha couldn't offer hair cuts, pedicures, or manicures and her clientele comprised of other homemakers who lived nearby. She told me that beauty products were unaffordable for her, so were facial kits, bowls, manicure sets and other tools and it was a losing proposition unless she opened a proper salon in a commercial area. That not being possible, she earned from mini facials, threading, and stitching blouses for her neighbours and kurta pyjamas for their husbands. 'The men never come for measurements or fittings. Their wives bring in samples. Gujarati men don't want to be seen giving measurements, their wives fight with me to get the fits right,' she added.

To boost her earnings, Vishakha also sold garments. She bought them on wholesale rates from the cloth markets of Ahmedabad, mostly salwar kameez fabrics, some ready-made stuff like nighties (which she called gowns), cheap printed saris in the range of Rs 300 to Rs 700, children's clothes and sold them in Nadiad from her one-room beauty parlour-cum-boutique. 'I mark everything up by 20 percent,' she told me.

'Why do so many beauticians in small towns double up as tailors? What's the link?' I asked.

'Fashion and beauty—aren't they connected in some way?' She asked me looking confused herself. She said she thought it was obvious that a beautician has good taste.

'How do you explain men's kurta pyjamas as fashion, Vishakha?' I asked her during one of our follow up phone conversations a few months after that long chat at Ahmedabad railway station.

'Everything is fashion these days, ben,' she responded. Ben is Gujarati for sister.

'Middle class and lower middle class people can't afford an army of designers, hair stylists, skin specialists, pedicurists, and tailors. But they also have wishes to fulfil and like to look good. People like me are all these things rolled into one,' she said.

Her neighbours not only sought Vishakha's advice in matching blouses and for shopping tips, but would come to her for a curious variety of clothes to be made for school fancy dress competitions for their children.

As her homework, Vishakha would look up advertisements and study 'Bollywood fashion' as she called it to catch up with all that was going on. Once in a while, she bought fashion magazines in English.

'Which ones do you buy?' I asked her.

'Any depending on who is on the cover,' she said. One of her neighbour-customers had recently brought *Harper's Bazaar* to her to copy some designs for a sister's wedding and Vishakha had asked if she could keep the copy after the wedding was over.

'It costs Rs 100 and they show the same things again and again. So I just keep old copies of magazines to show a variety of patterns to my clients,' she said.

'But fashion is about new trends, don't you worry that you are showing old designs to your clients?' I asked.

'Arre, ben, what will we do with new trends every month, who cares, do we have the money? It is filmi heroines that my customers want to copy. They want their eyebrows threaded like Anushka Sharma and now her Patiala suits have become famous too. I also make special Katrina Kaif blouses,' she said looking proud.

'Katrina Kaif blouses? But Katrina hardly wears saris,' I argued.

'You don't understand, ben, you have to popularize a pattern by calling it something. So I have Katrina Kaif blouses, Aishwarya Rai salwars, and my special line has names of different heroines. I change the names of my clothes when a film is a hit and rename it accordingly. That's how my tailoring business runs. During Diwali and festivals, I give a discount on Katrina blouses,' she explained.

Vishakha's most recent innovation for the festive season of 2011 was *Don 2* cholis.

'*Don 2* cholis? But who is wearing cholis in *Don 2*?' I asked.

'How would I know?' she responded and sounded like she was losing her patience with me. 'Ben, it has nothing to do with who actually wears what, we have to give it a Bollywood name and I go by whatever is a hit or is well hyped,' she repeated.

'Now see, the serial *Bade Acche Lagte Hain* on Sony is a hit and everyone is looking at Priya's blouses (the character played by Sakshi Tanwar), so I plan to make Priya cholis too, they are almost backless and have nice, sexy strings at the back. My customers don't want such plunging backs but still I can copy,' she said.

'How much do you charge for such cholis?' I asked.

'Rs 60 for a plain blouse, Rs 100 if it has lining, Rs 120 if it has a pattern at the back or a tie-up tassle. Bollywood blouses for Rs 150 and TV blouses for Rs 125,' she told me explaining that if *Don 2* is not a hit, her customers will bargain with her to give them a discount.

'I tried Chhammak Chhalo blouses from *Ra.One* also, but they didn't work out. Gujaratis don't like see-through chiffon as blouse fabric and the few blouses I made were tearing up very quickly at the seams,' she said. 'Customers are such kanjoos (miserly) people; they keep bargaining and nagging to charge less. They put pressure on me to give them a discount for the next piece they bring for stitching if their former one is not stitched to their satisfaction,' she said, moaning about the troubles of her trade.

'What about your masterji? Is he good?' I asked.

'Yes, but he never makes clothes on time, he is smoking all the time, he is a loser. He cuts very well but doesn't believe in working hard and bunks work a lot. My former masterji was very good, he was Muslim and you know how Muslims are with their cutting and embroidery. But after my husband read in the newspapers what Narendrabhai Modi had to say about Muslims, he asked me to dismiss that guy.'

'Narendrabhai may say what he likes to the public but the inside news is that he doesn't like Muslims. So my husband thinks we should not employ a Muslim masterji,' she went on.

'Who gave you inside news about Narendra Modi's dislike for Muslims?' I asked.

'My husband,' said Vishakha simply.

'And you believed him?' I asked befuddled by her ignorance. I had barely digested her concept of selling *Don 2* cholis for her customers without knowing if anyone in the film even wore cholis. And now this: she couldn't hire a Muslim tailor because of what Narendra Modi allegedly thought. Gosh, she seemed tailor made for irrationality.

Whether it was Narendra Modi's political views or Priyanka Chopra's cholis, the husband always had the last word in Vishakha's life. He was never ever impressed with what she did or the small money she consistently earned. He never lost a chance to bring her down. 'Everyone among my neighbours gives me credit for mini facials and Bollywood blouses but my husband doesn't care.'

Vishakha had come to accept that her marriage carried on because it had no real reason to break down.

Sheena's first marriage broke down when her children, a son and a daughter, were adolescents.

But long before her dream began to splinter, Sheena would hang out in Jamshedpur with a group of trendy girls called Jampot. Later, to pursue her ambition, she moved to Delhi and enrolled at the Institute of Home Economics for a BSc in Home Science. 'I had first touched a measuring tape and a pair of scissors on my sixteenth birthday and never wanted to keep them down,' she said.

She raved about her time at the Institute of Home Economics. 'My projects would be put up on display boards for others to see. I did very well,' she said.

After her Home Science degree, Sheena got married to a doctor who worked in Libya and went to live there with him. 'Libya was an excellent training ground for me as there was a lot of fabric available but no trained tailors,' she told me.

But it was only in Delhi in the year 1992 that she first started a small store from her home. It was called Expressions by Sheena Pal—that was her surname after her first marriage. She created a computer designed logo inspired by a sari border and advertised in the local Yellow Pages.

Sheena initially stocked only nightwear for women and bed linen. Her full-fledged darzi enterprise hadn't yet begun and she was trying to gauge if a store selling clothes from home would earn her some money. A cousin, settled in Chennai, helped her with the material and Sheena stocked the Madras checked fabric.

'A masterji from Lucknow, who was looking for work, randomly knocked on my door one day and changed my life,' she said looking locked in the past for a moment as we chatted. Sheena had invited me over for breakfast at her home and had got four types of cuisines cooked. This was a few days before Diwali and an assortment of sweets looked back from the table at me.

'That man insisted I hire him. I didn't know him from Adam but there was something in his manner that told me he knew what tailoring was all about. I asked him to stitch a few pieces as trial. The way his fingers worked, the way he cut and held the cloth told me I had the right guy and could finally launch a tailoring unit,' she recalls.

So Sheena finally started her tailoring shop. Masterji went on to employ a couple of karigars for finishing, sewing, stitching, dyeing, and sorting out fabric and other peripheral work.

Sheena's first marriage was falling apart day by day. The issues between her and her husband became non-negotiable and she decided to walk out. 'It wasn't as if my husband left me. We left my husband,' she said. Her two children and she took a collective decision to leave the house.

A divorce came through only to be followed by her first husband's subsequent death. Sheena went on to marry again, this time to a businessman who had a big house in Vasant Vihar. She moved both her house and her tailoring unit to where he lived. By now her daughter was an older teenager and her son a medical student. Both accompanied her.

Expressions by Sheena Pal became Expressions by Sheena Sachdev.

'My second husband wanted me to change my name. But that

marriage didn't survive either. Both my husbands had told me that they were attracted to me because of my ambition, and swore to support me in my business. But when the marriages started crumbling, they hit me below the belt, hurting my businesses. In their own ways, both made sure that my work suffered and that I had setbacks,' said Sheena. She wasn't sounding emotional anymore. She looked thoughtful about her truncated marital relationships but not shaken.

Changing relationships and booming retail have curiously defined the last ten odd years in Indian life.

'The word designer did not exist when we started off,' says Puneet Nanda of Satya Paul going back forty years in time. His father Satya Paul had migrated from Pakistan after the Partition and ran a restaurant called Punjab Vatni in Delhi's Sarojini Nagar. The man who would launch the Satya Paul label in 1985 with 'designer' saris first moved to Heritage, the garment and fabric store that is still successful and popular in Delhi's posh South Extension market.

'Heritage gave competition to handloom emporiums in that era; it became the place for connoisseurs to buy the finest of shawls,' says Puneet. He didn't know a shower curtain from silk when his father called him to quit photography and join the family business as a designer.

Today, Satya Paul is a 100-crore a year company, a growth that Puneet attributes to realistic assessment of the changing market. 'We gave women what they wanted; salwar kameezes at Heritage, then designer saris, stoles, scarves, gowns, saris, tunics, watches, bags followed by men's neckties, bags, belts, cufflinks, watches, and pens,' he added.

'We changed rapidly because we didn't want to be seen as an Aunty's brand,' says Jyoti Narula, Puneet's partner at Genesis Colors, the company that owns Satya Paul.

Retail grew infectiously in India. Once the 300 odd malls entered small towns and luxury destinations opened in metros in the late 2000s, 'fashion' and 'designer' were words bandied about in popular lexicon; like a cloud burst, splashing every nuance. Alongside, ladies tailors, too, went through several quick, glamorous transmutations. Those who had small corners in posh markets made hay and continue to do so. They also understood the importance of specializing. I often hear anecdotes about some tailor or the other from friends. If someone is a trouser specialist, another knows how to make the sexiest of cholis.

Neighbourhood shops promising 'designer wear' have mushroomed even in small towns. The darzi, who would once be called home every season or during weddings and special occasions to 'sit' and stitch a bunch of clothes for the entire family, from grandmother's petticoats to new style churidar-kurtas for young girls has climbed up the status ladder.

I remember Mahendrabhai, an attractive, bearded tailor in my hometown, who would 'sit' at my house as well as of many others in our community. In our adolescent rush for fashionable clothes, Mahendrabhai was a God for us. Very few stores sold ready-made garments, and everything had to be stitched, right from the school uniform to the 'nightie'. My friends, cousins, and I would nag our mothers to buy fabric from Cheap Cloth Store in Gandhidham (it is still called that but now stocks ready-to-wear as well as 'designer garments').

Mahendrabhai was a patient man. My mother and those of my friends' would chew his brains on minute tailoring details but he would simply smile and never get irritated. His terms were Rs 150 per day in the late Eighties. A cup of tea with biscuits and snacks at 11 am would be followed by a proper lunch whenever he was ready to eat it. Then, a round of tea or coffee with nashto (Gujarati for snacks) in the evening. At the end of a full working day that would conclude by 7 pm or so, Mahendrabhai would dish out at least one and half 'suits' (two salwars and one kurta or vice versa). Mahendrabhai was darzi and master rolled into one. When he got married to a fair, slim, giggly Gujarati girl, our hearts broke, also because he wouldn't stay back for lunch anymore and would start closing his foldable, hand cranked sewing machine by 5:30 pm instead of 7.

Things changed for Mahendrabhai's ilk in the Nineties. Like doctors who don't do home visits anymore, fewer and fewer darzis would agree to 'sit' as the years wore on. Today, if they are an immensely sought after breed, they have the fashion boom to thank. 'Tailor made designer wear' that much of India wears is like the vegetarian hot dog, the Jain pizza, the chicken tikka sandwich, or Punjabi Chinese.

The tailor is a living ghost in most of our lives and the word 'designer' one of the most overused words of the last decade. A shop selling miscellany in temple town Benares is called 'Designer Junction'. Garishly dressed mannequins in strappy blouses stand outside it like an army. A tailor in Anjar, in the Kutch district of Gujarat, calls himself 'Designer Tailors'.

Fashion has also spawned many ancillary vocations besides copycat darzis. Embroidery specialists, shops selling vintage borders, buttons, zips, block print fabrics, and hundreds of other small things that go into the making of 'Indian darzi couture'.

Being a masterji who works in a tailoring enterprise is a respectable profession now. Sheena told me that good tailors earned at least Rs 35,000 per month, sometimes a tad more than what the boutique owner may take home. If your masterji knows how to cut, you know you can make it in the business.

No wonder masterjis are the most wanted tribe in the underbelly of the fashion industry. Designers have often told me how the thousand export businesses that run from their factories in Noida in Uttar Pradesh depend on these 'masterjis'. They learn to cut and sew mass clothing—masterminding then the manufacture of everything from Zara tops to bikinis.

I was told about a certain Tara Matthews, a Sardarni from Sujan Singh Park in Delhi who gets bikinis 'manufactured' in a Noida factory. You can order them on the Net and can't even tell if they are from India. 'The fashion business is less about designers, it is more about tailors and what is available in malls,' Vishakha told me. According to her, women aren't just looking better because they have talented tailors to outfit them, but their approach to everything even under garments has changed. She was riveted by push-up bras as they improved her self-image. 'A number of my female friends discuss the difference black bras made in our lives. We grew up wearing white Libertina bras or cheap ones picked from weekly markets but the black bra is something else. It makes me feel sexy,' she said a bit shyly and hinted that she hadn't had sex with her husband for the last three years. 'A good bra makes an outfit better,' she said knowingly, adding that she often told her clients which bras to wear with their clothes.

Sheena, too, was a mini counsellor for her clients. 'People think they know it all but half of my clients don't even wear the right bra. I have to gently counsel them over their choices in fabrics and colours without hurting their egos. Many women have got their bust point all wrong, their boobs sag and then they blame me for badly fitting blouses,' she said reiterating how measurements were instrumental in her business.

'I may not have gone to NIFT to study, but even in my sleep I can distinguish a good fit from bad, a good masterji from a mediocre one,' says Sheena.

The word masterji cropped up every few minutes in every conversation I had with any tailor anywhere. Sheena seemed full of masterji anecdotes. I got tired of taking notes but her masterji tales never dried up.

'The relationship between a boutique owner and a masterji is nebulous, passionate, and very political. I have had far more intense and problematic relationships with my masterjis than with my two husbands,' Sheena told me. 'They know we are entirely dependent on them and exploit our situation,' she went on, adding that her tailoring instincts and her business had been shaped by the masterjis she had worked with. She praised Muslim karigars from Lucknow and said there was no one quite like them. But if she owed her understanding of fine karigari to some of her masterjis, it was also because of them that she had become temperamental. 'I used to be mortified about a masterji leaving me, I felt my business would sink and I would ground to a halt, but over the years I have learnt that they all play musical chairs. They threaten to leave us seemingly for offers they get from designers. At the same time, there are enough disgruntled masterjis in big cities who are frustrated with the discrepancies in income, recognition, and status between their designer employers and them. They come with resumes of having worked with designers, and we give them employment,' she said shrugging.

'Designers are power graspers; they want fame, name but don't want to share their fortunes with their tailors, leave alone giving them credit. Except Sabyasachi, who brings tailors and embroiders on the ramp while taking a bow,' said Sheena.

If flashy careers of designers have given confidence and ambition to tailors, they have also complicated their lives. People are spoilt for choice according to Sheena. Over the course of time, she has got frustrated with fickle clients who want designer copies at less than quarter of the actual price and then call to change their mind every two days.

'A client will bring me a designer choli borrowed from someone who owns it without even telling that person. That's the first sin, they then expect me to replicate it inch by inch but argue with me if I charge Rs 1000 per blouse,' she said shaking her head.

She has also realized that almost all of her customers in Delhi, much like Vishakha's in Nadiad, rely on films and magazines for patterns, so to counsel she has to keep herself abreast with who wore what and where. Katrina Kaif turns out to be one of the most followed Bollywood stars in the tailoring shops. That's why her posters are pasted everywhere from interiors of auto rickshaws in small towns to darzi boutiques. She is seen flashing her lovely smile, and you can't even see what she's wearing in most posters but she is still the Indian Ladies Tailor's biggest poster girl.

In cities, the mobile phone camera is the most important tool of plagiarism. Tailors themselves use it extensively, visiting designer boutiques and exhibitions, clicking away happily. Till she told me, I had no idea that Sheena even replicated designer saris. From lace to satin, from embroidery to brocade borders, from silk falls and printed linings to crystal embellishments, she could do it all. 'Bring me a piece and I will copy it for you,' she says laughing confidently.

Sheena researches markets, visits exhibitions by all kinds of traders including craft and textile revivalists. She drives her own car and uses Tuesday, the weekly off for her boutique to roam around in markets, looking at things and picking up fabric for her customers. She caters to the wedding market like any other designer, but also to what's now called TV fashion, theme parties, school and college farewell parties, kitty gatherings... the list is long and growing.

The blouse, she tells me, remains the item number of a darzi's creative life.

Tailors hired by stores also thrive because plagiarism is a serious and prosperous enterprise in India. Once, while researching a story, I visited a shop called Corner Matching Centre in Lajpat Nagar, Delhi. I was ostensibly looking for the Deepika Padukone white and indigo blue kurti she had worn for a song in *Love Aaj Kal* paired with a red churidar. I was told that the kurti had gone viral in street markets. True enough, there were dozens of Deepika kurtis in Lajpat Nagar, all priced around Rs 600. Similarly, I found copies of Manish Malhotra's salwar sets at Mumbai's Manish Market. The owner of the shop told me that they hired a team of tailors and would book a bunch of advance film tickets on the day of the release of any big Bollywood film and send the whole tailor sena (tailor army) there.

'First day, first show ji,' the Lajpat Nagar guy affirmed the process. They did the same. 'Our darzis should see how it looks on the big screen,' he said triumphantly, explaining how after sending their tailors to cinema halls, they followed it up by buying half a dozen DVDs. They had installed DVD players in their manufacturing units and tailors would watch films and copy patterns and fabric combinations. 'Isn't it good for Rs 600 only? You go to buy it from Manish Malhotra, you will get it for Rs 20,000,' he said. 'By the way, the same kurti is being sold in some big stores for Rs 2000. They buy from us on bulk and mark up the price,' he said and wrote down the names of the stores I could go and check his claim out.

'Darzi couture, madam,' muttered the suspicious looking sales person at a store called Geeta Circle in Kolkata. Darzi couture there meant a climb up to the first floor of a busy sari shop. There, original garments by Manish Malhotra, Anamika Khanna, Sabyasachi, Suneet Varma, even Abu Jani–Sandeep Khosla were displayed on trolleyed hangers. You could choose the designer you fancied and Geeta Circle assistants would show you its replicas, in a few colour combinations. I had gone with one of their regular customers, a high society Kolkata woman who regularly bought plagiarized stuff and because they trusted her, they told me that they had a team of tailors whose only job was to go, buy original designer pieces every season, including saris and then replicate them. If you didn't like the colour combinations they had in stock, you could ask for a copy in a colour of your choice.

Every city now has shops openly selling knock off 'designer wedding wear'. Sabyasachi and Suneet Varma are the two most copied Indian designers. Their knock offs are as easily found in Patna as in Mumbai. Suneet Varma said he can't decide if he should be flattered or insulted that stores like CTC Plaza, Bombay Selections, Meena Bazaar copied him so blatantly.

A strong subsidiary industry supports darzi couture. In Pydhonie market, a ten-minute walk from Chor Bazaar and Crawford Market in Mumbai, a shop announces Jean Paul Gaultier lace and embroidery swatches. Apparently Armani, DKNY, Moschino, Ferreti, and several others international designers source material from here too. Manish Malhotra too. Everything in the fashion industry comes full circle.

The behemoth word 'darzi' that infuses meaning and money to Sheena's life makes fashion designers bristle. Also because 'darzi' is what many of their families thought about them when they first set out to cut cloth for a living. Manish Arora, one of the country's blazing talents and the only Indian designer with international name and fame, gladly called himself a Ladies Tailor in a programme on *Discovery Channel* but only after his stupendous success.

'Darzi banoge?' asked designer Rahul Mishra's shocked Malhausi based father after investing every single penny he had on his son's education. He was too shocked to be told that his talented son wanted to join NID in Ahmedabad.

When I narrated these anecdotes to veteran designer Ravi Bajaj, one of the first in India to start his own fashion store, it brought a big smile to his face. 'I have always said we are glorified tailors but my contemporaries don't agree,' he said over a frothy cup of coffee at Soak, his restaurant and bar in Delhi's posh Greater Kailash Market. The 47-year-old designer has the body language of a surgeon. He is unhurried, clear, and realistic. Sleek spectacles and greying sideburns add to the urbane charm of this London-educated designer. Bajaj told me he had one of the most flamboyant lifestyles but nobody would be able to see it in a lifestyle magazine. He wore white trousers and a fine lime green linen shirt from his own men's line, which sat proudly on a well worked out body. 'We make and earn from Indian clothes—saris, salwar kameezes, lehnga cholis, yet many designers show Western garments on the ramp. Ninety percent of Indian designers make traditional clothes and 75 percent of our revenues come from Indian garments, so let there be no illusion that we are here to give any competition to Armani or Zegna,' said the designer.

Sheena on her part continues to dream of getting an international bank-like office where she will be designer at large. She has hired yet another masterji after firing her former one for swagger and sloth.

It was actually Akhtar bhai, the tailor from Noida, who surprised me by his sudden call while I was finishing this chapter.

'Can you please help me with Sabyasachi dada's number?' he pleaded.

'Why do you want it, Akhtar bhai, and anyway I will have to ask Sabyasachi first,' I said, quite perplexed.

'I want to take a tailoring class from him to improve my business—everyone wants a Sabyasachi copy these days. Isn't it better if I learn from dada himself? I can pay for my training from my savings. Will he agree?'

*Names changed

In the Red

'If we don't wake up to our own textiles, we will soon have a Benarasi made in China.'

—Rajeev Sethi

Rahul Salvi's voice on the phone was polite but guarded. A 32-year-old architect who had given up his job to become a full time handloom weaver, he spoke fluent English with a Gujarati accent. Piqued by a snippet in the Ahmedabad edition of *The Times of India* of February 19, 2010, I decided to visit him and his family, descendants of an eleventh century weaver community, in Patan. The Salvis had reportedly regretted Gujarat Chief Minister Narendra Modi's request to dress up filmstar Rekha in a Patan Patola sari for the Vibrant Fashion Week that month.

'Is this true that you didn't want to lend the sari for a fashion week?' I asked Rahul.

He didn't respond to my question but invited me to come to Patan and stay with them. He added that his cousin Savan would wait for me on the outskirts of the town to escort me to their home.

Patan, an old city with a rich, historical heritage and a population of about thirteen lakhs, is a five-hour smooth car drive from Ahmedabad. As expected, I found Savan leaning against his parked bike outside Rani Ni Vav (the Queen's well), an old sculptural monument, the architectural patterns of which are often replicated in Patola saris. Rani Ni Vav is outside the main town of Patan and visitors must climb down hundreds of small, narrow, steps carved in stone to reach the dark and engulfing bottom of the well.

A tall, thin and bearded young man, Savan, smiled warmly, revealing his gutka-stained teeth. His shirt wasn't tucked into his trousers and he reminded me of 'outshirt', an unfashionable word in dressing but commonly used in Gujarati English.

'Go ahead, take your time,' said Savan emphasizing that I should walk down to the depths of Rani Ni Vav to observe its patterns and to understand how they had been interpreted into weaving by their family. I began my trudge but felt discouraged after walking halfway down. Besides, to advertise how strongly I felt about Indian weaves and not give the impression of a city fashionista to the Salvis, I was dressed in a sari and tripping on the stone steps wasn't just an imaginary fear.

So I came back in less than half an hour, breathless with the climb back up to ground level and told Savan that it was enough for me. He laughed and asked the driver to follow his bike.

Patan was ingrained as a stately place in my memory of school textbooks on history, but it turned out to be a town with a languid air. People seemed unhurried, and although the traffic was sparse the horns honked loudly all around. Unperturbed cows sat by the wayside, and women wearing saris with the Gujarati ulta pallu, worked in front yards of houses. I smiled at them as we drove by and they smiled back.

The Salvis live on a street named after them—Salviwado, Patolawala street. The Patola made here is an unparalleled weave in the textile history of the world. But those who weave it are rapidly shrinking in numbers. I had been told by my designer friends who had studied at NID that Rahul Salvi and Savan were the youngest among Patola weavers. In stark symbolism, I had visualized a weaving cluster with deserted looms. What I saw instead was a modest house.

In keeping with Gujarati tradition, the footwear had been left outside. The weaving area was large and was flooded with natural light and brightened by tubelights. The centrepiece was a huge loom, holding in its jaws, a partly woven turmeric yellow Patola sari with a fuchsia and brown border. The walls wore blue paint, peeling in places. Framed pictures of master weavers in the family receiving awards from heads of the country hung on all the walls. Award citations and trophies sat in a glass showcase. Old wooden cupboards, an odd wall calendar, and a well-worn sofa made the place look like a set from a Gujarati play.

After Savan's warm and smiling demeanour, I was a bit taken aback when the three older men working at the loom in white pyjamas responded to my namaste with wariness. There was no lady in sight. Rahul trooped in soon after. A slightly built man about 5'2" and a bajra (muddy brown) complexion, he wore a sports jersey and camel-coloured creased trousers. He was courteous but there was no mistaking the distance in his eyes. The awkwardness of our new acquaintance hung heavy for a couple of minutes till Rahul's uncle Bharatbhai crumbled it by talking about the Patan Patola weave. It was as if he was reciting by rote.

It was in the eleventh century that Raja Kumarapal of the Solanki Dynasty brought 700 weavers to Patan from Jhalna in Maharashtra. Founded in 746 AD, Patan became an Ikat centre only after the weavers came here. According to folklore, the king would wear a new Patola for worship everyday as it was considered to be a holy cloth with miraculous powers that protected the wearer from evil, ill health, and bad luck. Hand-woven Patolas were exported to Indonesia, Thailand, Malaysia, and other South Asian markets. Most valued in Indonesia, the Patola was worn there for Ram Leela renditions.

The economic instability of post-independence India forced many weavers to shut shop to seek alternate livelihoods. India had textiles instead of tailored goods. The industrial and technology policy of India in the Sixties and Seventies was inward looking and instead of investing knowledge and technology in weaver centres to help them move beyond creating traditional textiles as opposed to stitched garments, the government ignored weaver clusters initially. But despite the many ups and downs, Kantilal Salvi, a master weaver and national awardee (1978) held on to the family legacy. Now only four families with three of them living in Patan that consist of about thirteen weavers make the authentic Patola with the double Ikat weave.

Ikat, an Indonesian word which means to knot, bind or tie around, is found in many ethnic cultures. In India, it is woven in Saurashtra and Patan in Gujarat, also in Orissa and Andhra Pradesh. Ikat was the flag of the craft movement of the Eighties when cottage industries and ethnic wear ruled 'Indian fashion'.

What many of us may wear or have seen our mothers and older sisters wearing is single Ikat, the simpler and more common form of Ikat weave. In this, either the warp or the weft is tied and resist-dyed whereas in double Ikat—like in Patan Patola—both the warp and weft are dyed. Resist-dyeing first requires tying, knotting, stitching, or using wax with extreme precision to prevent the dye from seeping into the entire cloth. This differentiates the motifs and patterns from the field of the sari. Later I would learn that women of the Salvi family helped with tying the cloth into knots (the process requires extreme attention to detail and patience) but were not involved in dyeing.

Minal, 28, is Bharatbhai's only child. She is Rahul's first cousin and the only unmarried girl of this family. She came across like a stand-alone motif in the mono-coloured story of the Salvis, entering the weaving area where I was chatting with her father and Rahul, wrapped in the aroma of asafoetida and mango pickle.

Born and raised in the Kutch district of Gujarat, I associate the smell of asafoetida very strongly with Gujarati cooking. Our next door neighbours were Gujaratis and I had grown up on asafoetida wafting into our home from our neighbour's. Minal's entry was like a punch of nostalgia. A vegetarian meal had been served in Bharatbhai's living quarters and she had come to call us.

Minal had completed an engineering degree in computer science for which she had studied in the neighbouring city of Palanpur. She now lived at home and taught a Bachelors course in computer science in a local Patan college. Alongside, through a private correspondence course from Bhopal, she was studying for an MTech degree. She was also waiting for Mr Right. She wore silver framed glasses and a nondescript brown salwar kameez. No frills and fancies, no nail polish or accessories, no L'Oreal tints in her casually tied back, dark hair.

She looked a bit impatient. Not with me particularly but there was a sense of fatigue in her towards people visiting them. When I later heard about the hundreds of people who visited the Salvis every year, I didn't blame Minal at all. Yet, it was difficult to miss her impatience, interwoven with wariness, of the same texture that her cousin Rahul and father Bharatbhai had.

When we walked over to Bharatbhai's residence, just across the weaving quarters, Minal's mother, Kalpana, smiled wanly at me but didn't utter a word beyond namaste. She wore a handloom kurta with white stretch leggings, her coloured hair strained at the roots for a touch up and like her daughter, she too wore spectacles.

Over lunch, I asked Minal if she read fashion magazines and if she was driven by any trends. 'Sometimes a *Femina* pops up here but nothing else. Not that I care,' she added a little too sharply. 'Everything—fashion, make up, dieting, modelling is about film actors and Bollywood. Not one magazine wants to know what regular, non-celebrity women want or how they want to look.

Magazines think we are fools that we will listen to anything they say and follow them. Admiring Hindi cinema and its stars is one thing but following them for everything from tooth paste to wedding wear is an obsession. I detest this overdose of Bollywood,' she said. That brief tirade was cathartic for her. Her taut nerves seemed to have relaxed a bit and after that, every time I would look up from my thali to glance at her, she smiled. She even told me that she favoured ethnic dressing and mostly wore salwar kameez or a kurta with leggings instead of a pair of jeans. 'I love Indian clothes. Of course, no fashion magazine cares what ordinary girls like me wear.'

Chit-chat had helped thaw the ice in the modest eating area (there was a small dining table inside the kitchen) and I assumed that I could carry the small talk further with Minal's mum. Without preamble, I asked Kalpanaben whether the salwar kameez had become an acceptable garment for married women in Gujarati households, replacing the sari, which was traditionally considered 'compulsory' post marriage. I remembered my Gujarati neighbours, a family with nine sisters, who would start wearing saris at home as soon as they got engaged to be married. Their mother told us that she wanted her daughters to get used to managing household chores and sleep in the six yards.

Kalpanaben clearly thought that my salwar kameez question was a dumb one. She didn't respond. Her husband answered on her behalf, saying they didn't impose 'restrictions' any more. 'As it is, women don't want to get married in this town and if we place restrictions on what they wear, it will dissuade them further,' he said candidly.

'Don't you want to get married?' I turned to ask Minal.

'Yes, eventually maybe but it's not my priority,' she said. 'I want to complete my MTech studies properly and shine, not do it just for the heck of acquiring a post-graduate degree,' she added, telling me how her commitment to teaching was growing. She had been teaching for a year when we met. 'Initially I began teaching in the local college because there isn't any other employment opportunity for a computer engineer in Patan, but now I really enjoy it. This is what I would love to do in the future.'

Bharatbhai listened, but with a non-committal attitude. Having made his position clear on women's dress codes a few minutes ago, he was only too happy to echo his daughter's disdain for the glamour industry. 'The money-propelling, hedonistic nature of the film world is contrary to our weave, which is about sustaining family traditions and work as worship,' he said. Kalpanaben didn't tell me so but Minal did about how her mother spent all her spare time weaving the Patan Patola. 'Over the years, my mother has developed reverence for this dying art and helps in whichever way she can,' she added.

The pieces of the puzzle had begun to fall in place. The Patan Patola has never been seen on the catwalk or on a young celeb. TV serials like *Kyunki Saas Bhi Kabhi Bahu Thi* that narrated the lives of rich Gujaratis with all rituals and fanfare, didn't ever zoom in on it. Nor did Sanjay Leela Bhansali's *Hum Dil De Chuke Sanam* or Mani Ratnam's *Guru*, films that revolved around affluent but traditional Gujaratis. In *Guru*, Aishwarya Rai is seen in a red and white gharchoda, the traditional, Gujarati wedding sari, in the wedding scene with Abhishek Bachchan (they were still not married to each other) but there was no sign of Patan's Patola.

Fiercely protected by the Salvi family as a private legacy, the weave remains out of sight even in the richest retail markets of the Middle East and India, where multiple lakhs are routinely spent on couture. The Patan Patola is bespoke, limited edition luxury in the way only the finest, handmade artisanal products of the world are. Each piece—woven from silk yarn—takes four to six months to make, if four people weave it for six hours a day. The Salvi family collectively make about four to five saris a year, provided all of them assiduously work and weave through the year. Even if one person falls ill for a longer time and takes time off, the annual production suffers.

For an authentic, autographed (the inside corner has the weaver's name and the date of completion) Patan Patola, the usual waiting period is three years or more, longer than for a Hermès Birkin bag. All orders must be placed at the Salvi residence or on their website. Ninety percent orders are from affluent Gujarati and Maharastrian families in India and abroad. The rest are requests from museums or private collectors.

Each piece costs above Rs 3.5 lakhs, going up to Rs 8 lakhs given the design intricacy. Now, patterns are first sketched on paper and colour schemes planned on charts, but in the olden days in the absence of paper, master weavers would give weaving instructions verbally. Entire sari patterns and colours were imagined in the mind of the weaver and techniques passed down generations by demonstration.

'Originally, the Patola was woven in four styles by the Salvi community,' writes textile historian Rta Kapur Chishti in her book *Saris: Tradition and Beyond*. 'For Jains and Hindus, it was in flowers, parrots, dancing figures and elephants. For the Muslim community, wedding sarees were woven with geometric and floral designs. For Maharashtrian Brahmins, narikunj (feminine figure) sarees of plain, dark-colour body and borders, with birds were made.' The geometric square, the core of the Patola sari, symbolizes security, while elephants, parrots, peacocks and figurines stand for saubhagya (a woman whose husband is alive).

In the last thirty years, the Salvis have revived indigenous vegetable dyes by using turmeric, marigold flowers, onion skin, pomegranate bark, lac, and indigo. They dye the yarn in bright hues of traditional Gujarati attire like yellow, rani pink, parrot green, often contrasted with black. Vermillion red is auspicious and remains a bestseller down the centuries. The saris are lined with slim, gold zari borders. The only one sample in natural white cotton that the Salvis have is a trial piece made a hundred years ago. It depicts a scene from the Mahabharata and for anyone fascinated with the intricacy of weaving, it's a jaw dropping piece.

Unlike other expensive weaves like Benarasi, Jamdani, Dhakai or even the Andhra Upaada, which even now are brought to the homes of discerning urban customers by weavers or their middlemen, or sold in craft bazaars, an authentic Patan Patola is difficult to find and acquire. Even prominent sari stores do not stock it because of its prohibitive price. Kala Niketan sari shops in Mumbai and Ahmedabad—owned and run by a Gujarati group—do have some saris, as do Garvi–Gurjari, the Gujarat government emporium in Ahmedabad and the Central Cottage Industries Emporium, Delhi. But these are very few pieces and their authenticity (whether they have been made by this Salvi family from Patan or not) is doubtful.

Moneyed Gujarati families, which commission such a sari like a piece of precious jewellery, revere it as an heirloom. Stored in white muslin, it is worn as a prestige symbol during religious functions, festivals and weddings and passed on to the daughter or the daughter-in-law. Sometimes it is draped over the bride as a bidaai shawl (a blessing) over the wedding costume after kanyadaan. But modern brides don't consider hand-woven and handspun weaves as luxury. At least that's what 29-year-old Ravina Chhaya told me.

'Who cares, darling? Look at how busy the design is; a Patan Patola will only make me look shorter,' said the attractive Mumbai girl, daughter of an influential businessman. Bandra boho in her look, she wore a black Mango tee, shorts, silver gladiator sandals, a stack of thick wooden bangles (nine, I counted) and silver hoops. Unlike Gujarati girls who live in Gujarat, Ravina's nose wasn't pierced. When she made a call on her i-Phone with a funky orange cover, she identified herself as Ravs.

Ravs had been introduced to me by a former colleague and she had sportingly invited me to join her on her trousseau shopping trip with her mum and two aunts. A former student of St Xavier's, Mumbai, she had fallen in love with a classmate, the only son of a Maharastrian family. Marriages between Gujaratis and Maharashtrians are quite common and those who live in Mumbai don't consider such liaisons to be cleavages in tradition. Ravs and her aunts chatted away in a seamless mix of Gujarati and English. I speak fluent Gujarati and loved this language combo, which I had never really tried. The ladies could barely wait to lay hands on Anamika Khanna ensembles with antique gotapatti borders, Suneet Varma saris in net and crystals and, predictably, a Sabyasachi lehnga with gara embroidery. Back in their car, a sleek, black Audi, they showed me their shopping list, a very detailed one with little notes on the fabrics for blouse pieces, pipings, and linings written in a different coloured ink from the rest. It had been made with the help of a personal shopper who had been hired at Rs 4 lakh for wedding shopping and packing services.

The list included a multi-coloured monogrammed LV bag, two pairs of Ferragamo shoes ('I will have to fly to Delhi for them yaar, unless Dad allows me to dash to Milan'), two pairs of Jimmy Choos, a Cartier watch—one each for bride and groom, a Roberto Cavalli Spring/Summer prêt dress that Ravina would pack for her honeymoon, jadau jewellery from Rose (she had seen Cindy Crawford sport it in a fashion magazine), make up from M.A.C., Raakesh Agarvwal sequined palazzos, a Judith Leiber clutch for the reception, and many other small and big things. I was informed without any air of show-off (full marks to Ravs's mother for that) that her daughter's wedding would be solemnized in a five star resort in Bangkok in Thailand and more than 400 guests and relatives from India and other parts of the world would attend it.They had six functions for the wedding, each with a different theme and dress code. The wedding programme was more than elaborate. Sample this:

An 'initiate celebrations' lunch called the Polynesian Paradise had Elegant Casual as the dress code.

The same evening, there would be a welcome dinner for guests checking in later than afternoon. This was titled Nostalgic Glory for which the dress code would be Retro Magic.

For the mehndi ceremony, the Chhayas wanted their guests to dress 'Tropical'.

The Ring Ceremony had been called Water, Wind and Fire and the dress code was 'Fusion'.

The wedding ritual required the baraatis to be in traditional wear.

And finally, the reception, with the event titled as Moroccan Kiss spelt the dress code as Glitz, Glam and Galore.

I politely pointed out that 'Tropical' denoted climate not

clothing and you couldn't have 'Galore' as one-third of a theme with Glitz and Glam as its other two portions.

Ravi ignored my comment and told me that they had emailed the themes of the different ceremonies to all their guests well in advance so that people could shop and plan their costumes accordingly.

'What a colossal waste of money,' I remarked. She was a young, Mumbai girl and I assumed she wouldn't mind my comment.

But she did, 'Waste? What do you mean? I am the only child of my parents, when else will we get an opportunity to spend like this and show the society what we are worth? How odd of you to call it a waste! Even my grandmother doesn't say that, you are so old fashioned, Shef,' she retorted.

I shut up and listened as she told me how fashion magazines had been her bible for the last two months and how much time and effort had gone into preparing a shopping list for all that she would wear for the different ceremonies. Everything 'obviously,' she said, rolling her eyes, was 'designer—Armani to Anamika Khanna.'

The Patan Patola didn't make it on the list.

Back in Delhi, Rajeev Sethi of the Asian Heritage Foundation, an internationally noted cultural exponent, design guru, and curator of numerous global craft and textile exhibitions would tell me how bling obsessed rich Indians find it difficult to accept Indian handmade products as luxury. Textile researcher and writer Rta Kapur Chishti, echoed a similar sentiment. Both Sethi and Chishti, like William Bissell of Fabindia and LailaTyabji, chairperson of Dastkar, were also dismissive about the contribution of fashion designers to the cause of weavers. I had noticed how designers found it comforting to regret the weaves and crafts they dropped from the repertoire of their work because these didn't bring enough money initially. Traditions were boring in the first few decades of a liberalized India and even traditionalists had dumped them. Those who were occasionally drawn to traditional finery would just pull out their mom's piece to wear.

Now there is a wave of revival in Indian fashion and all stories are changing towards revivalism. Almost every designer—veteran or young—works with Indian crafts and textiles in some form or the other. This includes the highly modernist Manish Arora. Partly it is because the rest of the world is enamoured by what India makes. In response to the market's needs, designers have begun to give a renewed impetus to traditional fabrics and crafts with little or no support from the Government of India.

Ironically, this new wave has led to a curious outcome. 'Designer revival' has begun to attract customers, but the same work done by original revivalists languishes for want of similar attention. Chishti, who started Tanbaan in 2011, an indigenous label, for which she works with khadi spinners and weavers in different clusters in Andhra Pradesh, Maharashtra and Uttar Pradesh, has been trying very hard to retail handspun khadi saris. But she finds it difficult to market them to a republic, which depends either on bling or on brands to make a statement of wealth and style. It is important to wear wealth, whatever else we may wear as most people I interviewed for this book told me.

Last year, Chishti put out these saris for sale by participating in an exhibition of woven saris in Delhi. More were taken than she had anticipated but they certainly didn't sell like hot cakes. Her khadi saris are stunning, their minor weaving inconsistencies make them unique, and cost above Rs 10,000. They can eclipse a Tarun Tahiliani garment or a Sabyasachi sari with their simplicity but very few people want them. Chishti knows only too well that she is a losing champion in a battlefield where her competitors, ironically, are crystals.

Chishti, who wears the sari in different drapes but never in the usual front pleated way as is worn in urban India, would become intermittently exasperated as she showed me khadi and special Benarasi wedding weaves in her basement studio in Delhi's Jangpura colony. Khadi, once the symbol of Indian swadeshi, a weave that stood for more than organic handmade produce, has now to be 'explained and justified' to the rich and ignorant.

Hand craft is a production process and important as indigenous technology. At the same time, everyone who works with the craft or weaving sector knows that just packaging and selling it dramatically like Italians and Parisians do with their brands is unlikely to work as a magic wand. Uplifting handmade artisanal goods and weaves has to be backed by making their production faster, vigorous, and economically viable. At the moment, most weavers and crafts persons can't even manage to send their children to schools or afford an acceptable quality of health services for their families. For instance, Fabindia works through public–private partnerships to bring welfare to the doorstep of weavers. As part of this, a fixed percentage of whatever you will buy from Fabindia goes directly to the weaver or craftsperson or their cluster. Some other sturdy organizations do the same—Dastkar essentially focuses on upliftment of underprivileged weavers and craftspeople. With complexities of poverty roaring in the underbelly, it is impossible for organizations that support handloom and handicraft to rationalize the overhead costs if they convert display, sale, and visual merchandizing to international standards. Economic sustainability is the top priority in India to sustain crafts or weaves. Or as cultural activist Pupul Jayakar had said more than once: 'Craft is an economic activity before it is a cultural activity.'

Even as some Indian, hand crafted products compare in their ingenuity with the best luxury products in the world, they lose out in the hierarchy of irresistibility for a string of reasons, some bureaucratic, others because of the way the weavers have been marginalized in the bigger march of fashion. 'They (the government) lump us with potters and cobblers,' said Parmeshwar Acharya, a veteran shilpi (artisan) at an awards gathering in Delhi.

The tapestry of people interested in or dependent on Indian weaves and textiles—grassroot level weavers, urban fashion designers, fashion media, the Ministry of Textiles and private entrepreneurs who support handlooms is split at the seams. All of them have their own plans but they are divergent, though ostensibly everyone is trying to contemporize textiles. For the handloom division of the Ministry of Textiles, working in association with designers could not only mean a Maheshwari dupatta turned into a bubble skirt and a Chanderi sari into an evening gown , but will lead to an association of bolder fashion photographers, stylists, and internationally trained window dressers who could change the way textiles are displayed. It is crucial that designers, especially those who now make entire collections from textiles, are invited by the handloom commission to work with weavers to help make their products relevant to the needs of Indian consumers.

It reminded me of Ravs. 'Anything we wear must show what we are worth. When you wear an Indian weave, you don't look as if you are with-it in the world of fashion,' she said. Ravs would be embarrassed to wear even the gharchoda (the white and red checked Gujarati bridal sari) for her wedding pheras. Instead, she had dreamt of 'something either by Tarun Tahiliani or Anamika Khanna in gold or beige as red was too common and rani pink doesn't suit me'. For the reception, she would wear a Lanvin gown that she had bought on a special shopping trip abroad.

Even Aishwarya Rai wore a woven Kanjeevaram sari for her wedding, I said to Ravs, asking her if she had noticed Aishwarya's non-designer Benarasi sari she wore during her pregnancy when she visited a temple with her father and mother in law during Durga Puja this year.

Ravs had noticed—all the newspapers had splashed the picture in their colour supplements but she couldn't be bothered. For her, it would be designer all the way.

During the shopping trip, the group—Ravs, her mum, and aunts—said they would first go and check out prices of designer copies at a store in Juhu, before heading to the boutiques for the original stuff. 'Just so that we know the price difference,' said Mrs Chhaya. We took a break and ate lunch at Mahesh Lunch Home in Juhu in Mumbai. None of the ladies were vegetarians and over prawn curry rice and a side plate of fried pomfret, they discussed why diamond solitaires made more sense for elegance and status, than old-style ear studs with a cluster of five diamonds.

Nobody even mentioned the Patan Patola. When I asked Ravina's mother if she would wear hers (she had an original one made by the Salvis, which had been handed down two generations), she looked at her daughter and said, 'Ravina will kill me if I wear a Patola sari for her shaadi.'

Rahul Salvi endorsed this realization that the Patan Patola was less and less wanted by younger Gujarati girls. The orders the

Salvis got were still from the senior ladies of traditional families. It wasn't the most aspirational thing for women in his own family either. 'My cousin sisters didn't want it for their weddings,' he said, a bashful smile flitting across his face. 'Now after reading stories in the press about us, one of them wants a sari. But we don't have the time to make it for her,' he added.

Minal was different. Unlike her older cousins, she wanted a Patan Patola sari. She did not want designer products or Swarovski-laden costumes for her trousseau.

'It's my dream to get married in a homemade Patan Patola. But I have no idea if my brothers, father, and uncles will manage to weave one for me. It takes so long to make each sari; they can barely finish the orders. Will they make one for me?' She wondered aloud but quickly added, 'They might actually.'

Like most other girls of her town, Minal knew she wouldn't marry in Patan. 'I am not going to settle down here, that's why I didn't learn weaving. What's the point of learning something and then not being able to do it consistently?

'I will have a stable career if I teach computer science; as a weaver I would be wasted,' she added.

The irony of her wish to 'settle' outside Patan and to have a 'stable career' after marriage had, in another way, come home to visit her cousin Rahul. He is a full time weaver 'settled' in Patan and no upwardly mobile Gujarati family would wed a daughter to him. 'Educated girls find it below their dignity to marry a weaver who lives in a small town,' Rahul told me, realizing that in the arranged marriage market he was an ineligible bachelor ever since he quit an architect's job in a city.

By noon, it had become obvious that the Salvis were not the usual gregarious Gujarati family. No chuckling women, no 'nashtas' of gathiya phaphda. Cutting chai, yes, but tea breaks were presided by thoughtful silence instead of back slapping post-mortems of the morning newspaper, a pet indulgence of small town Gujarati men.

The woefully insular Salvis seemed to be thwarting their own goals by refusing to be a part of cultural and craft activities in the mainstream. Rahul quit his architectural job because he was haunted by a gnawing guilt after the other sons of the family flew the nest to work as professionals in cities. 'If none of us from the young generation weave full time, it won't be long before the Patan Patola will be extinct.' So he and his cousin Savan, who learnt weaving by coming home every evening after engineering classes in Palanpur now take turns at the loom.

His passion though is constantly thwarted by the disappointments that have come his way after he chose to be a full time weaver. 'Even the Calico Museum of Textiles in Ahmedabad run by the Sarabhai Foundation doesn't welcome people like me,' he said bitterly. 'One of the most intricate Patan Patolas woven by my ancestors hang there, but every time I have gone for a museum visit, they have asked me to return later, giving priority to important visitors and foreign tourists,' he said, adding why he isn't interested in going there anymore. The Calico Museum takes a certain fixed number of visitors every day, twice a day and this has to be booked in advance. Rahul felt he could be at least accorded the privilege of arriving there without an advanced booking and taken in, but even after finding out who he was, they ignored him. He is generally miffed with the bigger picture. 'I don't live up to India's modern expectations from weavers. We have some expectations too and they are clearly being ignored,' he said.

Most of us would expect Minal, Rahul, Savan—three well-educated young people with fire in their bellies and passion for Patan Patola—to find new, smart ways to market their weave as a luxury product to new markets across the world. Instead, they sit back, simmering with cynicism. In 2002, when the Shilpguru title was introduced by the government to commemorate 50 years of Indian handicrafts, Rahul's father Vinayak Salvi, was decorated with it along with a national award by President Abdul Kalam Azad. The government released a commemorative stamp of Rs 5 with the Patan Patola sari on it.

The spurt of interest in the weave got them a lot of media attention. Over the years, the Salvi home in Patan has turned into a tourist destination. I had visited them in the peak of summer but even during the sweltering afternoon, I saw many people walk in, to look around and listen to a sentence or few about the Patola. After observing it all, I understood why Minal was initially wary when she greeted me and looked openly disinterested in the task of bringing me hot rotis from the stove while her mother rolled and baked them.

'We spend about four months a year explaining the weave to visitors,' says a family member. Bharatbhai—--now in his late fifties—said that as long as he can remember, politicians, scholars, revivalists, curators, journalists, student groups, and filmmakers from all over the world have visited them. Each person's name and address has been documented in the dozens of visitors' books that the Salvis own. This deluge of people could have easily helped them network and explore new business strategies. Yet they chose to keep designers, trainees, even technological modifications in process or patterns at bay.

The Salvi story has paradoxes in its warp and weft. Barring

exceptions made for some visitors, the family does not display vintage pieces, which are instead kept under lock and key. They shield them from what they suspect are prying eyes of plagiarists in the guise of researchers. The Shikarbhat sari, for instance, could be used as a model to teach antique sari patterns to inquisitive textile students. Woven 150 years ago, it was exported to Indonesia. About ten years ago, the Garden Mills management from Ahmedabad reclaimed it and brought it back to the Salvis. The family then made a replica—on a rich, red-coloured field with a vibrant elephant across the vertical length of the sari surrounded by flowers, birds and animals, reflecting a scene from a royal procession (Raja ki Savari) of King Kumarpal in the eleventh century. Each motif is unique. The sari took three and a half years to weave and is a museum piece.

A private Patan Patola museum is a dream for the Salvis and soon it will become a reality. 'We haven't found the commitment and integrity in young generation weavers who come for training. This is not business for us, it is our dharma and karma, a tradition we wish to keep alive as art not commerce,' they say defensively. So instead of contemporarizing their work, they are busy archiving its past in a private museum for which they haven't sought any government grant or subsidy. It is being made entirely from the family's savings over the decades. All vintage sari pieces, looms, threads and silk yarn, vegetable dyes, motifs, designs, sketches from the time paper began to be used have been carefully stored for centuries will be displayed at this museum, which should be ready this year (2012).

In complete divergence, their feuding relative Kanubhai Salvi who moved to Vadodara more than forty years ago runs a Patola loom there and has made a business out of the legacy. Salaried weavers make the saris while women in his family sell to elite sari stores in the cities. A third generation enthusiast in Kanubhai's family—Hetal Salvi—now vows to bring the Patan Patola to the fashion ramp to make it attractive to a younger market. She may just pull it off. The sari that walked the ramp at Vibrant Fashion Week on Gujarati model Priyanka Shah (Rekha didn't go) was sent by Kanubhai's family.

Over the years, the Patan Salvis have also severed their creative partnerships and do not travel any more with government sponsored exhibitions or those organized by NIFT. They have withdrawn from trading with emporiums and weaver's centres. 'Patola saris in government handloom houses are not ours; we haven't done any business with them for years,' asserts Bharatbhai. They have little respect for India's political figures, the only exception being Sonia Gandhi. They believe she is a true textile connoisseur who supports and wears hand-woven textiles more beautifully than anyone else they know. They gifted Sonia Gandhi a Patan Patola with great warmth and respect.

Apart from her, the Indian 'government' is best not spoken about. Bharatbhai showed me a government letter informing him that he had been chosen as a national awardee for 2008. A day before he and his wife Kalpana were to leave for the ceremony to be held at Delhi's Vigyan Bhavan, another official missive told him that the award had been cancelled. No explanation or apology was ever offered. Bharatbhai has been unable to digest the insult.

The Salvis aren't the only ones disgruntled with the way the Indian government treats weaving traditions. In May last year, after I wrote a column in *The Indian Express* on the divide between handloom and fashion lobbies, I received an email from noted dancer and textile exponent Mallika Sarabhai. She told me about Tanabana, a set of two books and 20 videos she had produced for the Union Ministry of Textiles in 2007. The idea was to give these books to designers worldwide so that they and the government could work together. 'As far as I know, it languishes in the ministry. We also suggested that a single-window authority be created to ensure the smooth execution of orders placed, or products developed so that designers felt safe regarding deliveries and quality. This too wasn't put in place,' she wrote.

Tanabana: Handcrafted and Hand-woven Textiles of India commissioned to Sarabhai when Shankersinh Vaghela was the textiles minister is a memorably put together set. It documents—insightfully and beautifully—lesser-known textiles. With text by Romanie Jaitly, a textile expert from NID, photographs by Yadavan Chandran and Roopesh Maroli; the books, which have been edited by Sarabhai, were produced by Darpana (her Ahmadabad-based organization), before being printed in Singapore. The project took the team two and a half years of travel and research. It is a pity that it hasn't been marketed well or commercially sold.

When I contacted them, the officials at the Ministry of Textiles refused to divulge the production costs of the book (the volumes are not for sale), but insisted that the set has been gifted to political dignitaries and ambassadors who visited India. No one could answer why instead of 1,000 copies, as Sarabhai claimed, only 200 odd copies were printed. Out of those, if I could get one in April 2011, surely copies still exist.

In the process of locating Tanabana in the handloom division of the Ministry of Textiles, I ran into suspicious bureaucrats who see fashion journalists as bad news. What emerged was not only the disagreement between handloom weavers and the fashion industry, but a gnawing disconnect between government officials and top handloom experts.

Veteran designer Ritu Kumar, India's first designer herself, who has been on juries of master weaver awards for years told me that weaver awards given away by the government were indeed in a sad state of affairs. Kumar, who likens her early years in textile revivalism to that of a barefoot doctor who worked in the villages to sustain and revive fading crafts and weaves, believes that The National Awards Scheme needs revitalization. 'I remember being on a committee which once chose to give a National award to a Rajasthani weaver who had woven Indira Gandhi's image on to a towel,' she says adding that after six years of being on that board, she refused to sign the jury paper that year. She was never invited to the jury again.

While the Salvi's commitment to Patan Patola is not dwindling the business is. Though NID, Ahmedabad, has recently recommended that the Patan Patola be included in UNESCO's global list of intangible cultural heritage, the pessimism of the Salvis has put Patan Patola in the red.

'Textile traditions that survive today are those that are intelligent,' says Prof Aditi Ranjan of NID, one of India's most respected textile scholars and the co-author of *Handmade in India*. She explains why a dupatta or a scarf version of a sari textile is an important divergence, which doesn't denude tradition but actually sustains it. 'As is the use of textiles in homes as curtains, cushion covers or other décor items which could also become heirlooms,' she adds. The Salvis have reluctantly started making Patola table cloths and scarves but they can't connect with new markets that demand couture or ready to wear fashion in sexy, fluid and easy-to-drape fabrics.

In sharp contrast, some other weaver groups are willingly going through the trials of revival in the hands of designers. Like Wendell Rodricks nine-year project to save the Goan tribal Kunbi sari. Reviving the Goan sari is hardly as simple as beguiling the international tourist visiting Goa with a milder recipe for fish vindaloo. The sari banned by the Portuguese for 200 years had become an outcast in this state. But under Rodricks, the rural weave has been modernized with softer fabrics, pastel colours, and new designs while keeping its rustic character intact. In 2010, he sent the Kunbi sari down the runway in its basic form as a plain six-yard drape as well as loose flowing trousers, easy dresses, chic kurtas with long slits. The audience stood up to applaud him.

Designers have told me that the intimidating price of the Patan Patola and the closed attitude of the Salvis prevent new work on the weave. So while the Patan Patola remains marginalized, the single Ikat, also its closest cousin, has had a fashion makeover both in India and abroad. Bangalore-based Deepika Govind, who has worked with Orissa Ikat of Sambalpur and single weave Patola clusters in Gujarat, transported the weave on Silk Modal—a blend of Indian silk with modal, an ecofriendly, cellulose fibre made from tree bark. She also associated with the Silk Board of India to use Ikat on silk knit. Both innovations were made into fusion garments and Western separates.

Surprisingly, some global designers have found ways to use and display Indian textiles without corrupting them with surface embellishments. In a winsome moment for Indian weaves, the Andhra Ikat, also known as the Telia Rumaal, went on the Parisian ramp in 2010 sent by Belgian designer Dries Van Noten. His Spring Summer 2011 collection, which had printed Ikat pants, sari dresses, jackets, clutches, varyingly hand-woven in Bali, Sumatra and India, included a woven Andhra Pochampalli in yellow and maroon silk with geometric designs. The designer billed it as the Madras Motif. Casually wrapped around the model's waist like a half sari, with trailing fabric on one side, Van Noten styled it with a dull grey top, showing how an ethnic weave could be made trendy and non-fussy.

Rahul will have none of it. He doesn't want to be a Van Noten, thank you. 'I have no intention to live up to modern India's expectations from its weavers. A Patola may be good for fashion but fashion isn't good for it,' he believes. Film star Priyanka Chopra's stylist requested the family for a Patan Patola sari for the actor to wear for an event but they refused.

An haute future for the Patan Patola looks dismal. Disparate straps of the Salvi family's cynicism for the glamour world forms a fence of barbed wire around them. Even when I was saying my good byes to the Salvis, Rahul insisted that he will not be brainwashed into believing that the English speaking designers who can show in Paris are the solution. 'Fashion is not the only way,' he argued. Minal nodded in agreement.

'The Patola will come apart, but never lose its pattern' goes a Gujarati song.

It almost seems like a tag line for the Salvi family. A dirge for the Patan Patola.

Peanuts as Salary, Free Trips to Paris

'If I want to knock a story off the front page, I just change my hairstyle.'

—Hilary Rodham Clinton

'I quit,' she said suddenly as she ate her tomato and basil pasta. At first, I didn't believe Latha. Every move she had made in her career in the last few years had been with a single minded goal: to become a powerful fashion journalist. Now she wanted to give it all up. I must have looked blank and Latha—always wont to giggle—began to laugh.

Fashion's decadent shimmy had fascinated her since childhood. As a teenager, Latha would cut trend pages from second-hand glossies, gaze at photos of designers like Ritu Beri, Ritu Kumar, and Rohit Bal and dream of working in a fashion magazine.

An Andhra Christian, she had been born in Kakinada, a small town near Vizag. Her fondest memories of growing up were wearing the 'weirdest clothes to school', changing satchels and school friends every two years with her father's transfer through Andhra. Her fashion icon was her grandmother, who headed the 3rd Andhra girls' battalion, NCC, and wore a large, traditional gold nose pin as her only accessory. 'She had no frills or flounces but she looked awesome. Both for her and my mother fashion was about being pleasant and modest,' said Latha.

A bright, ambitious girl, she had begun with a few small jobs in lifestyle media before joining *Marie Claire*, which I then edited. In a matter of years, she rose from being a desk writer to entertainment editor and would soon leave *Marie Claire* to join *Vogue.in* as its editor. At 28, she had done better for herself than many others in the fashion media.

Parmesh Shahani became editorial director of *Verve* in 2008. Hysterical divas, warring designers, fashion week politics, craftsmen, rough, hewn khadi contrasted with smooth, creamy silk, this was the just the trope the thirty-something Mumbai Sindhi boy was looking for. 'Indian fashion is a microcosm of modern India. Old guard vs new guard, modesty, morality, fabric innovation, the coming together of small town and big city behaviour, politics, power games, disparities between weavers and wearers—this churning reflects everything else happening everywhere else,' the MIT media studies graduate said, explaining why he was drawn to fashion.

On paper, Parmesh is an unlikely candidate to run a fashion magazine. He is the founder of freshlimesoda.com, India's first online youth site, and has written a much talked about study on homosexuality called 'Gay Bombay: Globalisation, Love and (Be) Longing in Contemporary India'. His first job was in finance; he joined the Mahindra Group in Mumbai as a venture capitalist. The company loved his ideas and Anuradha Mahindra, editor-in-chief of *Verve* offered him the post of editorial director in her magazine. Only fashion could have seamlessly brought together all the strands of his life and Parmesh took up the offer immediately.

For him, the fashion industry and its media were 'awesome'. It was like Bollywood, he told me, it welcomed everyone—gay, female, short, androgynous, regardless of race, creed, and religion. 'I know more gays who are nuclear scientists, lawyers, authors, and chartered accountants than there are in this industry but other professions do not absorb the gay identity as one of its own, unlike fashion,' he said.

Parmesh thrived on fashion's flexible world view, while Latha had begun to feel that this broad-mindedness of the industry was a charade. Fashion had seemed 'awesome' until she became a part of it.

25-year-old Garima Sharma felt at home though. A fashion hack with *Delhi Times*, the city supplement of *The Times of India*, she said she was absolutely delighted with her job. We had chatted in the cheerful and busy canteen at the TOI office on Bahadurshah Zafar Marg, where Garima told me that she grew up in Shalimar Bagh, a middle class Punjabi neighbourhood in Delhi. The world of her childhood was like Dibakar Banerjee's *Khosla Ka Ghosla*. I tried to imagine a young Garima growing up amid Punjabi bling, dholak beats, sofas wearing garish printed covers, boisterous mummies and aunts preparing festival food, loud exchanges across the wall with neighbours, and everyone assuming the privilege of interfering in everyone else's life. 'There was no fashion icon to look up to, but I loved fashion,' she said. A student of Ramjas College in Delhi University, Garima wanted to be fashionably dressed but couldn't, as she didn't have the resources then. Yet, like Latha, she was certain she would end up doing something in the fashion industry.

When I had first seen Garima at a fashion week a couple of years ago, I noticed she looked different from fashion magazine journalists who came to fashion weeks wearing branded sunglasses (often pulled up as hair bands), designer clothes, the 'it' bags of the season, hair styled at salons, and busy punching their phones even when the shows were on. Garima wore spectacles. This was before Tom Ford glasses became trendy and being bespectacled was considered cool. She came across as a sweet-faced, smiling and well-mannered girl, pen in hand, notebook open, dressed in regular jeans and tops, conscientiously taking notes. 'The first time I sat in the front row, I felt I was part of a movie scene. I have never felt such dramatic emotions in my life. When the lights suddenly came on at the start of the show, I was captivated,' she said.

Many girls from middle class backgrounds feel inadequate when thrown into the world of leggy models, rich fashionistas, socialites and celebrities who breeze in and out wearing designer labels on their sleeve. This is true Vanity Fair after all where everyone tries a little too hard to look like they were born with fashion spoons in their mouths. Since no one can really keep up with the frenetic pace of fashion, its fickle, chameleon nature, the inadequacy you feel upon not wearing the latest shoes or the most glamorous garment prods you to convert quickly to its cause. It's all about looks and unless you look the part, you are not made to feel at home. Instead of observing and enjoying the spectacle, many young fashion correspondents, both male and female, who come from ordinary families where shopping budgets are limited, say that they get a stab of self-doubt the moment they walk into a fashion event. They worry sick about their wardrobes instead of what they would write and report. It can be an unnerving experience if you are not confident without labels and get easily overwhelmed by glamour.

Latha initially did give in to this undefined pressure. She kept up by dressing trendily, updating her wardrobe with her jobs, cannily mixing street with a few choice labels. She might wear a Victoria Beckham kind of short and tight dress picked up from a nondescript shop in Hill Road in Bandra and pair it with Gucci shoes. When she lived in Delhi, she shopped smartly at Sarojini Nagar. The magazines she had been reading since adolescence had taught her the tricks of mix and match and you couldn't really make out if she was wearing Mango, Zara, or Sarojini Nagar. Her bags would be as big or small and as hip as the season's trend dictated, but you couldn't pin down their pedigree. Her accessories never looked cheap; well they didn't look luxurious either. But she managed to look like one of the 'fashion girls' soon enough and I had observed this change in her in the last few years, admiring the way she worked on her look. Latha is a short girl, about 5'2", has brown complexion, raven black hair, skin that needs much care because it gets easily blemished and she would tell me she had to watch what she ate otherwise the kilos piled upon her without warning. Her warmth and frequent laughter gave her an endearing presence.

But despite her skills and her evolving style, she wasn't considered 'snobbish' enough for an entertainment or fashion editor by her peers.

In most of the offices she had worked, colleagues wore luxury labels to work, changing their wardrobes with each season, including pre-fall. 'Does pre-fall even mean anything in India?' Latha asked me rhetorically rolling her eyes. 'So what are you wearing?' was a question she had learnt to dread. Even trainees in fashion magazines were hired on the basis of what they wore, she said. She would have loved to wear fashion brands all the time but with her salary, she couldn't afford to buy them every month. 'I was judged for my clothes. And I fell into the trap, prioritizing Giuseppe Zanotti shoes over a washing machine that my husband and I needed so badly,' she said.

Parmesh turned out to be a natural fashionista even though he hadn't grown up in a fashion filled world. His style reflects his free-spiritedness. He accessorizes like a magpie wearing cashmere shawls from Delhi, Jodhpur bazaar silver, electric coloured socks, leather florets tweaked into brooches and military medals. I remember him coming to Lakme Fashion Week in Mumbai in khaki shorts, a tucked-in saffron linen lapelled shirt with army war medal brooches pinned on the collars and pockets, gold epaulets on his shoulders, and a large belt on the waist and a beret. He was unforgettable, simply the most stylish man on the floor. Any given day, his look is irreverent. He can wear Jil Sander and Gucci with Indian labels like CellDsgn 11.11, Abraham and Thakore, and Fabindia. Many of his clothes are custom stitched by Chhotobhai, his favourite local tailor in Mumbai.

I joined the world of Latha, Parmesh, and Garima—different parts of the Indian fashion media—almost by accident in 2005, when I became editor of *Marie Claire*. Before that, I had worked with *India Today* for five years. My reporting beat, as Aroon Purie, the editor-in-chief of the group would teasingly say, stretched from 'sex to tortured women'. In short I wrote on lifestyle, health, sexuality, and gender.

By 2005, I was looking for a change. I sought an appointment with Vinod Mehta, the editor-in-chief of the *Outlook* Group. Except when he is on TV, Mehta can be cryptic. He says 'okay' to everything, whether he agrees or disagrees, and especially when he wants to dismiss a person. I loved his gossipy candour the instant I met him and though he said okay to me within five minutes of our first meeting; I wanted to work for him. 'I will call you when we have something. Okay,' he said and turned his back before I could walk out of his office. It was the oldest line in the book, but I felt he would call me.

He did, four months later, and offered me the job of the editor of *Marie Claire*. Instead of jumping for joy, I got mildly suspicious. Editor of a fashion magazine? Me? Did he really mean it? 'Are you sure? I don't even party,' I blurted. He said he knew.

I joined the *Outlook* Group in July that year and on paper my designation was Editor, New Project as the company didn't want to announce *Marie Claire* till the deal was finalized with their international partners. I was fine with it. I went ahead and hired a secretary and the two of us set to work from a small office in Delhi's Safdarjung Enclave area, a stone's throw from the *Outlook* headquarters. The walls alongside the staircase in our office building had paan stains and dirty black shoe imprints of people who probably went up and down kicking walls, but in my heart, there was a promise of new things to come.

My working life would soon change into a perfumed garden but only after some thorny realizations. The *Marie Claire* international team rejected my first editorial proposal on the Indian edition. Group *Marie Claire*, a conglomerate of fashion, accessory and décor magazines as well as books, has its international editorial, marketing, and finance headquarters in Paris. A central editorial team that comprises senior journalists with years of international media experience, fashion and creative directors, stylists and copy editors conversant with multiple cultures and languages, mentors editorial teams of its forty odd editions. They are a talented and hardworking group, unrelenting over professional processes. They train editors-in-chief as well as fashion, beauty, styling and design teams for weeks or months before a new edition of *Marie Claire* is launched in any country. Nothing is left to chance, certainly not to presumptions about an editor's capability to handle it all.

The editorial director who leads this team sent an official note disapproving my proposal. But the detailed feedback they offered on each of my ideas with every sentence analyzed from the perspective of the *Marie Claire* brand buffered my disappointment. I hadn't seen anything so meticulously explained before. They felt my conceptual note had too little fashion and beauty, that it was too features-oriented and needed more glamour to attract advertisers. A number of lights went on in my head. Here was good mentoring, I felt.

Things were not as clear around me in the *Outlook* office though. I found myself at the receiving end of snide comments from former colleagues. 'Fashion? Why are you wasting your time?' I was asked. 'So when are you launching your women's magazine.' 'One more *Cosmopolitan*, eh?' and worse, 'Listen, the *Outlook* Group hasn't even signed any deal with a media house abroad, they are just using you to see if something works out. It might take a couple of years before anything comes through.'

Before accepting Vinod Mehta's offer, I had actually asked him if he would transfer me to *Outlook*, the news magazine if the 'women's fashion magazine' business bombed. He had said yes, so I wasn't entirely worried about being jobless. But, the many intrusive remarks that came from 'serious journalists' clearly indicated that fashion journalists were seen as flighty and frivolous by the rest of the media and this irked me. I wanted to be taken seriously.

An ignored beast in the early-Nineties, the fashion media used hype as a broomstick to fly into the reader's eyes. I was part of the launch team of *Cosmopolitan* in 1996 and sensed that fashion assumed power. But when I looked around and read, it seemed that fashion writers barely knew the difference between ombre and Studio 54. Also, where was fashion? Were the few stores of Hauz Khas village and South Extension in Delhi and Tarun Tahiliani's Ensemble in the Great Western Building of Fort, Mumbai, supposed to speak for the entire industry? Some celebrities wore fashion but it meant densely embroidered ensembles by Abu Jani–Sandeep Khosla, Tahiliani's drapes worn by a few rich trophy wives and Ritu Kumar's garments created for contestants of Femina Miss India.

Outlook journalist Sunil Mehra's April 1998 story 'The Great Indian Fashion Hoax' strengthened my assumptions. People called Sunil's story an exposé of sorts. He used phrases like 'media's transparent fashion illiteracy' and quoted designers in his story from Tarun Tahiliani to Rina Dhaka, who appeared to despise each other. Sunil wrote about plagiarism and the way PR companies dressed the non-existing resumes of their clients. The fashion media was beginning to earn notoriety even before earning notice. After the first India Fashion Week in 2000, designers began to figure that cultivating fashion journalists made sense. *Elle* had launched a couple of years after *Cosmopolitan* came to India in 1996 and with it young fashion had officially arrived. Newspapers sniffed serious competition. From cheekily written Sunday fare, hyped fashion news became an everyday newspaper beat; the best new way to catch attention, both of the glamour starved reader and the advertiser.

Over the next few years, regional papers launched Fashion Fever sections and hype became synonymous with fashion journalism. Everything was gush. How right designer Suneet Varma was when he told Sunil Mehra: 'We don't need to advertise. The media does it for us.' Fashion and parties were presented as one and the same. The only way to sustain these frothy pages was unverified socialite gossip and Bollywood news. At fashion weeks, initially once-a-year affairs titled Lakme India Fashion Week, the front row was being groomed. The 'slim, well-dressed girl who could report on parties'—the first caricature of the fashion journalist—began to be minted.

Today, seven sturdy fashion titles sell in the Indian market, they all rake in hefty advertising revenue but for the rest of the media, fashion journalists still carry the image of flighty people who change clothes all the time and flit back and forth from Paris and Milan. Or, lifestyle correspondents, who could help 'soften' the front page. When Pakistani Minister Hina Rabbani Khan arrived in India in July last year, wearing south sea pearls and a Hermès Birkin bag, the fashion hack had her day. During Lady Gaga's first trip to India in November last year for her performance at Formula One, fashion journalists inside newspaper offices acquired temporary swagger. They had the inside information about who did Gaga's tri-coloured hair, what time she would visit Dilli Haat, how she chose Tarun Tahiliani's garment to wear for her performance.

Despite these quick to disappear halos, do fashion writers influence readers in this country of billions where the majority does not see clothes as a priority? Where a minority doesn't even have clothes to wear? This was a tricky question for me then and remains a tricky one even today.

Everyone from A.R. Rahman, Shah Rukh Khan, senior journalist Karan Thapar to MP Jyotiraditya Scindia attended the *GQ* Men of The Year Awards 2011. Such events give the impression that the fashion media is an important lobby and must be indulged. So while it seems that fashion magazines now wield some clout through their award functions, seldom are the views of fashion magazine editors or writers sought on prime time TV debates or in stories of national importance other than fashion.

I remember when Arnab Goswami of *Times Now* refused *Marie Claire* an interview. Latha was the one chasing him and after a few months, many emails and a couple of phone calls later, he regretted it, adding that his brand team didn't think it would be most appropriate for him to be featured in a fashion magazine. He wasn't the only one. We sent many requests to Priyanka Gandhi

Vadra for a cover interview. But we never heard back from her office. Somehow, politicians and government officials clearly don't like to be associated with fashion magazines even though the premier fashion body of the country, NIFT, is a government-run institution. I got nowhere when I tried to get an interview with Renuka Chaudhary. Formerly, the Minister of Health and Family Welfare who then served on a central government committee for Empowerment of Women, she made an important interviewee for a women's magazine but she was obviously not keen. I requested Vinod Mehta to recommend us to her, but in vain. Same was the case with Kamal Nath, the Union Minister of Commerce and Industry in 2009. The CEO of *Marie Claire* and I went to invite him to attend the *Marie Claire* fashion awards function as the chief guest. Fashion fell under his ministry and we thought it would be a significant collaboration. He received us very cordially in his office but we would never hear from him again.

Media houses that publish fashion magazines together with other political and business titles themselves discriminate between journalists of one kind from another. Fashion scribes are often labelled as 'babes' and 'chicks'. Good to bring in ad revenue and for appearances at parties and brand events but otherwise to be taken with a pinch of salt or malt, depending on what the occasion demands. No fashion journalist's views on anything else, be it euthanasia or Narendra Modi are taken seriously.

We have only ourselves to blame.

Seldom do analytical or sceptical stories about fashion make it to the press. Designers have got used to a review-less culture. Editorial policies in most fashion magazines are toothless. There is no enquiry into the daily wages that designers pay their karigars, labour union problems, number of people employed in factories where beautiful clothes are made, the working conditions there or enquiries into child labour. Most designer factories are situated in dumps in the metros, but all we see are photoshoots in five stars hotels or inside glowing studios. Bad news is conspiratorially buried and what gets represented is a boisterous bunch of people always partying.

Though designers seem to love toothless journalists, they are harsh about the media after a couple of drinks or during 'between you and me' conversations. They question voting processes of Best Dressed lists in magazines; others say that the Bollywood obsession of the industry has led to exhaustion. Some angrily ask why junior reporters are given the freedom to 'critique' without any training in fashion. Few of them had anything nice to say about fashion journalists.

At *Marie Claire,* even before the Paris feedback on my proposal, I knew I would be done with this job in about three years or so. '3MoreYears' was my first password when I was given the Outlook email account. Every time I changed my password, I would subtract the months that had gone by from my self-assigned three years.

A few months after I had joined *Outlook*, I was sent to meet the international editorial team at Groupe *Marie Claire* in Paris. After the debacle of my proposal, I wanted to prove that the *Outlook* Group hadn't made a mistake in hiring me. Driving past the Eiffel Tower to my hotel in Paris that early October morning, I felt an adrenaline surge in my veins. An almost irrational self-confidence coursed through me and I had a strong feeling that I would get to see the Eiffel Tower many times.

My hunch proved correct. I had done my homework for the presentation, relying primarily on my communication skills and understanding of the urban Indian culture and women's issues to make an impression. The editorial team as well as the director of international editions liked me and I could see their resistance to me thawing from the first day on. I was accepted as editor and taken for the first of many enjoyable working lunches to a stylish Parisian restaurant, where I learnt to break my baguette on a white tablecloth and not be worried about scattering the crumbs.

That evening, we raised a toast to *Marie Claire* India, and the deal between *Outlook* Group and Groupe *Marie Claire* to launch the Indian edition. Back home, *Outlook* published an announcement in its Glitterati pages and I officially became a part of the fashion media.

Marie Claire was launched in June 2006 with a tagline I had suggested: Let Me Be Me. The line became an instant marketing success. It was symbolic of the magazine content. Fashion was a powerful cultural matrix to explore modern India, women, disparities and urban lifestyles, an incredible instrument and I wanted to use it to make nuanced statements.

In the mid-Nineties, The Body Shop owned by Anita Roddick, hailed as a social reformer, feminist superstar and angel of green beauty, hired a powerful legal team in Britain to weed out all critical media stories about her company. Fearing a legal onslaught from her lawyer, *Vanity Fair* magazine killed journalist Jon Entine's brilliant investigative piece on The Body Shop's unethical practices carried on under the cover of idealism. Titled 'The Stranger Than Truth Story of The Body Shop', it was eventually published in *Killed: Great Journalism Too Hot to Print* by David Wallis. Entine's story was so accurate and well-argued that it led Roddick to deride her own creation as a 'dysfunctional coffin'. The point it also made was that lifestyle journalism wasn't just gloss; it could reveal the ugly face of fashion and beauty brands.

These were the kind of stories I was keen on publishing in *Marie Claire*. In one of the first reportage campaigns that we undertook in 2006, we focused on the needs of Bangalore-based acid attack victim Haseena Husain, who had been burnt by a spurned admirer and gone through 26 surgeries, to live with the scars. Hers was an extraordinary story of survival and emotional resilience.

We first ran a single story. It was noticed by *Marie Claire*'s international editorial director who suggested we turn it into a campaign. She was speaking after my own heart; I picked it up instantly and the magazine raised not just a strong reader empathy and interest in Haseena's life but also Rs 5 lakh as funds for her future medical treatment. We followed Haseena for three years through her attempts at corneal transplant to restore her lost eyesight, her psychotherapy, and later her training to live life as a visually challenged person. Fortunately for Haseena, her life changed for the better after *Marie Claire* met her. She even found a government job. But I am not sure what it did for the magazine as it became associated with strong feature journalism and 'causes' instead of fashionable froth.

'I Could Have Been Dead' was the headline I came up with for a piece written by a surgeon against female foeticide, the design of which showed a row of little girls holding hands. It was turned into a poster that was later put up in Max and Apollo hospitals all over by our marketing team. But was this what a fashion magazine should be doing? I suspected if the editorial director who had suggested Haseena Husain as a campaign regretted her own brilliant idea later. I would never find out.

Needless to say, the industry saw me as a fashion greenhorn. Worse, I had no contacts. I was aware of the designers but they were not on my speed dial and no one invited me to their bashes, which is seen as a mark of importance. When I attended my first fashion week as *Marie Claire* Editor in 2006 at the Grand Hyatt in Delhi, I felt uncomfortable with all the glamour around me. I had worn a deep green crepe sari from Nalli and an artisanal paper necklace but among the models chatting with designer Manish Arora in the coffee shop of the hotel (one of my first sightings) and the beautiful people everywhere, I looked like a behenji.

Who wears what and 'oh isn't it awesome': these two clichés define fashion as a genre. Sometimes they are taken very literally. Take this interaction a *Zoom* TV anchor had with film star Hema Malini on the red carpet of an awards function in 2010.

'What are you wearing, Hemaji?' the reporter asked her.

'A sari. Can't you see?' responded Hema Malini rather stumped.

'Whose sari is it?' said the reporter.

'Mine, of course. Why will I wear anyone else's?' said Hema Malini, a bit put off this time. The TV anchor had clearly not recognized Hema Malini's Kanjeevaram and driven by the script of the show, wanted the name of her designer.

The actress on her part wasn't even thinking labels.

I continued to wear my saris (often Kanjeevarams too) to the front row and a sense of individualism (as well as middle class mentality I suppose) prevented me from investing in luxury bags and shoes just to fall in line with my peers. Some people, I was told, laughed behind my back at my obviously non-trendy wardrobe. Yet, when I began to know people more intimately in the industry, quite a few would complement me on my saris. International brand heads appreciated the fact that my first photo in the editor's letter was in a sari; Indian designers didn't find it very impressive. My sari was an ordinary Bandhini in chiffon bought from Gujarat my homestate. It was photoshopped from red to pink by our art director who felt pink suited me better.

But this is not all. There are other subtexts in fashion media besides 'those who wear labels and those who don't'—something that had begun to bother Latha a lot. English journalists are treated differently compared to those who write in Hindi. Also, stylists and editors in magazines are given much more attention than those that work in newspapers. On any given day, Latha would be treated better than Garima.

Parmesh and I as editors were treated even better. Among fashion magazines, the *Vogue* team is considered royalty. Others visibly resent that. Much of fashion gossip in the days after *Vogue* launched in India was about the high and mighty behaviour of its team. The arrogance of the English media and the clash of those trained in fashion with those who report just because they are thrown into a newspaper's fashion beat is a catchy side story.

There are no references in Indian popular culture to terms such as 'trends'. This is mostly a Western idea. Interpreting Studio 64, Seventies glamour, or Twiggy for the Hindi belt readership leads to a circus of funny words. A regional reporter from Meerut, sent to cover the Delhi fashion week for the Sunday edition of her newspaper remarked, 'Jab salme sitare hi lagaane hain toh itne bade bade shabd kyun use karte hain?' (When all they make is bling fashion, why do they hide behind intellectual words?) She had been excited about coming to fashion week and had spent the last few days planning her clothes and accessories. Her mother had given her Rs 5,000 as pocket money to shop. She had visited the parlour for a beauty package and the beautician had promised her that the treatment would remove her tan and make her look fairer. But when she arrived in Delhi, she didn't like the 'atmosphere' and said she found fashion magazine editors 'odd'. There were other differences. She was staying at the YWPC while girls from fashion magazines had been put up in five star hotels.

Editors and stylists of fashion glossies have little patience for 'untrained' newspaper hacks. Some hold them responsible for hackneyed, misinformed stories that have forever blurred the lines between the fashion and party journalism. 'Newspapers make our lives difficult. It is because of them that in the big picture, fashion journalism appears vacuous,' says Sujata Assomull Sippy, former editor of *Harper's Bazaar* in India.

I feel this is true to some extent but before the glossies arrived to tell us the difference between spring-summer and autumn-winter in fashion, designers made headlines only because of their parties, drugs and flamboyant lifestyles, and rarely for their work. Tarun Tahiliani, Malini Ramani, and Rohit Bal were splashed across colour supplements as party revellers who made fashionable garments, not as designers who also partied.

Garima wasn't pleased when I mentioned that magazine editors saw hacks like her messing up fashion content. 'Fashion magazines only cater to the rich. But newspapers reach the masses and designers are happy to be a part of newspaper articles,' she said, adding that being better dressed did not make magazine journalists better informed.

Nevertheless, Garima's own sense of dress was changing. She no longer wore jeans with a hoodie top to the front row and seemed very comfortable in the fashion crowd.

Latha on her part had become increasingly uncomfortable with the fashion world. The discriminations inside the industry had begun to unnerve her. Magazines were not looking for talent or competitiveness, she felt. They liked girls who knew their wines and steaks and brought branded bags for interviews. I knew what she meant.

While interviewing for *Marie Claire* in Mumbai, I encountered a girl who presumed her bag would be enough to get her the job. I remember she carried a tiny canary yellow laptop to show me her resume, saying printouts were no longer 'in'. When she walked in, she first put her Dior bag on the table. I couldn't have missed it; it was obscuring my view of her and I had to politely tell her to shift it to the side. After an 'awesome chat' as she called it, she asked me what I did at *Marie Claire*! I was taken aback and thought it would be embarrassing to tell her that I was the editor, so I left her question unanswered.

Parmesh would tell me similar stories. Though I would meet him regularly at fashion weeks, we only really got talking when both of us were invited in 2007 on the jury of Young Fashion Entrepreneur of the Year Award given away by the British Council. He, too, was the editorial director of a fashion magazine but didn't have French, Italian or American bosses, unlike the Indian editors of *Elle, Vogue, Marie Claire, Harper's Bazaar*, or *Grazia*. Working closely with the international editorial director is an officially signed and sealed part of the agreement between the local publishing house and a global title. Parmesh however was free to take risks, and interpret or change the editorial mix without having to worry about upsetting an internationally baked brand. He once produced a black and white issue of *Verve* (no colour on any page) without a single cover line and invited artists, Indian English writers, performers, models and designers to write or pose for it. The edition wasn't even limited to fashion and lifestyle; he brought many other relevant aspects of modern life into it. I could see that he was a person of bold new ideas, while I was confined by the expectations of the brand I worked for.

I was obliged to follow the international template of *Marie Claire* as is the case for all other international magazines in India. In the first six months, every page, including those with products, had to be sent for editorial approval to Paris. Covers had to be discussed threadbare with them—which celeb to feature, what they would wear, and so on. But it was a learning experience too as clearly the brand had to be carefully safeguarded. The Paris team knew how to get their way without stepping on my toes. They would not make irrational or whimsical intrusions. Their inputs amounted to better results and I didn't mind them as ghost editors. If there was a clash, I would get to do what I felt strongly about and they would, after graceful arguments, recede. I was told that in time, their interventions on every page would fade but not their expectations.

Once, during a dinner hosted by an international brand in Delhi, the editor of a fashion magazine jokingly said that she had so many bosses that she forgot which one to please first. 'Every single page with every blush-on and moisturizer has to be sent to 'them'; they are finicky and untrusting. Why don't they understand that if they have hired us, they should accept that we know our jobs,' she said adding that after all that 'nonsense' with Italy, she had to get budget and strategy approvals from her publisher in the India office. I felt a sense of vicarious relief. My Parisian counterparts were rather nice and no one breathed down my neck from *Outlook*.

Yet the noose was tightening in other ways. Once when we were discussing a cover look, celebrity make up artist Mickey Contractor of M.A.C cosmetics said to me, 'You and your stylists have no idea what you are doing. Your teams bring beauty references pulled out from international editions, double guessing what your Paris, Milan, or US would say afterwards.' Mickey was sick of trial and error. 'Now when I work with an international magazine, I ask the creative director if he has got editorial approval on the "look" from his bosses abroad. Otherwise, I tell them not to waste my time. You may not know your job, but I do. I won't pander to your double guessing tactics,' he added.

Mumbai photographer Farrokh Chothia, too, was blunt and abrupt but had a point. 'I never look at references. I know what I am doing, if you want to work with me, great, otherwise no problem. But don't tell me what to do,' he said. Whose idea, whose vision, whose creative direction was it after all? Was it the editor's? Not really.

Latha was a foot soldier in this game of chess. As editor, I could argue, agree, or disagree with make up artists and photographers, and even with 'Paris' but, in her first few years, Latha was too small in the hierarchy to voice the dissent she felt. She was expected to 'love' implementing the vision of four different types of people. Slowly and steadily, I began to feel strongly about the impressions we handed down to our teams and protected my staff from editorial confusions. There was, after all, a cultural clash in this saga of producing an international magazine. I took clear decisions and if there was a serious debate between me and Paris I would tell my team which side I was on and why.

The reality is completely different for newspaper reporters. Correspondents like Garima rise because they dish out little fashion scoops—who plagiarized whose designs, a fashion malfunction on the ramp, why a star staged a walk out of a fashion event. Newspapers largely report fashion as a wasteful bubble.

Ask designer Rajesh Pratap Singh. He recalled the coke scandal of the Nineties and Rohit Bal's heart attack in 2010 that were turned into front page headlines in newspapers—one unverified, other very personal but both symbolic of the way newspapers treat fashion. Much later at *The Indian Express*, I would be told that the correspondent who missed the news of Rohit Bal's heart attack for the front page had been sharply pulled up for being shoddy with information.

For this book, I interviewed more than 300 people from the fashion fraternity—people from small towns, students and faculty from fashion institutes, retailers of non-fashion brands, social commentators, and psychologists. Not one person could remember any headline or fashion story except that Rohit Bal had suffered a heart attack.

The fashion–PR-media lobby in India is a complex battlefield. We were all co-dependent, yet at loggerheads with each other. Designers were disgusted by journalists yet most continued to oblige them. Journalists would say that most designers were just glorified darzis, yet schemed to sit in front rows at their shows and expect freebies from them. PR executives of design labels chided reporters whose reports could be 'handled' with gifts and meals yet chased them 24/7. This attention can be heady initially. I see the difference in reactions to PR phone calls in my team at *The Indian Express* every day. The middle level journalist bangs down the phone on PR executives (or does not take the call at all), while trainees listen and question: yes, who, where, what.

The PR industry laughs at how easy it is to manipulate the fashion media. Anshu Khanna, a former journalist and now head of Goodword communications, a PR firm, says their firms are the big Fix It companies. 'The PR machinery writes columns for designers, fusses up a wry piece of news, organizes events, creates fake events, fixes reviews, and even writes the script of an interaction with a journalist. We bring Moses to the river,' she says, talking about the W factor in fashion PR. 'It is about wine, women, and wannabes. Everything is fair in this game. There are people in Delhi and Mumbai society so keen to be seen in party pages that they are willing to pay Rs 15,000 for a Page 3 photo. Sections of the media of course oblige,' she added.

The rise of the PR industry as an aggressive part of The Great Publicity Machine is complicit with the laziness of newspaper journalists. Designers allege that press releases are copied word by word by fashion reporters. They fall into the pit they dig themselves. Sample this from designer Rahul Mishra's Butterfly Effect, Autumn Winter 2010–2011. 'The collection seeks to portray the journey of the human race and the process of Metamorphosis our planet has undergone in the last century.... It is an outcome of engineered art works inspired from one of the greatest Graphic Artist MC Escher's work and Urban landscape (sic).

And this:
Rahul Mishra Flies High
Written by ameliavega27 on August 13, 2010 1:51 pm
From: youstyleit.blogspot.com

'Rahul Mishra showcased his WIFW NW 2010 collection the "Butterfly Effect", portraying the journey of the human race and the process of metamorphosis our planet had undergone in the last century. It shows global warming as our biggest concern. The collection is an outcome of engineered art works inspired by M Escher's Work and Urban Landscape.'

Very few young correspondents are interested in the story; they are interested in celebrities instead. It's just so much easier; PR companies send a car to pick them up, feed and indulge them, give them gifts and top it all by sending everything in a well-worded press release. All they expect from a journalist is that they show up at an event, so that they can tell their client who all came. They don't need reporters to work; they need them to be acquiescent suckers to the system. A lot of celebrity and party coverage—also recognized as Page 3—makes newspaper pages look pretty, and the caption is the story itself.

Page 3 continues to be a hook even though its character has completely changed. What was once the playground of well-known people in society is now a bags and shoes declaration page. There are groups of people who want to run away from it and they plot hard not to be spotted on Page 3. When I interview some socialites for my stories in *The Indian Express*, they make requests not to be termed as socialites, even though that is their primary mainstay. They are unable to make up their minds whether Page 3 is good or bad publicity. Publicity it is, that much everyone agrees. They may find it fatiguing to party as part of their jobs but most of them say it is a necessary evil as a photo on Page 3 does propel business.

TOI's Medianet is an open declaration of publicity through payment. 'Once a person deposits the said amount of money and becomes a sustained "client", certain sections of some publications find ways to feature the photographs of that person frequently. So, he or she would be invited to shake hands with a celebrity or a film star somewhere, or asked to pose in a group picture with important people at an event. Slowly readers start seeing that person more often on Page 3; it is a way to become a wannabe celebrity,' he said.

My wariness for the PR lobby—both local and international—began a few months after *Marie Claire* was launched in India. A representative of an Italian luxury brand who wanted to 'explore media relationships' had come to see me. Now she was entrusted with the task of representing this iconic brand—also a powerful advertiser all over the world—which was to be launched soon in the country.

Lady Y breezed in more than an hour late without a word of apology. She placed a beautifully wrapped gift on my table, but didn't say it was for me. She looked stunning in a mauve dress revealing a lacy white tube top inside and a mix of several gold and silver chains with tiny pendants. She was a tall girl and her sky high heels, very Italian in design, made her tower over me. Her face had been highlighted by expertly applied make up and she looked like a model from one of the fashion pages in magazines I pored over all the time in those days. Her perfume reminded me of duty free shops at international airports. Her nails wore a nude shade and her lipstick was a glossy mauve. She looked me up and down and if she was shocked by my handloom sari, she managed to tone down her reaction to sophisticated surprise. 'It is such a pleasure to see a young person wearing a sari, not many wear them these days I am told,' she said. I replied that I wasn't very young and hinted that since she was late I would have to truncate the meeting as I had another commitment. But she paid no heed to what I said. She assumed that I would put everything on hold for her. She picked up a copy of *Marie Claire* India lying on my desk and flicked through it.

'This is where I expect our brand to be featured,' she said pointing at the product pages.

'I suppose the editorial plan is the same as in all editions of *Marie Claire*, right?' she went on, advising me why brands like

Lakme, Himalaya, Ponds, Ayur should not be featured alongside the beauty products of her brand and told me to make sure not to mix lesser known Indian designers with fashion from her brand.

'We have a wonderful working relationship with *Marie Claire* editors all over the world,' she added.

I didn't understand the politics behind brand hierarchies then. Why couldn't Armani, Dior, Louis Vuitton, Chanel be featured alongside Ponds, Lakme, Himalaya, or Ayur on a beauty page? Wasn't the reader smart enough to make the choice? Besides, I wasn't prepared for her assumptions that she could tell us where to feature what. She asked me, patronizingly, where I had studied.

'Nowhere abroad,' I said.

'Oh, so how did you get into fashion?' she asked.

'I have been a journalist for many years,' I responded.

'Good, *Marie Claire* has very strong editorial content, it needs people like you with a lot of experience,' she said suddenly becoming kind. We sipped our coffees. I bristled.

After that first meeting Lady Y sent me numerous emails, each more presumptive than the other. We bumped into each other at fashion events but she steadily kept me out of her circle of friends and editors, inviting me only when it was absolutely unavoidable to have *Marie Claire*. Then, she would do her best to look happy upon seeing me. We would both indulge in hypocritical air kissing though my colleagues warned me that our mutual dislike was no secret.

Lady Y wasn't the only one. Take Lady Z. She headed the Indian communications division of the watch and accessories division of an international luxury brand. She was a stunner to look at, very articulate, wore diamonds in her ears and a big watch from the brand she spoke for.

One day she walked in to my office in a little black dress. Very little.'I am here because I have a problem,' she said, painfully polite but stiff.

'We have been supporting your magazine ever since its launch, it is nine months now and not even a single watch from our brand has been featured on your cover,' she said. 'How long do you think this one-sided support can go on?' she asked as if she was ticking off an errant high school kid.

She found nothing odd in sitting across an editor in an editorial office and stamping her feet for coverage. The tyrannous idea called 'editorial support' had since long entered my life but it was now becoming a powerful ghost editor. That's how I labelled it in my own head. The term perhaps requires a bit of deconstruction.

Editorial support is for those who advertise in your magazine or those you want to please whatever the reasons may be like hotels, transport agencies, restaurants, or any person or property that gives you space, food, or conveniences pro bono for any magazine event or fashion shoot. If you count, there are so many individuals and agencies to thank each month that a news list can be constructed just with 'editorial support'. A smart marketing person can bring out a fashion magazine without any help from a journalist. International brands bring big monies so their voice is suitably arrogant and their insistence on coverage directly proportional. But it isn't as if Indian PR executives, who do not have similar money or clout, are benign players in this game which must end as Love All.

Working as editor of a fashion magazine is like living with in-laws in an Indian joint family. You have to keep so many people happy. In my case it was Paris, seniors in the local office, the PR industry, advertisers, designers with fat egos, Bollywood, their photographers and make up artists.

Nowhere does this politics get stickier then when it is for the cover. Once, a noted Mumbai fashion photographer shot for a *Marie Claire* cover with Sonam Kapoor. It was a smooth shoot. Sonam knew her mind about the clothes and styling and was professional about it all. She did her fittings, came for the shoot on time, and did everything that was expected of her. She preferred a Viktor & Rolf outfit to a LV one but added that she knew we would put LV on the cover. She had been a cover girl too often to be fooled.

Two days later, our fashion stylist was called by Sonam's publicist to say that they did not approve of the selected cover images that the photographer had been given for post-production.

I had to intervene.

'How did she get those pictures?' I asked our stylist.

'He sent it directly to her for approval,' I was told.

'How can he send it without asking us? Is he the editor of the magazine?' I asked furiously.

I explained to Sonam that covers were work in progress till they were finalized by a magazine and no photographer had the professional right to directly send images to a celeb. She understood. I followed it up with an email to the photographer saying the same thing and requesting that he should not send out an unfinished cover shot without the masthead, cover lines, and editorial work. We managed to defuse a potentially difficult situation without upsetting anyone.

Brands that vie to be on the cover don't just insist on 'editorial support'. They keep fashion magazine teams happy in various ways. Ask Latha, she felt indulged and spoilt in her working life till she felt that editorial gifts (an elegant term for freebies) were diluting her point of view.

Many freebies came her way. 'Brands expect journalists to accept gifts, sometimes they force us to because it is a sure way to remind you that you will be followed up, called, and asked whether the story was on its way; it is a silent deal,' she said.

Latha admitted the gifts could make a person slip, but it was the doors that a job in a powerful fashion organization opened for a journalist, which was a headier experience. When they indulge you, they create an illusion of power and success, she said. 'I would get calls from offices of some of my most loved Parisian designers inviting me to experience their brand, visit, and meet them. This was VIP treatment. I did consider that I would miss it all before I quit my job,' she told me candidly.

I knew what she meant as I had waded through these issues myself. I came from a news magazine background where accepting gifts from brands or from anyone else was against the code of journalistic ethics. Yet, I was unable to take a consistent stand on it. In the first year of setting up the magazine before the launch, five people from my team including myself had been sent to the Paris *Marie Claire* office to be trained. We learnt to style fashion and beauty shoots, edited pictures, and were taught how to respect brand hierarchies. The communications team of Chanel in Paris had invited us all to visit Coco Chanel's famous apartment at Faubourg St Honore.

That very evening, after our visit, the person in charge of Chanel's India operations sent each of us a bottle of Chanel No. 5 perfume as welcome gifts. I discussed it with my team saying we should return them as it was *Outlook* policy. Besides, we were too new in the game to even decide how to play it. They agreed reluctantly. I sent all five bottles back with a note saying 'We Love Chanel'.

Editorial gifts are common practice. I would give them away in what we called the 'kitty' in my office and the team would take out chits for the products. A lot of editors do this anyway, because they have the problem of plenty. I was doing it out of rebelliousness. I gave the best of brands like Fendi, Chanel, or Roberto Cavalli that came for me only to the senior girls in my team and the rest were put in the kitty that was open even for interns to dip into.

But my inconsistencies were beginning to catch up. I would refuse gifts sent to me by luxury houses but kept what came for reviews. If I would accept something from an Indian designer, I would send back an art piece, usually a Buddha head carved in stone. As far as my personal khaata (accounting system) went, no favour was left unreturned. But it was not as if too many Indian designers plied me with clothes. Most had probably ticked me off their lists, seeing my saris.

Information about our office 'kitty' slipped out. 'How can you put a luxury bag into your silly kitty?' one Indian representative of a European luxury brand called me to say. 'Who told you?' I asked. 'I have my sources. You guys don't respect good things,' she said, clearly angry.

'I don't like logo bags,' I said, adding that I didn't buy even a small piece of luxury with my own money as I was worried people would think it was a freebie.

'You have no idea how much I fought to get these bags for all my India editors, and you gave it away,' she yelled but broke into laughter the next minute.

'Kitty! Shefalee Vasudev, you are so stupid you have no idea. I think I like you,' she said laughing very loudly. I laughed too, glad somebody had seen humour in it.

'If I send you cookies from the best bakery in India, will you give them away to the kitty too or will you eat them?' she asked.

'I will eat them. But please send me salted nuts instead; I don't have a sweet tooth.'

We became friends.

Once, right in the middle of an edit meeting in my room, my secretary interrupted to say that a huge gift box had been sent by one of the most powerful luxury brands and whether he should accept it or not. It was tied with a pink ribbon and came with a perfumed note. 'Dear Shefalee, don't make a fuss this time, this is no big deal, your counterparts across the world get these every season.' It read.

My colleagues couldn't see the note but they all recognized the label on the box and started murmuring. Would it find its way to the kitty, they wondered. But I was determined to send this back. I phoned Vinod Mehta to take his advice again. 'We are going to upset someone,' I said. 'Return it,' he advised, 'but be very polite.' I sent it back with a bunch of yellow roses.

The gentleman—Mr D—who had sent the box (it had a plus sized handbag from the last season) and the note, later told me that I was looking at the wrong end of the stick if I believed that press gifts, pencilled into marketing costs of all brands were bribes. We spoke more openly only after I quit my job. 'Try to see the story for what it is, instead of what you think it is. Even if the freebies didn't come, editors have no choice but give us editorial support. Besides, Indian journalists have no idea of luxury, unless they get to try these products, how will they understand the DNA of a brand, how will they even write about them?' he asked, adding that he was 'educating Indian journalists' not bribing them.

What largely parades as stories is a clever placement of products for editorial endorsements. Jointly planned features between rich luxury brands and fashion publications are over-the-table agreements. 'The systemic dealing off, of editorial photographs against pages of advertising is an invention widely attributed to Franco Sartori, managing director of Condé Nast in Italy,' wrote Nicholas Coleridge in *The Fashion Conspiracy*. 'This effectively leaves the fashion editor impotent, since the pages no longer reflect her own taste and choice but the merchandizing strategy of the advertiser. From the Eighties, the practice was increasingly copied in America going on to become a sturdy strategy in converting new markets to the cause of luxury they had never beheld.'

In India, powerful advertisers sponsor entire fashion shoots. Editorial crews from fashion magazines are flown to exotic global destinations for fashion editorials that are co-created between the brand and creative directors. Which celebrity will wear the brand, which photographer will shoot and how many pages would be assigned to it, is all predetermined.

Latha was caught between polarities that leapt out of her love for fashion and her growing abhorrence for its truths. In her stints with fashion publications, she was invited by fashion and beauty brands with headquarters in Europe or the US. They were always a paradox for her. 'Peanuts as salaries and free trips to Paris. Flights by business class with sushi rolls and caviar, then back to Bandra boho,' she said. We laughed loudly.

'Indian journalists are not the torchbearers of luxury. We neither wear designer garments all the time nor can we afford luxurious lifestyles. Yet we are drawn into understanding and writing about luxury, compelled to nod our heads and agree that we have been converted. You end up writing the good things and debate the misgivings—never the other way round,' said Latha.

Once, Fendi invited me to join an editors' trip to Rome in 2008. This was to show us the brand, its DNA, and its beliefs in its home country so that we could write about it authentically. During the planning, the PR representatives sought minute details about us. Do we eat non-vegetarian food; is there anything we were allergic to? Would we like a window seat on the plane? Other questions followed. 'Can you send me a brief about the story you will do? How many pages would it be? I have to send these details to headquarters.'

I refused to commit to what kind of story I would do after the Fendi trip, also refusing to commit the number of pages for it, arguing that they couldn't take away a journalist's privilege. Yet I went on the trip like all other editors by business class and ate and drank for four days at Fendi's expense. In retrospect, this was a half-virgin stand.

Luxury brands strategized the colonization of the mind of fashion journalists and through them those of Indian customers. 'The media has converted India into a seller's market. The buyer is damned. Press consciousness here is stronger than fashion consciousness,' says designer Hemant Sagar. 'Those who can't buy luxury brands buy a magazine which features them. It looks hip in the armpit,' he went on.

Indian fashion magazines obliged generous brands like LV by putting strolleys and trunks on covers. The September 2008 cover of *Verve* (with Parmesh Shahani as editor) had Ameesha Patel dressed in wedding bling outside a French castle on the cover. Alongside, sat two pieces of LV luggage. This was repeated in the September 2010 (after Parmesh quit) bridal issue of *Verve* with Deepika Padukone on the cover wearing an Anamika Khanna lehnga with a strolley and hand luggage bag beside her; both LV.

Between the two, Dior and LV have notched the highest number of magazine covers in India since they arrived in 2003 and 2006 respectively. Dior got 20 covers in 2010. But it would be the July 2008 issue of *L'Officiel* magazine that would go down as a classroom lesson on What Not To Do in fashion media. It featured Dita Von Teese in a LV scarf sexily draped as a boob tube worn with a Suneet Varma lehngna, holding a LV clutch. Diffused patterns of the LV monogram were splashed on the cover background and on the magazine's logo—something no publication in the world had done so far.

I had many interactions with the marketing teams of luxury brands when I worked with *Marie Claire*. For European brands, the higher powers work from Milan and Paris. It is not unusual to see editors-in-chief or CEOs of fashion publications waiting to meet the top executives of these brands. Some of the most powerful people in fashion media from all over the world go to meet important executives at the headquarters of various brands in Paris or Milan. Most brands have persuasive representatives—used to openly asking editors and publishers about editorial plans.

Fashion magazine covers mirror the deals between them and their international advertisers. They usually show celebs dressed in international fashion and accessories. Some do eight issues in a year with foreign labels, others all twelve. The sari is robust and alive on the Indian ramp but not on magazine covers. Even *Femina* doesn't put the sari anymore on its cover. *Vogue* India's special sari issue in November 2010 had Priyanka Chopra wearing a Marc Jacobs sari dress. *Marie Claire*'s bridal issue of October 2011 had Paris Hilton on the cover but not in a sari.

An insider at Tag Heuer, also a LVMH brand, told me that brands were now shifting their gaze to news TV channels and newspapers. Ermenegildo Zegna's 2008 commercial, which showed a European groom arriving for a Rajasthani wedding in red tilak and a safa, left a warm recall. To reach new demographics, Zegna also bought 10 to 12 insertions in city supplements choosing Bangalore, Mumbai, and Delhi editions of TOI.

The Photoshopped world of high fashion is hostage to celebrity and the upper class. Bollywood on the one hand and luxury brand advertisers on the other—that's the ambit within which a fashion magazine must create a lust list, meaning, and money from. Occasionally though, the use of editorial pages as marketing tools brings in innovative ideas. *Dostana* the Bollywood film, which had John Abraham, Abhishek Bachchan and Priyanka Chopra with a subtle gay theme directed by Tarun Mansukhani, made a deal with *Verve* magazine. The magazine's logo was to be used in the film as a part of the script as Priyanka Chopra played a fashion journalist. In return, the magazine was to give *Dostana* a cover and many pages of special quid pro quo coverage. 'The story suited our magazine's core and we agreed because of the branding opportunity it offered in a year that *Vogue* was to launch in India with *Harper's Bazaar* to follow,' said Parmesh who headed *Verve* then. 'But as a product placement bid, *Verve* was side-lined. It didn't get the visibility we were promised in formal letters,' he adds.

With a Priyanka Chopra cover, *Verve* printed a relationship issue, called the *Dostana* special, roping in stories that wouldn't have seen the light of the day otherwise. *Vogue* India followed suit with the choice of the cover girl. In September 2008, it put Priyanka Chopra on the cover from a fashion story shot for and shown in Madhur Bhandarkar's film *Fashion*. The magazine carried a story on the film and the film showed Priyanka Chopra on the cover of *Vogue*. Also quid pro quo.

By 2009, I was beginning to feel colonized. I went on many editors' trips to see the headquarters of different brands and meet their core teams and understand their DNA. Estée Lauder, Hermès, Ferragamo, Dior, Fendi, to name a few. These would remain some of the most memorable professional trips I would make. The brands really knew how to spoil people and lend us the illusion of importance. Like other fashion journalists, I would return from these travels and convert my experiences into fashion reportage as I was expected to do. I believed it was genuinely significant for the Indian readership that was beginning to aspire for, appreciate and buy these brands at home, but at the end of the day these were all brand mandated trips and the end goal was clear: positive, pretty coverage.

The publisher of *Marie Claire* at *Outlook* did not tell me to choose between an editorial stand and an advertiser's interest, yet I knew by living in that environment that decisions had to be taken that made it easier for marketing teams to return to brands for advertising. A wish list was sent to me by the marketing team every month, which mentioned the brands (in order of priority) to be given 'support'. The marketing team never fought with me if I didn't play ball. One person from my team who had quit another fashion magazine to join us told us she had been taught to work through carefully made excel sheets that monitored how much coverage was given to which brand per month. This would give a bird's eye view to the creative director and the editor who would then strategize it during shoots.

It would be facile to consciously become a part of the revenue dependent model of journalism and then not abide by its rules. Anyone who believes otherwise is stupid. Or as Karl Lagerfeld said, 'If it's social work you want to do, why come to fashion?'

As for me, I wanted to keep writing on the social complexities of life in India. The editorial director who had first assessed my proposal in 2005 was right. I was not the right person for the job. She could perhaps sense how unprepared I would be for fashion's real face. I felt I was fighting a battle every day inside my head. Was I doing the right thing? I knew how to look after myself, but was I doing the magazine a disservice with my insistence on hard-hitting social reports as part of the editorial menu?

I envisioned a fashion world that rocked with the impulses of news journalism and mirrored the real India yet at the same time looked captivating and seductive enough for the advertisers to want to be a part of. I wanted to be a half-virgin. But sadly it doesn't work like that.

My knickers got really twisted as *Marie Claire* began to redefine itself internationally. From a fashion and beauty magazine with strong feature journalism, it was, across all its global editions becoming softer in its editorial stance, prettier, ultra positive, and geared to meet the advertising giants halfway. Recession had come and dug in, and competition from other magazines in the world, especially in China and India, was forcing a recasting of image. Increase in fashion and beauty coverage meant more strategized marketing initiatives. The message was not lost to any international editor. While no official mailer went out with a clear directive to change content, yet these issues were brought up in private meetings and international editorial conferences. 'Editorial strength' became a double-edged sword. You could be strong as long as the big picture was aligned to interpreting the world as a fashionable place and ignore its zits.

Most of us at *Marie Claire* India were retrained by a new creative director called Joseph Carle. A former fashion expert at the French *Elle*, he brought a compelling vision to the fashion pages. Yet, the slant was clear. Fashion had to be strengthened and the number of pages devoted to it had to be increased. And though he did it very intelligently, Joseph was never mistaken about the power of advertising brands.

An editorial decision of mine inspired by Joseph's free ideas led us to lose some advertisements. We had shot with Shilpa Shetty for a cover. Shilpa looked exactly as she did everywhere: dusky, glowing, her mahogany hair curled, her long lissome legs beautifully facing the camera, her bust partially uncovered to reveal the fullness of her cleavage just as a cover girl's should. But it was not an exceptional shoot and none of the images came alive for me. Joseph Carle agreed. He looked at all image options then looked at me.

'What do you want to do?' he asked.

I showed him a candid, behind the scenes kind of shot taken when the make up artist's assistant was holding a mirror before Shilpa and she was checking her face. You could see the camera in the frame. I wanted to run that as the cover. Joseph agreed as he loved it too. The cover went to press even though nobody in the Indian team was convinced whether it was the right choice. But Joseph and I were sure it was.

'I am reeling, shocked, my therapist says I will recover,' read a phone text from the photographer when the edition was out.

Shilpa had woken up the photographer the morning the cover hit the stands to ask if it was a mistake. It wasn't, I assured him. It was a conscious editorial decision. 'Look how different it is from what we do every month. People love surprises and she is so much the star in this shot. This is the magazine's interpretation of her celebrity,' I said defensively.

The readers loved it. Our mail box was full. I got more feedback on it within the industry than for our usual covers. Six months later, our marketing team informed me that Shilpa Shetty had categorically refused to allow a Puma sportswear campaign she endorsed to be published in *Marie Claire*. It was a multi-page, fully paid for advertorial that the magazine lost.

A fashion shoot in *Vogue* India's August 2008 issue would reopen the debate in my mind. The story was first commented upon by then *Mail Today* columnist Kanika Gahlaut and later picked up newspapers and fashion websites all over the world. A 16-page fashion shoot had a Hermès Birkin bag, a Fendi Bib, a Burberry umbrella, and many other luxury products modelled by poor people in an Indian village. Kanika wrote about the display as 'tacky and distasteful and an example of vulgarity'. In an interview to *New York Times*' Heather Simmons she said: 'There's nothing fun or funny about putting a person in a mud hut in clothing designed by Alexander McQueen. There are farmer suicides here.'

'Lighten up,' said *Vogue* India's Editor Priya Tanna when contacted by *New York Times* and other papers. 'With fashion you have to remember that we can't take it seriously. We were not trying to make a political statement or save the world,' she added.

Not everyone was amused. An ensuing debate in the media led Kanika Gahlaut to follow up her story. Surprisingly, no known Indian designer went on record with any point of view against the *Vogue* story. *Conde Nast* is a powerful group; nobody was willing to rub it the wrong way. Kanika even tried to speak to brand heads in Milan and Paris and was met with a 'no response.'

I couldn't lighten up. For me, fashion had become serious business and my notion that it is actually magazines devoted entirely to it that endanger it with frivolity was becoming stronger.

What I did not admit but had begun to also clearly see was that if some magazines were going head on with putting international brands on their covers, regardless of who really bought and wore them, *Marie Claire*, under me, was committing a similar crime by encouraging an ethnic sub-culture. I favoured Indian, artisanal, hand-woven work by local designers, especially the younger ones who brought with them the zeal to put India on the global fashion map with its Indian textiles not modern silhouettes or Swarovski crystals. I wasn't holier than thou; if *Vogue* and *Harper's Bazaar* supported one kind of capitalism of thought; I supported another. *Marie Claire* became as associated with 'Indian' wear and had the stamp of an 'inward looking, India oriented magazine' as the others were with pleasing international giants. Theirs was at least a commercially sound loyalty; mine was idealistic, commercially unviable.

Marie Claire Fashion Awards, instituted in 2008 as the first KPMG accounted formal fashion awards of the country were tagged 'Made in India' by me making the magazine's stance clear. It miffed some of our international advertiser friends. To strengthen the property, for the fourth anniversary of *Marie Claire*, I worked hard with the support of veteran craft and textile expert

Laila Tyabji, also the Chairperson of Dastkar, to bring weavers and craftspeople associated with the Dastkar society on the same platform with select young designers. It was the first ever such project where a rural artisan took a bow with an urban designer after jointly created clothes by them walked the ramp at a fashion show that gave the audiences goose flesh and *Marie Claire* many new admirers.

At the same time, it only drove home the point further, that *Marie Claire* favoured India and that was not perhaps the brightest of strategies. It gave us distinction in a market but did that distinction sell our magazine more to the readers or to the advertisers? I am not sure.

Now fashion publications, TV channels, city supplements and brands have, astutely perhaps, joined hands. So Garima Sharma, Latha Sunadh, Parmesh Shahani, me as well as Lady Y and Lady Z must all be on the same side of the fence. It is an incestuous game. Fashion award functions of magazines like *Marie Claire* invite anchors from *NDTV Good Times* to emcee the evening. *Zoom* TV has editorial arrangements with magazines to interview Bollywood stars during fashion shoots of magazines. The telecast credits the magazine bringing it free publicity—the best last word anyone can have in this industry.

Now jointly hosted events by various brands and magazines are a trend. So a Tod's lunch with *Harper's Bazaar* would be covered by *HT City*. A *Vogue* evening with LV would be covered by Mumbai *Midday*. *Elle* with Ferragamo, *Harper's Bazaar* with Armani or Suneet Varma, *Vogue* with LV or Mirari Jewellers, *Cosmpolitan* with Ranna Gill, *Grazia* with Tod's. They would all be covered by Night Out, *Zoom*. The same 500 people rotate on guest lists; readers learn to recognize the hostesses and the guests through their pictures as fashion royalty, tinkling glasses, and gossip in glossies.

Fashion glossies have willingly trapped themselves in a few big editorial ideas and they repeat these every year. Bridal issue, Shape and Age Issue, Best Dressed issue, Party special, Resort and Vacation special (with models in swimsuits on the cover), September issue, Jewellery and Watch Specials or a Power Issue. With themes locked in and pre sold to advertisers, exploration of stories is neither news based nor necessarily in tandem with the big changes in society. Like anyone else conversant with the way the industry works, I can pick up any issue of any fashion magazine and point out which ad has been supported by editorial endorsement. Or vice versa.

Parmesh was disappointed both with marketing teams of magazines as well as with sponsors who brought in the biggest money to fashion events. 'Marketing teams sell magazines for what they are not. Instead of harping upon the distinction, they sell similarities which one product has with another, in a bid to outdo each other in the race for advertisements,' he said. He also felt strongly about the way fashion sponsors brought money and power to shows of established designers but did nothing for younger talent. 'The eco system is so unfair. Can't they see that the avant garde will be a market in the next decade?'

Are readers fooled? Fashion magazines claim that their sale and readership figures are between 70,000 and one lakh. But often these are highly exaggerated claims, sometimes hyped by more than forty percent. Since only a couple of such magazines are audited, there is no way to pin down the real figures. In the Indian magazine market, *Vogue*, *Cosmopolitan*, and *Hello* clearly sell more than others.

Fashion begins to look like a small place once the ideas it provokes become bigger. Parmesh quit his job at *Verve* to pursue academics again. He now heads the Godrej India Culture Lab, a global think tank that explores textures of modern Indian society. But he isn't cynical about fashion and opted for a consultancy with *Verve*.

The PR industry emerges as the resilient survivor in this story. By the end of my tenure, I came to feel a grudging admiration for some PR chiefs, including Lady Y and Lady Z. But it was Mr D who really surprised me. Four months after I quit my job he told me: 'Frankly, I am quite disgusted with the way editors and journalists ask for freebies and favours. Some even ask for money from designers to write about them, though not with my kind of brand because we are too powerful. It is not as if I can't give a shoe here or there, but it is so crass. And what do they write anyway, it is so frustrating. I feel like quitting my job!'

I laughed aloud. Mr D quitting his job because he was sick of corrupt journalists. Now that was a story.

Garima Sharma had become very sceptical too. 'Initially fashion fascinated me, but as I got involved, I realized that it's like groups in school—the language may be sophisticated, but the issues are the same. There's insecurity, jealousy, talent, affairs of the heart, all Seven Sins, dangerously played out. Politics is rampant and it can make one forget the respect you have for designers in a matter of seconds,' she said, adding that her rose tinted glasses have come off. She has moved to Mumbai now but continues to work for TOI. She wears contact lenses and makes sure to dress up and do a bit of make up for fashion events.

I lost interest because I wasn't sure what an editor's job meant in a fashion magazine except for being the smartest cookie in a team. This was brochure journalism and you had to figure out the least common denominator between advertisers, Bollywood celebs, the marketing wish list, the personal obligation list, put seven cover lines out of which three had to be international and get it right. Even so, I loved it passionately, and was unfaithful to my original 3MoreYears password. I stayed out three months short of five years.

Latha shrugs, she is okay, she tried this and that and came back to fashion media on her own terms. I met her in February this year at the Wills India Fashion Week. She now edits an online style and beauty magazine called www.strut120.com. 'It is totally about keeping fashion real and gritty, not the glossy kind I used to dream about. I have made it my personal mandate that 'price on request' is not the fashion I want. Nor do I want to work on fashion that only a handful can afford or what's only available to those who travel abroad, the trust fund babies and rich brats. I don't want to buy Photoshopped opinions anymore. But I do want to be buried with the Birkin.'

In the Wings

'There are some things one remembers even though they have never happened.'

—Harold Pinter, *Old Times*

'Fashion is in a desperate place right now. It is not a clean, decent industry. If you are looking for truth and honesty, it doesn't exist. If you are looking for money, best of luck. For those who want to hold on to values, fashion is not the easiest place to be in.'

Coming from Rajesh Pratap Singh, one of the industry's most respected designers, this wasn't idle rumination. Reticent, erudite, ponderous, Pratap has little use for swagger. Representative of minimalism, one of the three dominant genres visible in Indian fashion alongside wedding couture and dramatic kitsch, his personality reflects his brand. He is quietly irreverent—shuns fashion parties, doesn't have Bollywood stars on his speed dial, firmly avoids the media and unless his show is sponsored by a corporate giant, doesn't even hire a PR agency to sell himself and his clothes. The creation and management of hype that the glamour industry lives by is anathema to him. Yet his shows attract committed craft revivalists who are otherwise unflinchingly critical of designers and don't want to be seen at fashion weeks. Pratap's label has a strong, original signature. His garments are non-fussy, classic, structured and 'solid', to use a favourite cliché of Indian customers.

Interestingly, Pratap has never made a wedding lehnga in his career. The dazzling world of crystal bling and wedding couture hasn't kissed his creative flurry yet. For him it is his white and black cotton shirts with fine pleats or deconstructed bandhgalas made out of textiles, which hang in the most important wardrobes in the country. His clothes have a loyal clientele abroad and sell the most in Japan and the European markets. 'New York, Paris or Delhi, my customers have the same mindset. They are men and women who enjoy clothes, are independent minded and interested in how they are made instead of just the influence of the finished product. They are certainly not logo bearers,' he said with a reluctant smile.

Ostentation disturbs Pratap's world view. Unlike many other designers who issue press releases when they as much as touch a yard of khadi, the last thing he would do is to make a song and dance about reviving textiles despite his commitment to them.

I chased him for more than six months for this interview. Enough people in the industry had told me that he avoided journalists like the plague. We had had a couple of phone conversations earlier when I worked at *Marie Claire*, but he had maintained a studied distance that I admired. For a fashion exhibition curated by us for the annual awards event of the magazine, he had contributed by sending a bike made from a few hundred pairs of scissors for display. But he didn't turn up at the event. At the rare gathering that he would be spotted at, I would walk up and say hello; he would respond courteously but turn away almost instantly. It was always difficult to catch Pratap's eye. For this conversation, he agreed to meet me only after I sent a request through some of his friends. Once he agreed to be interviewed, he didn't hold back.

When you drive into Pratap's office and workshop near Surajkund on the outskirts of Delhi, it is like arriving at a quiet farmhouse for a relaxed weekend. The sense of having left the city far behind wraps you like a thin shawl and you want to keep wearing it as a layer. The waiting lounge in his large working arena is functional, well-lit, pristine, and uncluttered. I was soon ushered into a front office that bore his spartan stamp: a single imposing sculptural installation besides a large table in wood and comfortable seats all around. He came in to sit across me and it took a good amount of warm up time for Pratap to look directly into my eyes as we chatted. He is a tall, good looking man and wears his more pepper, less salt hair usually long—sometimes tying it behind in a ponytail. Born and brought up in Rajasthan, Pratap, now 42, looks his age and his cautiousness only adds to his thoughtful demeanour.

His sister-in-law Sapna manages the finances of his company. People in the industry often talk of her as a 'fabulous business aide'. Pratap's wife Payal who recently launched her own fashion line manages the manufacturing of her label from the same premises. Inside this workshop, Pratap weaves his own khadi on ambar charkhas (hand cranked machines). As he took me for a guided tour, I saw huge swatches of Ajrakh and other textiles strewn around and he told me he was designing his next collection. He works with handlooms in villages in Rajasthan and Bengal to create authentic, hand-spun yarn for his clothes. Since his childhood, Pratap has been influenced by Rajasthani men's garments.

'Seventy percent of the men wear white in Rajasthan. I also like women in men's clothes,' he said, explaining his love for minimalism and the silhouettes traditionally worn in India's desert regions. He said he is interested in cutting edge research and development to challenge his creative boundaries as he showed me his experimentation with double-sided textile jackets. 'Fashion is not pure art, yet the demand on creativity is not less than any other trade. The beauty of working in fashion is the opportunity to make something new. It is a rush in itself. R & D is of consequence to me, showing myself or my wares at fashion weeks soaked in fashion politics is not,' he said.

I asked him why he had discontinued showing at Paris Fashion Week after a couple of very successful shows there. He was frank about his reasons.

'I can't afford it. A single show costs a crore of rupees and Indian designers don't make so much money,' he said.

'You are successful as well as one of the most influential designers in Indian fashion. It is easy to assume that you make money,' I said.

'I don't know how you measure success. But the barometer must include actual earnings that swell each year, and no, I can't say I am commercially successful,' he said, without the slightest hint of embarrassment.

Most designers I had met so far had tried to convince me how good their business was and how sought after they were by the rich, famous as well as 'real people'. And here was this self-deprecating designer trying to do just the opposite.

Pratap's elusiveness is no secret in the industry but I didn't know that he was a rebel. His views on the fashion industry would as I soon realized turn out to the most scathing of them all.

'Designers don't make money worth their salt. For most of India, we are only entertainment. It is the smaller towns that are evolving as stronger fashion markets, with sub pockets of a niche clientele coming up in every region. I see Jaipur and Cochin as emerging markets, that's where Indian fashion must move. The scale and success of urban fashion is largely hype.'

'Hype' is a hot air balloon inflated by the fashion media that rises above talent and fact. Frequent publicity—often without good reason—keeps *some* designers always in the news. It lends consumerism crazy readers the illusion of a large, booming market where clothes sell like cakes. 'Publicity' can be a ferocious beast especially when it is allowed to roam freely and hunt who it pleases; as Pratap would come to realize through his brush with fashion politics. He had been turned into a front page 'item' for an alleged wardrobe malfunction at his show at Wills Fashion Week in March 2008. A blue cowl-necked Pratap dress had slipped off a Belgian model's shoulder revealing half a boob. While she had quickly slipped it back on, 'Wardrobe malfunction mars designer Rajesh Pratap Singh's show' became a catchy headline next day.

Pratap was out of the country when this happened but most newspapers and TV channels suggested that he had orchestrated this for publicity. 'Scandal is the only time that we are on the front page. Otherwise the media dumps us into city supplements as a side dish in the larger context of news and views. When I woke up in Paris, my phone was inundated with missed calls and my message box was more than full. I had no idea what could have happened,' he said.

The usual spate of denials, counter denials, and accusations followed. Not one of his colleagues stood up for him in his absence. The FDCI, which could have called a press conference and issued an official statement, did nothing. Sunil Sethi, now the FDCI President, a close friend and supporter of Pratap was not in the power seat then. Had he been, say those who suggest solutions (only in retrospect), he would have saved the day. 'Sethi tries hard to protect designers hunted for the wrong reasons. And Pratap, oh, Sethi is especially fond of him; the whole game would have played out differently,' an insider told me. But that was not to be. Instead, insinuations ran amok provoking fodder to already rampant internal politics in the industry.

Fashion politics in India is a melting pot of unhealthy rivalry inside a disorganized industry. There are lobbies and clans united by vengeance and commercial interests instead of a larger cause or commitment. These clans comprise designers, sponsors, powerful people from fashion week bodies, a model or two, even make up artists, photographers, and journalists. They perpetuate each other's cause when it suits them and become turncoats when it doesn't. The altering formations of such clans replicate what Indian politicians do, shifting political loyalties depending on the situation. Fashion politics is like any other politics. Some have opted out of the race, wary forever, like textile conservationists Pranavi Kapur and Madhu Jain. Others like Abu Jani–Sandeep Khosla, Suneet Varma and Ravi Bajaj, all mighty names, have decided to cast it aside like a badly fitting costume to make their own way. They have studiously kept themselves away from fashion weeks as much as they can.

In India's fashion industry, unprofessionalism is dressed up to look like a fascinating conglomerate growing by leaps and bounds. Fashion does have a visible market now and the industry is bigger than it ever was with more than 300 designers participating in the various fashion weeks either through stalls or shows. This year, a dozen designers celebrate 20 years and more in fashion—JJ Valaya, Suneet Varma, Abraham & Thakore, Madhu Jain, Abu-Sandeep, Tarun Tahiliani, Rohit Bal, Ashima and Leena, Rina Dhaka, Wendell Rodricks, and Ravi Bajaj. Yet even now the FDCI, the apex body of Indian fashion, doesn't lay down any guidelines or industry codes of ethics. If the industry has grown in size and popular influence, its complexity and confusion, too, has multiplied. It may seem like a logical trajectory of growth and evolution, but it is far too complicated to fit into any logarithm of 'progress'. There are no specified codes on copyright issues, plagiarism, professional conduct, disclaimers of profit, no guidelines for quality control of merchandize, no unifying rules on how garments should be labelled for the local market versus a foreign market and little logic on pricing.

Do Indian designers hire child labour? This all-important question is just brushed away conveniently under the carpet. Every week there are fashion events in cities; but I have never been to a fashion seminar that enlightens us on labour laws in fashion's sweatshops, on import policies, or on what is authentically organic vs what is 'labelled as organic'. Neither designers nor fashion stores are expected to declare the details of the textile or weave they use, the geographical denomination of the craft used on a garment or where it was created. Fabindia has been successful in creating and standardizing the Craft Mark label bringing credibility to its goods. Good Earth explains the fabric it uses in its cotton and silk garments on its labels. Now even the design industry is lobbying actively for an India Design Mark but a fashion garment gets by with just Made in India, Dry Clean Only.

Although fashion is a labour dominated industry there is an absence of guidelines on how to deal with errant labour in workshops, what to do with pressing issues of VAT or other taxes that push up prices or how to handle rampant plagiarism that is visible in the mass market. A formlessness lurks even in the selection criteria for designers who apply for fashion shows. At best, it is vague. A phone call, a personal friendship, or a bitter rivalry can influence the final list made by any jury. No accounting firm is brought in to scrutinize the decisions of sponsors and fashion week head honchos. Shows are given out on a range of unspecified reasons—empathy or sympathy; favouritism or eccentricity. Sometimes it is obvious success; sometimes irrepressible vengeance for another lobby. There are numerous under-the-table dealings between fashion week bodies and the show sponsors. These are almost never raked up openly.

In exchange of favours and front row seats, even journalists allegedly write only what the powers that be want them to. They are used as pawns (not unsuspecting) to play dirty fashion politics. Rajesh Pratap agrees that the industry's lack of conviction and commitment perpetuates politics. 'We don't know how to take any kind of stand, good or bad. Some journalists blackmail us for favours and freebies and yet we call them and give them front row seats,' he said, adding that the presence of those who spread the rot and provoke internal disagreements would sooner than later be a reason why he will opt out of showing at fashion weeks.

I could hardly disagree. Resentful rivalry is common and designer egos can be difficult to deal with. During an edition of *Marie Claire* Fashion Awards, I had got so many feelers about seating arrangements—'who doesn't want to be seated next to whom'; 'who will not hand over a trophy to whom'—that I had to work with the event management team myself to avoid unpleasant encounters among our guests. Most of us know about the clans as I would learn to call them and we worked hard to put the clans together in groups and separate the bitter rivals from each other.

'Who am I sitting with?' one designer phoned me to ask when the awards property was first launched.

I said I wasn't sure and asked if he had any concerns. He gave me three names that he shouldn't be placed with at a table, come what may. 'Also, make sure that I sit at the same table where your chief guest is. Otherwise, my dear, I will have to leave. Don't take it personally. It is not about you. It's about my status,' he added.

Half an hour before the show was to start in 2009, the last time that I would be part of *Marie Claire* Fashion Awards, I got a call from a senior designer. We had invited him to give away one of the trophies. 'Who am I giving the award to?' he asked.

I told him the name of the designer who would receive the trophy from him, again asking why to make sure that we were not making a political mistake. 'You see I can't be giving an award in a category where we are obviously the best,' he said.

The calls didn't stop there. A designer who I called to invite personally for the awards asked me if he was one of the winners. 'It is mandated by KPMG the accounting firm that we don't announce the results till they do it themselves during the ceremony,' I said. He bristled, calling me naïve.

'I am not a fashion student anymore, Shefalee. If I am not winning, I can't attend,' he said.

For organizers of fashion events, this ego war is unnerving. Bollywood celebs who routinely attend film award functions without the promise of winning a trophy secretly insist upon some kind of award through their publicists when they came for fashion events. It suddenly becomes beneath their dignity to attend a fashion event without being decorated. This holds true for many successful designers who crave the spotlight like moths. Unless you invite them to give away a trophy or win one themselves, they don't want to be seen applauding for their own industry.

Consider these political potshots.

'The richest people want the biggest discounts on clothes, Bollywood wants them free,' some designers would tell me.

'The most well known designers want awards that they don't deserve, those that should rightfully go to the younger generation,' I would retort back.

'Fashion editors only come to fashion weeks to be seen in the front row; they are not interested in fashion. They are busy texting on their phone even when the show is on. I will show you a video of my show to prove how disinterested the divas are,' I was told.

'I will show you a video to prove how designer A, B, C wanted his seat changed because he didn't want to be seated next to X,Y, Z,' I offered.

There are no winners in these slanging matches. Everyone stands to lose something. Camaraderie and trust are the first casualties.

Powerful designers, established enough in their business to get sponsors for their shows and film stars as special guests or show stoppers, give pretty interviews to journalists. Those who don't, fret and fume, finding their creative pursuits diminished in the larger mess. They often end up toeing the line to do whatever it takes to remain a visible part of fashion weeks. A fashion week which is essentially a business event, defined by the number of buyers and trade, is now a big party as everyone knows. In the absence of clear categories and minimum quality of work required to get a show, it can sometimes mimic the theatre of the absurd.

Curiously, the great fashion split of 2005 is where this all started. Acrimonious fights, disagreements and mudslinging among head honchos and designers of the former Lakme India Fashion Week (LIFW), gathered momentum. LIFW was a collaborative effort between FDCI and Lakme, the cosmetics division of Hindustan Lever. There are many small and big anecdotes around who should take the credit for starting Indian fashion weeks. But most point unerringly towards Anil Chopra, the CEO of Lakme Lever, and designer Wendell Rodricks who was one of its first architects. Chopra, who quit in 2011 after 12 years with Hindustan Lever, envisioned an India fashion week with Wendell Rodricks and Sonia Singh the then marketing head of Lakme on the steps of the New York Library. Since international talent company IMG had proposed the event,

Wendell, who was a consultant with Lakme, suggested that the company should get visibility with its sponsor logo in the backdrop and a Lakme Grand Finale. The first fashion week took place in New Delhi in the autumn of 2000. Initially floated as a once-in-a year event, it was a pioneering platform for the business of Indian fashion jointly created by FDCI, its title sponsor Lakme, and international talent agency IMG. Wendell presented the finale of the first season with fellow designers Tarun Tahiliani and Raghuvendra Rathore.

In 2005 a fission led to the formation of what are now the two most recognizable fashion week properties. One is the Wills Lifestyle India Fashion Week (WIFW) promoted by FDCI and sponsored by Wills, which is held in Delhi twice a year. The other is called Lakme Fashion Week (LFW) sponsored by Lakme and jointly backed by Hindustan Lever and IMG and is held in Mumbai, twice every year. Ostensibly, the split happened for two reasons. One was the inordinately high marketing fee being asked of Lakme by FDCI. The other was the disagreement over the venue of the biannual fashion weeks, whether it should be Mumbai or Delhi. Things weren't so innocuous—there was also an internal power struggle. FDCI was then headed by Rathi Vinay Jha, a civil servant now retired who had served on many important posts across India. She was also the founding director of NIFT. Chopra and she allegedly didn't see eye to eye.

With two major fashion week bodies, the fashion industry should have become organized with a proper charter for business and sponsor collaborations. Instead, it is bursting at the seams with creases of fashion politics. Political disagreements on juries have sometimes turned into disgusting personal affronts; there have also been loud and uncouth slanging matches between designers. A string of emails that smacked of dirty vendetta and ganging up against one another were leaked out from FDCI in 2008. Power politics broke out inside the organization between Executive Director Sumeet Nair and now President Sunil Sethi.

I was forwarded some emails by one of the senior designers who was on its Board of Governors. The demeaning language was appalling; it also revealed what the designers thought of each other and how poorly they felt about their own industry. Those fights led to Nair quitting FDCI where he had been working as an important and senior member. This was the second major split in the Indian fashion industry. In retaliation, Nair formed a breakaway faction called Delhi Fashion Week, (DFW) dividing the designer lobby further. The industry hit a new low. DFW was organized on the same days as of Wills Fashion Week, which was FDCI's property, and manipulative strategies were unleashed by both sides to sabotage each other's events. The big question was: Where would the two mighty crowd pullers Tarun Tahiliani and Rohit Bal show?

DFW wound up soon enough but the hatchet between Sethi and Nair has never been buried. Multiplicity of fashion weeks has split the industry further in terms of loyalty and creative focus. Same collections are shown at different events and every motley group with half a sponsor in tow boasts of a fashion week. On last count, India has Wills Fashion Week (twice a year in Delhi), Lakme Fashion Week (twice a year in Mumbai), Men's Fashion Week (once a year in Delhi), Couture Fashion Week (twice a year, one in Mumbai, one in Delhi), Resort Fashion Week (once a year in Goa), and Jewellery fashion week (once a year in Mumbai). Now there are city specific fashion weeks—Jaipur, Kolkata, Chennai, Bangalore, Hyderabad, even Bhopal. These do not include travelling fashion shows sponsored by Blender's Pride and Chivas Regal. There is no commitment to a singular, united fashion week that showcases the fashion of this country. In a bid to be 'different', fashion bodies name their events by what suits them, paying no heed to international norms. LFW changed the name of its Spring-Summer shows to Summer-Resort and that of Autumn-Winter to Winter-Festive. This is against international norms of showing collections six months ahead of their arrival in stores. That's the only way buyers can order for the next season and designers have enough time to meet the orders placed. The titles were changed without any internal industry dialogue and the new localized fashion calendar has thrown Indian designers in a tizzy. Those who want to participate in LFW have to be ready with their collections to hit the stores immediately after the show. But those who participate in WIFW have six months to deliver their consignments. Those who participate in both need two sorts of collections each year—an impossible feat given the production logistics and costs.

To plod through these inconsistencies, designers often disregard fashion week themes and show what they want or what's ready and available. Some show couture collections during Summer-Resort, others show Spring Summer collections during Winter-Festive. Swimsuits and bikinis, prêt, diffusion, formal wear or wedding garments—everything is game in any season. The themes announced by fashion week bodies are a sham. If a designer has a sponsor, even fewer questions are asked.

The 'best' and most established names manage to rope in powerful sponsors. Sponsors look for headlines in city supplements of newspapers and Bollywood is the easiest shortcut to publicity. The fashion media ignores everything if there is a film star around and more such publicity pulls in a stronger sponsor who wants to return the next time. 'For five days of crass publicity, sponsors ignore young talent and the most innovative collections, crushing dreams of the younger generation,' a young designer told me. For a person watching this as a spectator sport, sponsors appear short-sighted. They support established names and avoid taking risks with those still testing the waters.

In 2009, Sunil Sethi, the President of FDCI, had allotted a prime time show slot to Sanjana Jon at WIFW in Delhi. Sanjana is the sister of convicted Indian designer Anand Jon, currently serving time in an American prison for proven charges of sexual misconduct. She is neither a designer nor does she have retail stores in India. But she pulled in a mighty sponsor and got a show while other deserving designers had to taste disappointment. Her theme was Save the Girl Child and she got Bollywood stars Salman Khan and Sushmita Sen to walk the ramp for her.

For a piece I wrote on this for *Outlook*, Sethi gave me a schlocky quote. 'It's a sponsor show, who am I to say no if they bring in stars as well as money enough to pay for ten shows?' he asked. 'Don't forget, the only question journalists ask me every day is which star is going to walk the ramp today?' he countered.

Termed as the undisputed leader-politician of the fashion industry, Sunil Sethi's fame is warped with critical ideas about him. While his enemies grudgingly hand it to him for his indefatigable energy, and fruitful initiatives that persistently promote Indian fashion, his friends can't stop talking about how power hungry he can be. Considering he is the only person who has led the fragmented industry from the front and given it a presence, shape, and restive ambition in the form of the now formidable WIFW, which gets the most business, the most attention, and the most designer participation, I am constantly surprised at the mixed feelings he evokes in some people.

The 58-year-old Sethi is a fourth-generation Delhiite who was raised in a rich business family which dealt in automobiles. He studied at St Xavier's school (distinctly remembers all his catechism classes), before enrolling at Delhi's Sri Ram College of Commerce. One of his closest college buddies is Gulshan Grover who would later become Bollywood's bad man. The two were the livewires of the Yuva Manch theatre group in college and retain a friendly bond even now. Grover is a front row fixture at WIFW. 'In those days there was a divide over clothing on the Delhi University campus. News anchor Rajat Sharma who led the Hindi debating society wore kurtas and jholas and all those with 'leftist' leanings did the same. Education and lineage were important—which college you went to and what your family did. How you looked took a back seat.

Sethi, who consistently appears on India's best dressed lists, is tall and enviously slim for his age. He is a classicist who combines a razor edginess of style in his sense of dress—he wears well-tailored Nehru jackets and shirts and you will suddenly notice a sketch of Mahatma Gandhi embroidered in a subtle thread in the corner of one of his Rajesh Pratap shirts or a blue lace on one of his shoes and a green on another. Sethi has generously salted hair and a thick moustache. He has obviously never flirted with L'Oreal.

In his college days, he was a hot favourite among girls and got a lot of female attention. He brushes it off modestly saying that it was all because of owning a Wrangler jacket in denim and a second-hand Fiat car with bucket seats in the front. This was one of the six cars on the campus during those days and the most fashionable, adds Sethi, because it wore tweed seat covers. 'In 1976 when I was barely 20-years-old, I packed suitcases with Indian clothes—glitzy saris, printed T-shirts, and wigs from Janpath—and took to countries like Mauritius, Canada, and the US to sell as part of Merchants of India exhibitions. I was always carrying excess baggage,' he said laughing as he sat upright (he never ever slumps) on a straight-backed chair at his finely designed office in Okhla in Delhi. This is also where he runs Alliance Merchandising Company, a design, fashion, and lifestyle goods buying consultancy service and a dozen other related projects. 'My first order was of 10,000 T-shirts which I got from Crazy David in Canada,' he recalls. Sethi would stay in 5-dollar hotels or at YMCA and even at boarding houses of Hare Rama Hare Krishna congregations.

He claims that the credit for getting the first sponsor for a fashion event in India should go to him. 'At the very first fashion event held at ITC Maurya in 1978, where students participated as models, I convinced Weston Avis Jeans to sponsor the show,' he says. The 'Made in India' distinction as a label in fashion according to him was his idea when, in 1986 he founded Alliance Merchandising Company, which boomed as a financially successful project. From 1995 to 2000, Sethi took a promotional show called Best of India to Selfridges in London. He then worked as a sourcing agent for homes and lifestyle goods for the popular store.

Vittorio Radice, the then managing director of Selfridges who was visiting India with a curiosity to tap the energy of New India visited Jaipur with Sethi to meet Mahipat Singh, a member of the royal family of Moti Dungri who was the buying director for Selfridges. When Radice attended the decadent New Year celebrations and saw India's ethnic costumes (Sethi's bandhgala among them), he suggested another show with a Bollywood promotion. Seventeen designers took this Bollywood-themed show curated by Sethi to Selfridges. These included Abu Jani–Sandeep Khosla, and the big names of Indian fashion and textile. 'Designers would spend their own money on tickets to see the response to their products and clothes,' Sethi told me, smiling as usual from ear to ear.

'Till the mid-nineties few knew the concept of labelling garments, issues of quality control, international sizing or how to set up export licensing, the problems of international shipments that carried clothes. Alliance Merchandising Company managed it all including details like separate slips that were mandated to go with embellished garments or those that had vegetable dyes,' said Sethi.

If some designers are disillusioned with Sethi's controlling ways, he, too, is an equally disenchanted man deep down. Sethi manages WIFW almost single-handedly; he is there to organize and sort out all exigencies from certificates from fire departments to a 22-year-old journalist throwing a fuss about a seat. He personally seats the big and the small, makes place for bureaucrats and political guests, making sure that the youngest stylist too goes out smiling with a booze lounge entry pass. He hands out favours like biscuits, and runs around (even when he walks, his strides outpace everyone else) from morning till past midnight, smiling constantly. A lot of us journalists know about the defeats and frustrations of designers but few realize that Sethi also feels let down a dozen times at every fashion week. He told me stories of those who had become turncoats after taking his advice, practical help, money, and support for years.

Without a minute's debate he agrees that there is intense politics in the industry. Curiously and interestingly, he doesn't see himself above it. But says that politics emanates from insecurity and that a majority of 'big' designers may stick to their guns in making ornate couture but it is time they became realistic and sensed the competition that the young generation of designers is bringing their way. 'Either shape up or perish because the next generation is catching up. Very few people in this industry are professional. It is because of this that even the most talented designers are unable to reap the rewards, which should be theirs by now after twenty or twenty-five years of business,' says Sethi adding that it was after intense introspection that he decided to become an unflinching supporter of young designers.

Not everyone agrees with him. He is unmistakably the industry's Godfather, say people. Some say he is also its Shylock from Shakespeare's *Merchant of Venice*. I personally think these are lazy ways to describe a versatile man. He is not an old-style Don. He works on the modern principle of enlightened self-interest. He believes that his growth is impossible without the growth of his industry and his accomplices. He doesn't sacrifice self-interest but nor does he compromise the interest of fashion at large.

The internal realities at other fashion weeks too are beguiling. LFW for instance went overboard with sponsors. In the last two years, eight odd shows out of 25 were sponsored (a sponsored show takes away creative freedom from a designer who must design a collection to meet the sponsor's goals), many by brands which have nothing to do with fashion or clothing. If there was Killer Jeans and Levi's, there was also Grey Goose, Skoda, and Nikon. These brands came in for a fat slice of the publicity pie—whether they make fashion or not is another story. There may be an immense mismatch between a designer's sensibility and his sponsor, but who can refuse multiple lakhs to mount a show?

Consider this small side story about Swati Bhimte, a Delhi girl was chosen by Levi's for their GenNext Designer award at LFW in September 2007. GenNext shows, rightly called 'The Future of Fashion' and pioneered by LFW's Anil Chopra, give a platform to talented, fledgling fashion designers. Proper selection criteria is laid down for these shows with an advisory board comprising veteran designers, editors of fashion magazines, retail buyers, and heads of fashion institutes. LFW not only invites fashion greenhorns with a minimum production base to apply with samples of their work but supports the chosen ones for a collective fashion show with everything paid for. With veteran designers as mentors to direct and choreograph the shows (Wendell Rodricks was the mentor for about six years), the fashion kids have it all. The mentor guides them on how to make garments that best define their sensibility, how to put out a capsule collection and even the choice of music. A specially created mentoring team give these debutants a crash course in PR and media. LFW takes care of everything—the models, make up, and stylists. This is a dream platform. In five years from 2005 to 2010, 68 designers debuted here. Compared to 25 odd applicants in 2005, September 2010 saw 172 applicants. The entries came from 34 cities, from Kochi to Rishikesh. LFW celebrated with a special show called Five Years of GenNext.

Swati Bhimte became LFW's falling star. 'The Levi's award ended my career,' says Swati, who had to eventually shut shop. Her experience is a warning to those who assume that a sparkling initiation in a fashion week is followed by a smooth ride into retail. She signed a contract with Levi's, for which she was to be awarded Rs 5 lakh. The deal was for 125 odd garments, of which 35 ensembles would be displayed on the ramp; the rest would be stocked in Levi's stores. Then the tables turned. 'For reasons best known to them, Levi's pulled out as LFW sponsor the next season after I had invested money and made the garments. "No sponsor, no show" is what LFW told me a few days before the fashion week,' Swati said.

Swati had turned away smaller orders that could have helped her stay afloat and made her staff work on this collection alone. That was her biggest mistake. Star one day, struggler the next. 'No one in the media wanted to run this side of my story,' she says.

Swati is now a commercial stylist in Mumbai. 'Staid, non-creative work mostly, but thoroughly professional,' she says. Levi's did eventually sponsor her show but a season too late. Garments created for Fall-Winter showed in a week labelled Spring-Summer. By then, shutters had come down on Swati's Delhi unit.

Young designers say that market realities are an acid test. This is an intensely competitive and unforgiving business. To survive, a young designer needs a sound business plan, enough financial and psychological bandwidth to take repeated beatings in the market as well have a good product to be entertained by a retailer in the first place. Even if all these things are in place, the market is unfair to new designers and stores mark down 50 percent on their garment rates.

Ask Jasleen Kochhar and Jenjum Gadi, a young designer duo who make a label called Koga from a small unit in Delhi's Shahpur Jat. 'Supporting young designers is a coated word,' says Jasleen adding that no fashion body does anything to monitor how young designers are treated in the retail market. 'Stores mark down

50 percent on the consignments we give them,' she told me. Which means if a garment is priced at Rs 3000 by a designer, the store will give her only Rs 1500 and pocket the rest. While they pay big designers for the entire consignment immediately upon the delivery of clothes, they keep the clothes of young strugglers on credit. 'They only pay us when and if the garment sells,' said Jasleen. She also told me how stores seldom ever organized promotions for younger designers while happily hosting cocktail events and seasonal launch functions for the older ones. 'If an established designer's ensemble costs Rs 3 lakh, they will still pay for it and display it lavishly in the window, but they won't pay even Rs 5000 for an ensemble of ours. Stores should be investing in garments that actually cost less but shockingly stores which do better business start playing power games and pay younger designers really small amounts. Nobody is ready to take a risk. It's very tough to survive,' said the duo.

Fashion institutes and colleges are partly to blame for the disillusionment that young designers feel when they become a part of the industry, feels Rajesh Pratap. 'To make these huge institutions without appropriate faculty can only lead to disillusionment. Nobody prepares fashion students for the tough times that would challenge them in the market. They are just brainwashed by glamour and hype. Glamour doesn't redeem the industry's complexities,' he said.

Getting a show is certainly not a cakewalk. For the sake of formality, there are fashion juries to select and reject. When I asked Sethi about the criteria of selection of designers to show in a couture week, he told me 'There are no criteria. If there is anyone who can suggest a process we can all agree to, we will be happy to incorporate it.' He hinted at the disagreements that defined any process laid down by the FDCI. I had heard enough gossip about how designers on the board of governors usually disagree over everything and then Sethi gets to take the final call trying to maintain a balance sheet of keeping 'all sides happy'.

For seasonal prêt fashion weeks, a designer must pay between Rs 4 lakh for a solo show as participation fees and Rs 2.5 lakh for a joint show. The fashion week organization pays for models, choreographers, the venue, PR and hosting international buyers. If it is just a stall a designer wants to put up and not have a show, it would cost between Rs 1.5 to Rs 2 lakh depending on a double stall or a single one. These events too are rife with politics and rivalry. A designer gets judged by where her stall is located (tucked away in a corner or clearly visible in the centre); what time the show is slotted (prime time shows are considered more respectable); and of course, who the is sponsor, if there is one. Every season there is a racket over time slots and the benign, non-political ones lose the battle. They are given afternoon slots on working days. The big designers who participate backed by powerful sponsors not only get money for their collections and sets but also prime time slots on weekends.

The politics of couture is different. Money is big in couture so the game is headier. A couture show costs a participating designer Rs 10 lakh. Sethi told me that each collection goes above Rs 75 lakh and if a designer shows more than 40 garments, the investment would not be less than Rs 2 crore. A couture set being elaborate or ornate would cost the designer anything between Rs 3 to Rs 15 lakh. The event costs FDCI roughly Rs 5 crore.

Behind it lies a web of networking and desperation to woo the elite, the only customers of couture. It is like a Shakespearean comedy. Fashion politics has tension and deception between characters, multiple intertwining plots, more emphasis on situations than characters, separation and re-unification, a clever servant and a happy ending. But every happy ending leaves some people unhappy.

The FDCI board begins a couture week endeavour with two initiatives. It circulates an announcement among designers inviting entries leaving out newbies, or those whose resources do not facilitate couture production. All efforts are made to keep the names on the jury (a 10-member jury is formed) confidential to avoid decisions made by influence. This jury interestingly includes wives of a couple of rich industrialists, seen as true customers of couture. Every jury member must give two lists of 10 designers each. List A and List B. An average is done and a final List A is made. If some designer from List A is unable to participate, the top one from List B gets a chance.

Yet, when insiders claim that despite murky politics, furious midnight phone fights, accusatory emails, even emotional blackmail, the list of 10 finalists that the jury chooses usually has eight names that are common among all, the argument must be paid heed to. 'Try to understand that there are established names in Indian couture. If they apply, they can't be refused,' said a fuming Sethi to me. 'Do you expect us to ask Rohit Bal to send us one of his garments to examine for the sake of selection criteria?' he asked me outraged.

This 'no-criteria' process allows the freedom of selection to those in power. Even if eight out of ten names are predictable, I would imagine the choice of the remaining two can be biased without anyone to question the process 'Yes, there is usually a controversy around a couple of names, whenever a final list is out,' admitted Sethi, telling me there was no way to keep everyone happy.

'To be honest all this makes me sick,' says Pratap. 'I am not a hooker after all. I have seen a side to fashion that is debased, corrupt, and exploitative. We are answerable to our kids after all and we must ask whether the decisions we make are worth it. I am certainly a misfit in these equations,' he added.

Clinical detachment is Pratap's survival mechanism. I noticed its symbolism in the décor inside his boutiques. He has nine stand-alone stores all over India. They have walls painted stark white and dotted with lockers like those you would see in the doctor's scrub rooms outside operation theatres. Pratap's father is a cardiologist and the colour white denotes purity, cleanliness, and healing for the designer. 'Merchandize that is not displayed is placed inside the lockers so that it is hidden from view,' he told me. In one of his Delhi stores, a hospital steel stretcher has been placed in the centre and clothes are displayed on it. In one of his Mumbai stores, a Buddha made of scissors sits in the window.

Hidden from view and far from the madding crowd are numerous young talents in the Indian fashion market who do not want to be seen anywhere near a fashion week. They create funky, alternative fashion and will herald the Indian avant garde. Without Bollywood showstoppers or a booze brand to sponsor, corrupt or bully them, they do important heritage work and experiment fearlessly with new silhouettes that are anti-fit, anti-bling, why, even anti-fashion. It is this emerging gene pool of style creators outside what's known as the 'fashion industry', who might make fashion weeks redundant in the years to come.

Acknowledgments

* Chiki Sarkar who suggested that I write this kind of narrative on fashion.

* Raakesh Agarvwal, Imcha Imchen, and their families for allowing me to look inside the closets of their minds.

* The Salvi family in Patan for their patience and hospitality. Particularly Rahul.

* Jennifer and Nagma who allowed me to intrusively trail them over months.

* Sunil Sethi for his patience with a hundred scattered questions.

* National Institute of Design (NID), Ahmedabad and National Institute of Fashion Technology (NIFT), Delhi, for granting me access to their libraries.

* My deep gratitude to Sharda Ugra, Vir Sanghvi, Prita Maitra, Hemant Sagar, Parmesh Shahani, Simran Bhargava, Arti Sandhu, Ashdeen Lilaowala for their many suggestions and for moderating me by reading the manuscript in its different stages.

* Sanjay Nigam for his insistent reminders to reject, select, and rewrite. And, for sparing me his acidic reviews of this work.

A Note on the Author

Shefalee Vasudev was born in Gandhidham, a Sindhi resettlement township in Kutch which later came to be known as the New Sindh. As the only child of two Sindhi writers who had participated in the freedom movement and were deeply influenced by the Partition, she was raised to value reading above everything else. She did her schooling from Modern School, an English medium school in Gandhidham but her parents made sure she learnt to speak, read and write Sindhi along the way.

Shefalee wanted to be a journalist right from her school days and her first article appeared in the Ahmedabad edition of *The Times of India* when she was in Class X. After her post graduation from Gujarat University, she lived and worked in different cities before settling down in Delhi in the mid Nineties. Over the years she has worked with *The Navhind Times* in Goa, *The Asian Age* and *Cosmpolitan* magazine in Delhi, before scripting and anchoring a Hindi news feature show for DD News. During her *India Today* job, as part of an exchange programme, Shefalee was chosen to teach a course on India through journalism at the Medill School of Journalism, in North Western University, Illinois, US. However, it was at *Marie Claire*, as its founding editor, that she realized there was a genre in writing that remained unexplored in India: fashion journalism pursued like a cultural study with the same level of curiosity, research, enquiry and questioning employed in any other form of journalism. Currently, Shefalee works as Associate Editor at *The Indian Express* and writes Unfashion a popular column and blog. *Powder Room: The Untold Story of Indian Fashion* is her debut book.